# Making Asian American
# Film and Video

**Asian American Studies Today**

This series publishes scholarship on cutting-edge themes and issues, including broadly based histories of both long-standing and more recent immigrant populations; focused investigations of ethnic enclaves and understudied subgroups; and examinations of relationships among various cultural, regional, and socioeconomic communities. Of particular interest are subject areas in need of further critical inquiry, including transnationalism, globalization, homeland polity, and other pertinent topics.

Series Editor: Huping Ling, Truman State University

Jennifer Ann Ho, *Racial Ambiguity in Asian American Culture*
Jun Okada, *Making Asian American Film and Video:
    History, Institutions, Movements*
David S. Roh, Betsy Huang, and Greta A. Niu, *Techno-Orientalism:
    Imagining Asia in Speculative Fiction, History, and Media*

# Making Asian American Film and Video

## Histories, Institutions, Movements

JUN OKADA

**Rutgers University Press**
New Brunswick, New Jersey, and London

Library of Congress Cataloging-in-Publication Data
Okada, Jun, 1973–
  Making Asian American film and video : histories, institutions, movements / Jun Okada.
    pages cm. — (Asian American studies today)
  Includes bibliographical references and index.
  ISBN 978-0-8135-6502-6 (hardcover : alk. paper) — ISBN 978-0-8135-6501-9 (pbk. : alk. paper) — ISBN 978-0-8135-6503-3 (e-book)
  1. Asian Americans in motion pictures. 2. Asian Americans in the motion picture industry. I. Title.
  PN1995.9.A77O53 2015
  791.43'652995073—dc23
                                  2014023226

A British Cataloging-in-Publication record for this book is available from the British Library.

Copyright © 2015 by Jun Okada
All rights reserved
No part of this book may be reproduced or utilized in any form or by any means, electronic or mechanical, or by any information storage and retrieval system, without written permission from the publisher. Please contact Rutgers University Press, 106 Somerset Street, New Brunswick, NJ 08901. The only exception to this prohibition is "fair use" as defined by U.S. copyright law.

Visit our website: http://rutgerspress.rutgers.edu

Manufactured in the United States of America

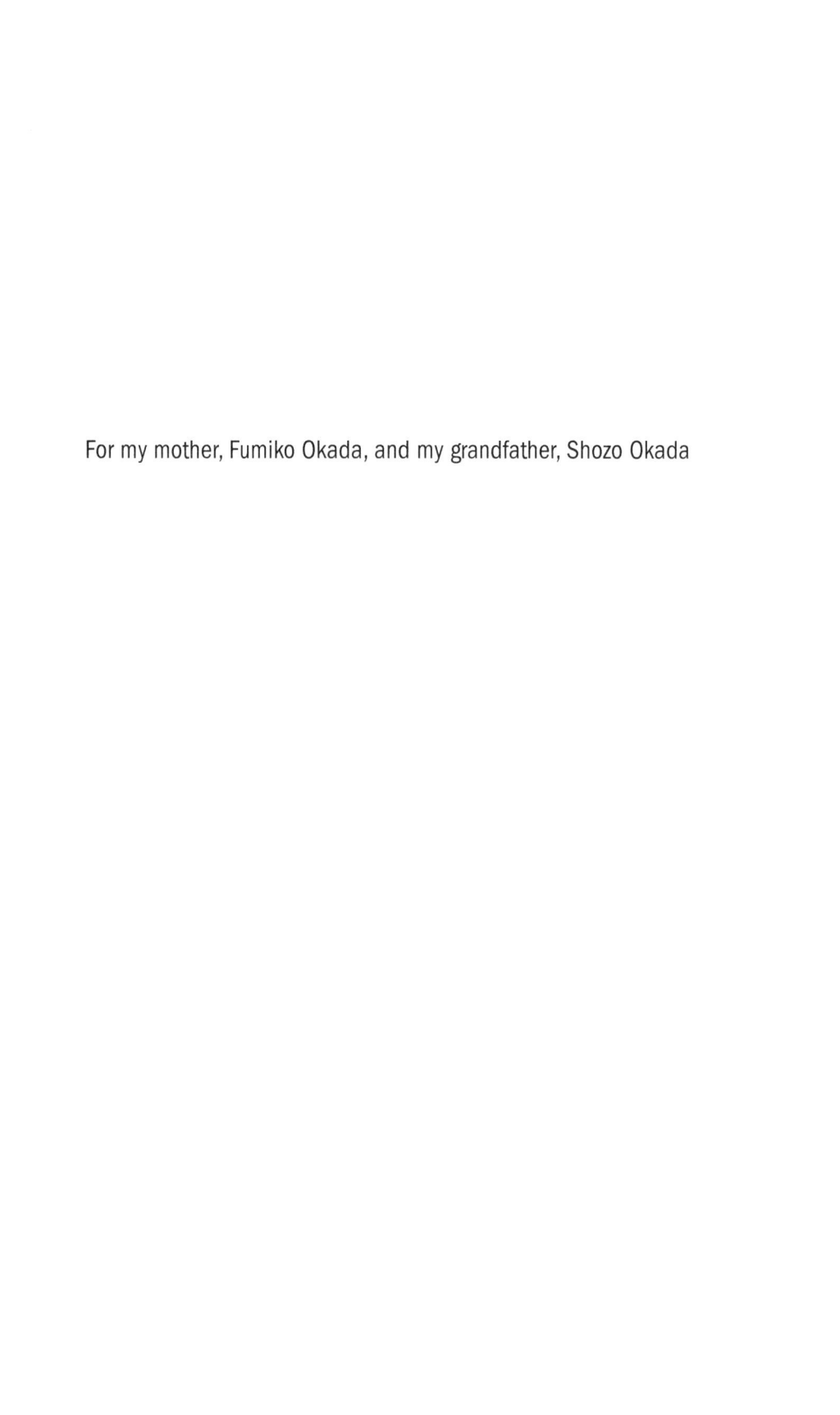

For my mother, Fumiko Okada, and my grandfather, Shozo Okada

# Contents

| | | |
|---|---|---|
| | Acknowledgments | ix |
| | Introduction: The Shared History of Asian American Film and Video and Public Interest Media | 1 |
| 1 | "Noble and Uplifting and Boring as Hell": Asian American Film and Video, 1971–1982 | 12 |
| 2 | The Center for Asian American Media and the Televisual Public Sphere | 39 |
| 3 | Pathology as Authenticity: ITVS, *Terminal USA*, and the Televisual Struggle over Positive/Negative Images | 55 |
| 4 | Dismembered from History: Racial Ambivalence in the Films of Gregg Araki | 79 |
| 5 | *Better Luck Tomorrow* and the Transnational Reframing of Asian American Film and Video | 97 |
| 6 | The Post–Asian American Feature Film: The Persistence of Institutionality in *Finishing the Game: The Search for a New Bruce Lee* and *American Zombie* | 124 |
| | Afterword | 134 |
| | Notes | 137 |
| | Bibliography | 145 |
| | Index | 153 |

## Acknowledgments

I would like to acknowledge the friends and colleagues who supported me as I produced this book. Research for *Making Asian American Film and Video* began at the Department of Film, Television, and Digital Media at UCLA, where my perspectives were informed by the work of my mentors, Teshome Gabriel, Chon Noriega, Kathleen McHugh, Nick Brown, Peter Wollen, Janet Bergstrom, Vivian Sobchack, Steve Mamber, and John Caldwell. I appreciate their instruction and sage advice about matters intellectual and material. Outside of UCLA, Peter X Feng championed this manuscript from its early origins, when he was a visiting scholar at UCLA, up to and including the last editorial suggestions of the final draft of this book. The seminars of the UCLA Chicano Studies Research Center's Race and Independent Media Project, especially, were a once-in-a-lifetime opportunity to learn from the most important scholars in the field of race and media studies—Chon Noriega, Peter X Feng, Eve Oishi, Richard E. Espinoza, Anna Everett, L. S. Kim, Michelle Raheja, Yeidy Rivero, Celine Parreñas Shimizu, and Jacqueline Najuma Stewart. At UCLA, I was fortunate to have my research funded by the Cota-Robles Graduate Fellowship, the George and Sakaye Aratani Graduate Fellowship, and the Institute of American Cultures Ethnic Studies Research Grant. And life would most certainly have been unbearable without my UCLA friends who sustained me through many evenings of talks, fantastic film screenings at Melnitz Hall and LACMA, as well as karaoke and shared dinners. Thank you, Andrey Gordienko, Sachiko Mizuno, Emily Carman, Lindy Leong, Sharon Sharp, Sara Vizcarrondo, Victoria Meng, Azadeh Farahmand, and Zinaid Meeran. I must also mention Dr. Wendy Belcher, who helped many of us publish our first peer-reviewed articles through her work at UCLA.

Later, when the dissertation began to take shape as a book and during the first years of my first real job in the Department of English at State University of Geneseo, my colleagues Beth McCoy, Richard Finkelstein, and Ron Herzman, were kind and supportive throughout my untenured years and helped usher in my new identity as tenured faculty. There, my provost and president and fellow English Department colleagues, Carol Long and Chris Dahl, continued to support my growth. At SUNY Geneseo, the Presidential Summer Fellowship and the Drescher Faculty Leave Award, awarded to me by my union, United University Professionals, generously funded my research and writing.

Beyond UCLA and SUNY Geneseo, Jean Ma not only encouraged my work but, more importantly, befriended me through our undergraduate years together at UC Berkeley and numerous meetings of the Society for Cinema and Media Studies conference. Guo-Juin Hong, my generous friend and colleague, helped me chair the Asian Pacific American Caucus of SCMS and invited me to share my work at Duke University. My colleagues on the member board of the Asian Pacific Islander American Association of Greater Rochester—Mimi Lee, Lily Lee, Greta Niu, Sharon Delmendo, Mar Doromal, Marilyn Ajavananda, and others—helped me to keep up my morale throughout my long adjustment to a new town. My other wonderful friends from childhood to the brink of middle age—Julie Baltzley, Robb Hillman, Adabel Lee, Pilapa Esara, and Alison M. Parker—saw me through bad times and good, and I thank you all for being there. Of course, I owe deep gratitude to my mother, Fumiko Okada, and brother, Ryo Okada, and to my extended family in Japan for always wanting the best for me. Most importantly, I admire the filmmakers and media professionals who are the subject of this book and who truly inspired me with their dedication to social change through art—it is to you that this work is ultimately dedicated. And last but not least, I would like to give a shout-out to a most unlikely suspect: the dynamic and amazing Latin dance community of Rochester, who miraculously nourished mind, soul, and body on harsh winter nights when I happily danced salsa, bachata, and merengue during breaks from doing the arduous work of manuscript revisions. Wepa!

**Making Asian American
Film and Video**

# Introduction

## The Shared History of Asian American Film and Video and Public Interest Media

In 1967, the Carnegie Commission on Educational Television published a report that showed a troubling lack of multicultural diversity on commercial television, the remedy for which would appear in the form of the Public Broadcasting Service (PBS). The report, titled *Public Television: A Program for Action*, not only described the absence of people of color on and in television but prescribed a highly ambitious yet vaguely articulated solution, stating that public television should "help us see America whole, in all its diversity." It "should be a mirror of the American style" and "should remind us of our heritage and enliven our traditions." PBS would be a place "where people of the community express their hopes, their protests, their enthusiasms, and their will." It should provide "a voice for groups in the community that may otherwise be unheard." Its programs "should help us know what it is to be many in one, to have growing maturity in our sense of ourselves as a people." It should, in short, be the "clearest expression of American diversity, and of excellence within diversity."[1]

At roughly the same time, Asian American film and video emerged to do the very things expressed as desires by public television's mission. Beginning with protests by the Third World Liberation Front against the University of California, Berkeley and San Francisco State College in 1968, the Ethnic Studies movement helped transform university film curricula at UCLA. At first, despite the effect of the Ethnic Studies discourse, UCLA's film school admitted very few minorities until protests in 1968 led to the establishment of EthnoCommunications, a pilot film program for minority filmmakers. Asian American filmmaking students from EthnoCommunications went on to form the film collective Visual Communications, which by 1973, produced the first Asian American films about the Japanese American internment, farm labor in Central California, and portraits of Chinese American immigration.

The two historical events—the birth of PBS and the birth of Asian American independent film and video, seemed to coincide auspiciously, but history had other ideas. Specifically, the utopian vision of multiculturalism set out by the Carnegie Commission continued to be unrealized. In fact, it took more than a decade for the independent Task Force on Minorities in Public Broadcasting to do its own research to find that "excellence in diversity" was not being served on the programs themselves or in the hiring ranks of PBS. The task force's report, *A Formula for Change*, enabled the creation of a number of consortia representing America's underrepresented minority groups: Asian Americans, African Americans, Native Americans, and Chicanos. These consortia were financed by PBS's main funder, the Corporation for Public Broadcasting, to reassert the promise of the original goal for diversity set out by the Carnegie Commission a decade earlier.

The Asian American consortium, National Asian American Telecommunications Association (NAATA), was one of the most successful of the Minority Consortia.[2] Yet, even before *A Formula for Change*, the Asian American film and video community was linked to public interest media, organizing in grassroots collectives and local groups such as the pioneering Visual Communications. These organizations have been responsible for the production of thousands of Asian American independent films and videos since the 1970s. The testament to NAATA's success lay in its steady growth over time and the development of an increasingly prodigious and influential international film festival, the San Francisco International Asian American Film Festival. Though similar to the other consortia in its funding and programming relationship to PBS, NAATA had a unique stake in the development of a genre—Asian American film and video—which depended on it to thrive, but with caveats. Without public media and its stance on diversity, the institution of Asian American film and video—films, film festivals, discourse—would not exist. The analysis of Asian American film and video as a byproduct of a much larger phenomenon—the rise of public interest media—illuminates our understanding of minority media production and its problematic yet necessary historical relationship to the state. This book explores precisely how public media and its intricate discourse of diversity enabled Asian American film and video while, at the same time, problematizing its purpose and transforming its goals.

Previous monographs and collections have established the field of Asian American film and video (Xing, Leong, Hamamoto and Liu, Feng, Mimura,

Ono, and Pham); however, *Making Asian American Film and Video* is the first book that foregrounds the role of the state—specifically, public broadcasting and its related institutions—in the development of Asian American media and, in so doing, establishes a new paradigm for the study of this movement.[3] Clearly, even this cursory history reveals how PBS, despite its intentions to serve the values of multiculturalism, provided both a boon and an obstacle to Asian American film and video. Asian American film and video is a complex topic to define because it contains a multitude of component terms that each deserves a book of its own—a film genre, a film movement, an ethnic identity, and a politics of identity. The common scholarly approach to Asian American film and video has been the discourse of film studies, which frequently focuses on subject matter or spectatorship. Rather than using these traditional perspectives as paths toward definition, I define Asian American film and video as that which is interwoven with the rise of public broadcasting and thereby identified intimately and inextricably with questions about institutional parameters, funding, programming, and artistic freedom.

Asian American film and video moves fluidly between movement and genre. This fluidity depends largely on institutional context, which itself has shifted from its political origins in the 1970s to its more commercially based production structure in the 1990s. Film cycles and genres develop as groups of films that have narrative and thematic similarities to each other, and often their success is negotiated between Hollywood studios and audiences. Film movements, on the other hand, often share a specific time period and a commitment to a style and an ideology. Examples include the French new wave, Italian neorealism, and Soviet montage movements, which were committed simultaneously to a new aesthetic in response to the old and to the political ideology that reflected this desire for the use of cinema in social change. Asian American film and video began in the early 1970s, most certainly as a movement, by young, politically engaged filmmakers committed to usurping the control of the image from Hollywood in representing Asians and Asian Americans. Aesthetically, these early films were rudimentary and extremely low budget. Yet, decades later, Asian American film and video operates much like a genre, responding to market trends such as the surge in interest in East Asian cinema in the United States in the 1990s. In many ways, the institutional history of Asian American film and video, particularly its relationship to the Public Broadcasting Service, is crucial to understanding its historical trajectory and multifaceted identity because the development of the Public Broadcasting Service and its support of ethnic media became the bridge for underrepresented minority films and filmmakers to achieve commercial, mainstream legitimacy. Yet, this road is also paved with deep ambivalence about whether Asian American film and video should become a distinct genre outside the mainstream or one that evolves to blend into the dominant culture. In many ways, public interest media represents a middle ground in which Asian American film and video has played out this ambivalence.

This book explores the significant symbiotic relationship between Asian American independent film and video and public interest media institutions as they both emerged and evolved during the post–ethnic studies 1970s to the era of "global cinema" in the 1990s to the consolidation of the independent Asian American feature film of the early 2000s. I demonstrate this multifaceted relationship through analyses of the prescriptive and critical discourse produced by filmmakers, activists, and critics that shaped what has become known as Asian American independent film and video. This contextual discourse appears in written form—in journals, film festival programs, and blogs—and it also appears within the text itself, showing how essential public media institutions have become for Asian American film and video.

The structure of this book follows the historical, evolutionary path of the relationship between public media institutions and Asian American independent film and video from its birth in 1972 to its peak with the production of Justin Lin's hit film, *Better Luck Tomorrow* (2002) and explores its aftermath, the "post–Asian American film." Although Asian American film and video has always been eclectic and diverse, representing all formats and genres, and is not in itself a linear movement, I emphasize that this arc traces the institutional mission of Asian American film and video to its ironic teleological destiny—the profitable commercial feature film. That this narrative trajectory is satisfied by capitalism's grand prize is also telling of the tensions between institutionally based public media and commercial media and the compromises of both. It is important to realize that this seemingly binary structure is in fact a spectrum, involving films and filmmakers that exist at various points along public, commercial, and independent definitions. In this way, the story of Asian American film and video is very clearly about the procurement of resources and of material necessity as much as it is about the progressive history of representation. Therefore, the first decades of Asian American film and video were completely in line with institutional objectives because, by virtue of marginalization by Hollywood, the public media institution was the source of material support. Once filmmakers were theoretically free from institutional obligations, that is, they had proven the market potential of Asian American film and video, the legacy and residue of public media remained as ghostly traces within the text.

What is public interest media, and why is it so significant to Asian American independent film and video? In answering this question, it is necessary to step back and revisit yet another question, which remains central: What is Asian American film and video? The answer: Films and videos made by and about Asian Americans. Given the tautological insufficiency of this answer, several books have sought to carve out a more nuanced response. In fact, the authors who have written monographs and edited volumes about Asian

American film and video have wrestled with this question, not only because it continues to be an unknown quantity and quality marginalized by area studies, literary studies, ethnic studies, and especially film studies, where it commonly resides, but because this question is also an extension of the larger question, What is Asian American?

In answering these elusive questions, it is important to establish the historical origins of Asian American film and video as one that was politically motivated out of necessity to "create our own stories" in the face of the institutional racism and invisibility within Hollywood and dominant media. Specifically, this meant the multitude of stories of people of Asian descent who have shared the familiar experience of immigration, racial discrimination, and alienation at various periods in the United States. Theoretically, Asian American film and video encompasses any topic that touches upon any issue having to do with cultures and nations of the Asian continent. Typically, Asian American film and video includes filmmakers and film subjects that reflect ethnicities from Cambodian to Indian, Pakistani to Indonesian, Nepalese to Thai. What brings these ethnicities together is their link to experiences forged in contact with US culture, policies, and history as it is represented in moving images. However, in practice, Asian American film and video, like any genre, has a center-to-periphery structure, with a preference toward groups who have been in the United States in larger numbers and for a longer period of time: Chinese, Japanese, Korean, Vietnamese, and Filipino. Additionally, since Asian American film and video emerges from a strong political context, the most visible films have been about social change centered on histories of discrimination: the Japanese American internment, Filipino and Japanese American farm labor, Chinatowns and Chinese American labor history, and stories surrounding the effects of World War II, the Korean War, and the Vietnam War on Asian Americans. Moreover, the larger context of the Asian American movement includes the formation of other Asian American labor groups during the post–civil rights era, such as Asian Americans for a Fair Media (1973) and the Asian American Legal Defense and Education Fund (1974), along with institutions such as Visual Communications.[4]

This is a book about Asian American film and video, but it also argues that there is no such thing as an authentic, organic, or autonomous "Asian American film and video." It is a concept invented by the network of grassroots, local, and national institutions that emerged following the civil rights and student movements of the 1960s and 1970s. Asian American filmmakers make films in the same way that others make films. The definition that "Asian American films and videos are made by and about Asian Americans" is not an adequate definition. It's not adequate because it is neither mutually exclusive nor collectively exhaustive. For example, several notable Asian American filmmakers make films that aren't about Asian Americans, such as the Oscar-winning documentary filmmaker Jessica Yu or Wayne Wang, who, despite making the iconic Asian American film *Chan Is Missing* (1982), has helmed Hollywood genre films (*Maid in Manhattan* [2002]; *Anywhere but Here* [1999]) as well as independent "non–Asian American films" (*Smoke* [1995]; *Blue in the Face* [1995]).[5] What is more, several noted documentaries, which would be considered classically Asian American in their sympathetic views and deconstruction of key historical events in Asian American history, were not made by Asian Americans. Examples include Eric Paul Fournier's *Of Civil Wrongs and Rights: The Fred Korematsu Story* (2000), about the famed activist who resisted and challenged the US government's internment of Japanese Americans during WWII, and Barbara Sonnenborn's *Regret to Inform* (1998), about her journey to Vietnam twenty years after her husband was killed there. Neither Fournier nor Sonnenborn are Asian Americans, yet both films were funded, exhibited, and continue to be distributed as part of the definitive collection of Asian American films from the central clearinghouse for Asian American media, CAAM (Center for Asian American Media), challenging the idea that Asian American films must be directed by Asian Americans, an idea that is a holdover from still another institution, the institution of film studies. Specifically, auteur theory, which holds that a film's author is not the screenwriter, but the director, has informed the way we think about authorship and identity.[6]

This book is one of a few on the subject of Asian American film and video and the first to focus on institutional history as its defining element. Several books and articles have sought to define Asian American independent film and video from extant models of film studies, such as authorship, spectatorship, and Third Cinema.[7] Jun Xing's *Asian America through the Lens* (1998) is the first of such examples of in-depth scholarship and offers a broad, comprehensive look at Asian American film and video as an important arm of the Asian American movement. Two highly useful and eclectic essay collections, *Countervisions* (2000) edited by Darrell Hamamoto and *Moving the Image* (1991) edited by Russell Leong, add necessary reflections on the growing genre of Asian American film and video. While *Countervisions* presents a series of scholarly essays on important films and videos that make up the genre, *Moving the Image* offers an eclectic mix of shorter essays and filmmakers' reflections to give an authentic account of the diversity and energy of Asian American independent film and video on the ground. Two later monographs focus more deeply on specific aspects of Asian American film and video. Peter X Feng's *Identities in Motion: Asian American Film and Video* (2002) derives its framework from theories of spectatorship, performing close readings of key Asian American films to argue that "identities are not located in movies themselves, but are mobilized within the spectator."[8] Alternatively, Glen M. Mimura's *Ghostlife of Third Cinema* (2009), gives a more historically contextualized account of Asian American film and video and attempts to find a specific cinematic tradition to contextualize it. In doing so, Mimura's book connects the genre to the aesthetics of Third Cinema and "post-1960s era of globalization." Like all of these works, my book explores text, context, and history. However, unlike these previous volumes, it suggests an alternative account to Asian American film and video's history as originating in the emergence of institutionalized public interest media in the 1970s.

Chapter 1, "'Noble and Uplifting and Boring as Hell': Asian American Film and Video, 1971–1982," examines the earliest discourse about the struggle to define Asian American film and video to reveal that what was assumed about Asian American media's overt and unquestioned social change agenda was highly contested during its origin years. Following the civil rights and Ethnic Studies movements, Asian American film and video emerged in the early 1970s and shared with that era a fundamental ideology of social change. However, a closer examination of its institutional history shows how this tradition conflicted with an equally important and at times contradictory discourse of aesthetics and form. The purpose of this chapter is to introduce the embeddedness of the institution both literally, as providing the first institutional home for Asian American films and videos, as well as discursively, through ongoing debates about its aesthetic direction. In one sense, this chapter aims to show that Asian American independent media had risen out of political necessity to fight institutional racism and invisibility within Hollywood and dominant media. Yet, the chapter also troubles this narrative by revealing the historical ambivalence about Asian American media's overt task. In other words, as Asian American independent film and video emerged with the message of resistance against Hollywood, it also seemed to exclude itself from the opportunities and possibilities that mainstream media offered. As much as the question of identity politics was evident, what was covert was a need to complicate the idea of a resistant, ideological cinema.

Chapter 2, "The Center for Asian American Media and the Televisual Public Sphere," explores the convergence of Asian American film and video with national public television and the Corporation for Public Broadcasting (CPB) through the establishment of the Minority Consortia in 1980. The advent of the Minority Consortia decisively steered the direction of Asian American media as a genre toward films that promoted the articulation of historical "injury." This relationship profoundly affected the kinds of films being made and being labeled Asian American. Because of the national identity and nature of public television as occupying a contemporary "public sphere," the contract between select Asian American films and PBS lent these films an "official" status. Many films produced out of this relationship are contractually obligated to represent a sanctioned Asian American identity, which ultimately becomes one of articulation of grievances, injury, and ressentiment. Consequently, there exists the historical inevitability of the transformation of Asian

American independent media into an overt ideological project for "positive" Asian American identity politics as a result of its relationship to PBS.

Chapter 3, "Pathology as Authenticity: ITVS, *Terminal USA*, and the Televisual Struggle over Positive/Negative Images," steps back from the concerns of institution building to examine the effects of the Public Broadcasting Act of 1989 and through it, the development of the Independent Television Service (ITVS) on Asian American film and video. The 1980s saw a spike in independent media production, both public and commercial. The larger debate in the world of public media was that independent producers themselves did not have enough control over programs that aired on PBS. This line of argument led to passage of the Public Broadcasting Act of 1989 and the creation of ITVS, an entity that was ideally free from bureaucratic control by nonproducers. After the Minority Consortia, ITVS emerged as yet another of the attempts at checks and balances of the PBS/CPB hierarchy, specifically attempting to produce more aesthetically and politically controversial films for public television. By looking at one of these films, *Terminal USA* (Jon Moritsugu, 1993), which was part of ITVS's first series on PBS, *TV Families*, I examine a key moment in the attempt to challenge established norms regarding race and representation on public television. One of the critiques of the Minority Consortia was that in choosing which films to show on PBS, it consistently chose "positive images" over other diverse visions. Chapter 3 asks, If the institutionalization of Asian American media was indeed flawed, what would a more "authentic" representation be? Although many decry ITVS as initially a failure, I argue that it created a window of opportunity to offer a more productive and culturally meaningful image of Asian Americans via the "negative image."

In chapter 4, "Dismembered from History: Racial Ambivalence in the Films of Gregg Araki," I continue the line of questioning begun in chapter 3 to explore the work of Asian American filmmakers whose work does not fall into the categories of social change media established through the requirements of public interest media. Specifically, this chapter looks closely at the work of Gregg Araki as an example of a high-profile independent filmmaker of Asian heritage who stands both within and outside the established institutional confines of Asian American film and video. Araki's career flourished as his independent feature films *The Living End* (1992), *Totally Fucked Up* (1993), *Doom Generation* (1995), and *Nowhere* (1997), were critically acclaimed and/or gained cult status in the 1990s. Though he is infamously known as the Asian American filmmaker who doesn't make Asian American films, it is ironically his very resistance to institutional forms of filmmaking that has reinscribed the institutional as the mark of the genre. In other words, because the stigma associated with Asian American film and video (as outlined in chapters 1 and 2) had become so entrenched, that resistance itself has become a constitutive discourse of the genre. Araki vociferously resists the label of "Asian American," and his films embrace both punk and queer aesthetics and alternative private funding systems that actively resist associations with public interest media. And yet, his involvement in and support of the Asian American media community in his public discourse has identified Araki as a meaningfully ambivalent figure standing both inside and outside of the institution, challenging its entire existence. In other words, his outspoken resistance to the limitations of Asian American film and video and his reluctant inclusion within the community have reinscribed him as an Asian American filmmaker even while the subject matter of his films trenchantly prove otherwise. But upon closer examination, Araki's films betray covert elements of Asian American identity issues that link his work inevitably to Asian American film and video. By revealing the seams of an institutionally constructed and problematic Asian American film and video, Araki's films emphasize the ambivalence at its heart.

Chapter 5, "*Better Luck Tomorrow* and the Transnational Reframing of Asian American Film and Video," explores Justin Lin's breakthrough feature film *Better Luck Tomorrow* as watershed text that both reflected and signaled a new era of global cinema's influence on Asian American film and video. Though Asian American film festivals have always included Asian films, at first as a way to compensate for the dearth of Asian American films, the "transnational turn" in the 1990s was a conscious appropriation of internationalization in the fashion of other major film festivals. Using *Better Luck Tomorrow* as the node in the transformation of Asian American feature film in the 1990s and beyond, this chapter explores the gradual shift in emphasis from social change filmmaking to a global discourse in the highly successful and renowned San Francisco International Asian American Film Festival. This transformation, as I argue in the chapter, is about the increasing tendency to globalize Asian American film and video, which entailed a gradual erasing of its institutional traces. Moreover, the chapter narrates the emergence of the Asian American independent feature film and competing discourses of institutionality and transnationality as a definitive aspect of the "Asian American feature film wave" of the 1990s.

One of the persistent problems of Asian American media has been the difficulty in making and distributing feature films. Besides *Chan Is Missing*, Asian American media had been relegated to PBS documentaries. In response to this problem, Asian American film festivals in the 1990s strategically encouraged the production of transnationality in Asian American media by piggybacking on Chinese-language cinema, which was experiencing an enormous surge in global popularity. Specifically, films of the "Fifth-Generation" directors from the People's Republic of China, as well as films from the Taiwan and Hong Kong new wave cinemas, influenced Asian American independent film and video during this time. In using the independent sleeper hit *Better Luck Tomorrow* as the latter turning point for the "successful Asian American feature film," I argue that it and its predecessors engaged in a "transnational aesthetic," which capitalized on the blurring of the lines between Asian and Asian American identity. Significantly, I distinguish between two tendencies in Asian American independent feature films of the 1990s, the transnational aesthetic, which emphasized globality and the more classic film of countermemory, previously the predominant strategy of Asian American film and video.

In chapter 6, I conclude *Making Asian American Film and Video* with a reflection on post–Asian American film and video, focusing my analysis on two fake documentaries, Justin Lin's *Finishing the Game: The Search for a New Bruce Lee* (2007) and Grace Lee's *American Zombie* (2007). These two films reflect the "post–Asian American," not in their having overcome identity issues, but in their direct commentary on Asian American film and video's institutionality or their ties to public media institutions while ironically being materially outside and beyond it. In other words, unlike the PBS documentaries and low-budget Asian American feature films of the past, both Lin's and Lee's feature films were produced through diverse fiscal strategies and for wider audiences, a pattern that has become more viable due to the success of previous independently produced Asian American feature films. Moreover, the term "post–Asian American" is used purposefully and problematically to refer to the issue of the neoliberal, "postracial" moment in which these two films were made.

The conclusion focuses on these two mockumentaries because the people who made them grew up within the institutions of Asian American film and video in the 1990s and reached success with their groundbreaking films about Asian American identity—Lin with *Better Luck Tomorrow* and Lee with *The Grace Lee Project*. That the two filmmakers emerged in 2007 with fake documentaries reflecting on the legacy of Asian American film and video is very telling about institutional history and institutional style, which has become the telltale sign of the genre. This is especially true in these films' use of strategies of paratextuality, intertextuality, parody, and others to uniquely identify the indelible stamp of institutionality on their work.

Both Lin's and Lee's films are about the problem of race and representation, but they also make fun of the never-ending nature of this problem as the plague that haunts Asian Americans. *Finishing the Game* is a fake documentary that takes place in the 1970s and which imagines what the audition and preproduction process would have been like in the real-life historical event of finishing Bruce Lee's last film after his untimely death. The fake documentary follows three actors who vie for to replace Bruce Lee in a series of bumbling auditions that parodies the race politics of that era while reflecting on the continuing saga of the problem of Asian American representation that remains today. The film nods to the absurdity of Asian American actors finding work in

1970s Hollywood—a trope that is identifiable from a mainstream perspective. Yet, in *Finishing the Game*, the frame of the fake documentary made for public television makes even a very specific intertextual reference to Asian American film and video's institutional origins. Certainly, the attitude of the film and indeed, its central joke is a deep ambivalence about the representational ghetto of public television and its alternatives. Likewise, Grace Lee's *American Zombie* reflects ironically on the film-within-the-film's serious attempts at examining the plight of "Zombie Americans" as a way of parodying the history of Asian American film and video and, indeed, Lee's own claim to fame through films about the politics of identity. Ultimately, I conclude the book with these two films because of their intertextual reflections on the inextricability of the institution from Asian American film and video. It was the goal of Asian American film and video first to remedy negative images with positive images and then to make profitable mainstream feature films. Ultimately, the goal was to be recognized as a genre. That Asian American filmmakers continue to be concerned with identity in a so-called postracial society is significant to understanding that Asian American film and video has had powerful residual effects. That these films make institutionality central to their discourse on the historical and ongoing process of making Asian American film and video underlines the idea that it is the institution that binds together, creates tension within, and gives meaning to the genre.

# 1
## "Noble and Uplifting and Boring as Hell"

Asian American Film and Video, 1971-1982

In his book *Identities in Motion*, the film scholar Peter X Feng marks the unexpected box office popularity of *Chan Is Missing* (Wayne Wang, 1982) as the beginning of a recognizable genre: Asian American film and video. The film "announced that Asian Americans could be artists, could be commercial filmmakers, and could support Asian American filmmaking, as well as successfully market Asian American films to wider audiences."[1] What this particular origin point elides is the fact that *Chan Is Missing*, a neo-noir film nominally about a search for a missing Chinese immigrant and more symbolically about Chinese American identity, began in the world of independent Asian American film as an avant-garde, "dialectical" work, originally called *Fire Over Water*. Wang reedited that version, which bewildered audiences at small Asian American film festivals, into the realist, narrative fiction feature that heralded the birth of a genre.

Yet another moment poses as an origin point of Asian American film and video: its sponsorship by public television. At around the same time in the early 1980s, filmmakers and activists formed the National Asian American Telecommunications Association (NAATA), which, with major funding from the Corporation for Public Broadcasting, supported filmmakers, set up an educational distribution catalog, and most importantly, programmed documentaries to air on national public television.² Both *Chan Is Missing* and NAATA gave greater mainstream visibility to Asian American film and video and exposed the subsequent need to conform the creative, filmmaking enterprise to the function of narrating the politics of Asian American identity. Yet, prior to institutionalization by the CPB and the growing indie film movement, Asian American film and video was imbued with much greater formal diversity, especially in experimental works. This chapter analyzes the complex history that led up to these apocryphal origin points of the genre. In comparing the diverse films and discourse produced by the original Asian American film collectives, Visual Communications and Asian CineVision, it demonstrates that the fundamental debate of Asian American film and video was over its function as a primarily ideological cinema. Contrary to the received notion that its function has always been to narrate a politics of identity, discursive analysis of Asian American film and video in its formative years reveals that it was also strongly shaped by questions of form and aesthetics.

## Asian American Film and Video in Context

This chapter extrapolates from extant scholarship on Asian American film and video, which has focused on either the textual strategies or the production histories of the genre.³ Whereas Feng theorizes Asian American film narratives by looking at how "Asian American makers construct Asian American cinematic identity by locating their subjectivities in relation to dominant cinematic discourses," David E. James understands the first Asian American film collective, Visual Communications, in the larger history of underground, "popular" cinemas, in which Asian Americans created "narratives of their own history, and participate[d] in the production of their own self-consciousness and public identity."⁴ By contrast, this chapter examines Asian American cinematic self-representation and its cursory history through discursive context, specifically, how Asian American filmmakers and critics perceived its direction and the shaping of its underlying purpose. In particular, it attempts to reveal the important yet forgotten historical debate over the place of abstraction, experimentation, and the aesthetic in a putatively "political" minority moving image culture.

Crucial to this discursive debate is the role that material factors have played in determining the predominance of the "positive image" in Asian American film and video. In other words, before "Asian Americans could be artists," they had to exist as subjects. In 1978, through pressure from independent producers regarding the lack of representation, both by and about minorities in public television, as well as within the management ranks of public broadcasting stations across the country, the Corporation for Public Broadcasting commissioned a Task Force on Minorities in Public Broadcasting. Its report,

*A Formula for Change*, predictably found a systematic lack of representation both in minority content and in personnel in the PBS world and made recommendations, the most important being the creation and funding of the Minority Consortia—strategic, ethnicity-specific groups of producers and media activists advocating for Asian American, Native American, Chicano, and African American interests. Today, each of the members of the consortia exists to support minority interests in public broadcasting. Since 1980, NAATA, the Asian American consortium, has continued to serve the interests of CPB's minority task force report, particularly in its educational distribution and public broadcasting divisions, that is, primarily to increase the representation of Asian Americans in public broadcasting.

By funding the production of independent films through a competitive grant called the Media Fund, NAATA was instrumental in the encouragement and growth of Asian American films that follow the ideological social change mission that can be traced back to the first films made by Visual Communications in the early seventies. Although NAATA and PBS have provided crucial support for Asian American film and video, they also brought about one of its underlying problems. Because of the PBS-NAATA mandate that Asian American film and video be explicitly "Asian American"—that is, narrative fiction and nonfiction films about Asian American history, culture, and politics— they have imposed on it what Wendy Brown has termed a "politics of injury" that has become the hallmark of its output.[5] Therefore, the material history of a necessarily political "cinema of ethnic identity" is the precondition of Asian American film and video.

Despite these preconditions, a debate still ensued about the direction of Asian American film and video, especially regarding the importance of aesthetics. Specifically this disagreement was between the emphasis on ideological filmmaking and one that embraced overt formal experimentation. On the one hand, the Los Angeles collective Visual Communications pursued a greater social change orientation in filmmaking, establishing the genre by making the first Asian American films, *Manzanar* and *Wong Sinsaang*, both ideologically charged documentaries about, respectively, the Japanese American internment and a Chinese American laundry worker, in 1971. Although these documentaries could in some ways be described as experimental, particularly in their creative juxtaposition of sound and image as an expression of the importance of uncovering a lost history and of critiquing historically embedded racist assumptions, they are resolutely ideological in their single-minded pursuit of the "positive image" for and of Asian Americans.

On the other end of the spectrum, people associated with the New York media organization Asian CineVision in the late 1970s and the 1980s, including the critic Daryl Chin, were adamant about the possibility of a more purely aesthetic inclination in Asian American film and video, particularly in its connection to American and international avant-garde cinema. Chin, one of the founders of ACV's Asian American International Film Festival and a longtime, outspoken art critic, curator, performance artist, and New Yorker, championed experimental video art. Specifically, he encouraged artists like Janice Tanaka and Bruce and Norman Yonemoto, whose earlier works have not traditionally been associated with Asian American film and video because they question the terms of realism as a style and the realist text as an ideological strategy.[6] Tanaka's early video art—for example, *Superhuman Flights of Submoronic Fancies* (1982), *Ontogenesis* (1981), and *Beaver Valley* (1980)— lay at the extremes of the formally abstract, a kind of "structural video" that uses varying degrees of degraded video images layered together to achieve the look of painting with electronic signals. The Yonemotos' work, which is more superficially narrative, is highly self-reflexive, finding its source material in the larger-than-life realism found in the cinematic codes of American film melodramas of the 1950s. In their video melodrama *Green Card*, the Yonemotos use video to deconstruct spatial continuity, among other conventions of realist Hollywood cinema. The works of all of these filmmakers—Wong, Yonemoto, and Tanaka—exist in a nuanced continuum of identity politics and art that was part of a vigorous Asian American film and video culture of the 1970s and 1980s.

## Visual Communications

Visual Communications (VC) was formed in the early 1970s to instill an Asian American filmmaking practice with ideas about collectivity, social change, and, particularly, opposition to Hollywood cinema and the mainstream art world. Begun by UCLA students Duane Kubo, Robert Nakamura, Alan Ohashi, and Eddie Wong in the early 1970s, VC produced posters, leaflets, and photographs for groups such as the Japanese American Citizens League (JACL), the national cultural and political organization for Japanese Americans in Los Angeles. Incorporating as an independent nonprofit organization in 1971, VC became a full-service, grassroots organization that produced various media to promote awareness of issues in the various Asian-descent communities of Los Angeles. The majority of VC's founding members were students of UCLA's alternative film school, EthnoCommunications.

EthnoCommunications, which David E. James calls the "chief crucible" of ethnic cinema in the United States, emerged as a response to the Watts Rebellion in Los Angeles in 1965 and the civil rights movement and in "immediate response to student complaints about racial exclusivity" of the UCLA School of Film and Television, renowned for graduating white, male directors, some of whom have become a part of the Hollywood elite.[7] Addressing the issue of racial and ethnic marginalization in the film school, Ethno was organized by the four ethnic studies centers at UCLA and admitted and graduated some of the most important independent filmmakers of the 1970s and 1980s including Julie Dash, Charles Burnett, and Haile Gerima. For the Asian American student body of EthnoCommunications—in particular, Bob Nakamura and Eddie Wong—the goal was to find a new approach toward filmmaking that wasn't based on the notion of individual authorship and instead addressed the importance of community and group collaboration. In addition to making their thesis films at EthnoCommunications, Nakamura and Wong founded VC, based on some of the same ideology that forged Ethno, as an independent collective with the purpose of making social change films in and for the Asian American community. Through funding that they would receive from varied local and national sources, including the Comprehensive Employment and Training Act, VC made several documentaries with the goal of educating the local community, schools, and other audiences specifically about issues facing Asian Americans, such as racism, cultural preservation, economic hardship, and the possibility for social change.

The problems of racial and social inequality that VC was committed to help solve naturally inclined it to clash with prevailing notions of film as art in the early 1970s. As their overriding goal was social change, "VC's films were almost all documentaries, cheaply made and screened in schools and other community centers, and the filmmakers understood their function in terms of their community origin and relevance."[8] As James correctly concludes, VC was ultimately engaged in an ideological, anticapitalist, populist worker's cinema, like other social change film movements in history. VC's "anti-art" stance was practiced through its ideological intervention in conventional notions of commercial and art cinema, especially that of authorship. Nakamura found that "on a larger scale ... it's not that we rejected art, but we really felt, at least some of us, I know Eddie, and we had long talks or discussions sometimes about art and being a very Eurocentric part of a system of elitism and very irrelevant to community and to what we were. I don't want to say we were philistines, but in our examination that art wasn't very relevant to what we were about, what our communities were about."[9] Though Nakamura resisted the artistic enterprise as the main purpose of Asian American filmmaking, VC's Project 1 and Project 2, otherwise known as *Manzanar* and *Wong Sinsaang*, exhibit an interest in formal experimentation, particularly as they straddle the overlapping distinction between an expository documentary, which "frequently builds a sense of dramatic involvement around the need for a solution,"[10] and an "essay film," which Jonas Mekas, in his review of the new nonfiction cinema of the 1960s, describes thusly:

> It tries new steps. It is not afraid to look ugly. It dares turn its back to art. There is not a single "composed" frame anywhere within it. No "nice" stills to put on your wall. No editing of ideas. Everything comes from the subject matter. The

FIG. 1 Visual Communications members (*left to right*) Bob Nakamura, Lawson Inada, Alan Kondo, Duane Kubo, and Eddie Wong preparing to shoot a scene from the VC film *I Told You So* (1973). (Courtesy of Visual Communications.)

truth is what matters. The new film-maker is a child of his times: He has had enough of prefabrication, false intelligence. Even the mistakes, the out-of-focus shots, the shaky shots, the unsure steps, the hesitant movements, the overexposed and underexposed bits are part of the vocabulary. The doors to the spontaneous are opening; the foul air of stale and respectable professionalism is oozing out.[11]

Both *Manzanar* and *Wong Sinsaang* are, according to James, "student films, technically and formally rudimentary,"[12] but they make "truth what matters" with nonsynchronous, autobiographical voiceovers that give access to a history and a representation that had hitherto been invisible—the internment and the Asian American immigrant experience. However, I would argue that regardless of what one finds in their aesthetic manipulation of sound and image, the two films are primarily concerned with the underlying ideological project of resisting racist imagery and historical marginalization. As expository documentaries, first and foremost, the two films "take shape around the solution to a problem or puzzle: . . . tracing the history of an event or the biography of a person."[13] In this case, the early films of VC sought a solution to the problem of racism, and their primary strategy was to provide the content for the exploration and experience of Asian American identity in the moving image.

## *Manzanar* (1971)

*Manzanar* opens with present-day, 16mm, color footage of the former site of the Manzanar Relocation Center in the Owens Valley desert of southeastern California, where Nakamura was imprisoned, at the age of six, with his family and where he returns to film what remains. Opening on an image of the white stone pillar monument that commemorates the camps at Manzanar, the footage goes on to reveal an innocuous scene of nature—fields of desert flora surrounded by dark, rugged mountains and no trace of current human habitation. The first sign of life is a shot of a line of barbed wire that comes into sharp focus against tumbleweeds. Also abandoned in this location are signs of a long-lost domestic life: archaeological remnants such as shards of pottery, rusted car parts, and building foundations, which contrast with the harshness of the environment. Then, cut in with the forlorn shots of mountains and grass of present-day Manzanar are archival images of newspaper headlines and black-and-white photographs of events leading up to and during the internment, images of adults and children standing or sitting outside with their belongings, which are shown in increasingly rapid sequence to match the austere musical score of traditional Japanese flute. Then, over a long montage of still images, which occupies most of the film, a first-person voiceover by Nakamura narrates the memory of first learning what forced relocation meant, and leaving his home for Manzanar as a six-year-old, saying, "I really can't remember anything—just vague impressions, feelings, smells, and sounds." Deceptively simple, *Manzanar* directly and guilelessly "summon[s] an elegiac wistfulness to hallow the historical memory that the Japanese American community shares but had so long repressed."[14]

The central concern of the film is to offer an archive of internment images, to memorialize what has hitherto been lost. However, the use of contrapuntal sound adds an important ideological dimension that is the hallmark of VC's repositioning of history. The long shots of dark mountains coupled with close-ups of desert flora suggest the space of an American Western, while the stark flute music is an obvious musical counterpoint that unobtrusively yet abstractly sets the mood for the central montage of black-and-white still images of and around the internment camp. The black-and-white still images contrast with the opening color sequence, as clear indicators of the past. They provide information about the racist sentiments of that past through photographs of signs that read, for example, "Japs Don't Let the Sun Set on You Here, Keep Moving." These photographs reveal not that they can necessarily ever fully represent what happened, but that they are what ultimately permits memorialization, unlike the location itself and unlike Namakura's own first-person narration, which he admits himself in the film as being unreliable and "vague."

"Noble and Uplifting and Boring as Hell" • 19

FIG. 2  Monument at Manzanar, from *Manzanar* (Robert Nakamura, 1972). (Courtesy of Visual Communications.)

*Manzanar* was less an effort to master the form of cinema than an attempt to use cinema as a device of preservation and documentation, with a decidedly ideological purpose: to redress the internment within the larger project of fighting racism. Since one of the most salient features of the Japanese American internment was the lack of photographic and cinematographic documentation of its occurrence, due in large part to the US government's restrictions on photographic documentation of what was later deemed to be an illegal incarceration.[15] Visual Communications' earliest goal was to address the public silence around the internment by building an archive of images, both still and moving. It collected those images for one of the first photographic exhibits of the internment, called the Camp Cubes Photo Display, which was the first, in the late 1960s, to publicly acknowledge the forced incarceration through visual documentation. Given VC's inclination toward the basic need for public commemoration of a collective trauma as part of the larger project of recognizing the history and community of Asian Americans, it seems only natural that an exhibition of still photographs (in a private living room, no less) would also be VC's first public event as a collective.

As the Camp Cubes Photo Display represents one of the first of such public exhibitions showing evidence of the Japanese American internment, it follows that *Manzanar* was largely an extension of the effort to provide the materiality of images in the public sphere, especially after decades of repression by both the government and in the Japanese American community. The straightforward documentary style of *Manzanar* takes into consideration the film as an extension of VC's larger archival impulse regarding the internment and by extension, racial injustice at large. Visual Communications' continued memorialization of the internment is evident in the larger purpose of this archive. In fact, several of VC's subsequent films—*Wataridori: Birds of Passage* (1974), *Hito Hata: Raise the Banner* (1980), and Nakamura's later documentaries such as *Something Strong Within* (1994) and *Toyo Miyatake: Infinite Shades of Gray* (2001)—dealt with different facets of the internment. Certainly, there was less emphasis on either personal reflection or formal cinematic rigor and more emphasis on collective remembrance. Nakamura recalls:

> We put together this first exhibit and it was amazing. Actually we ended up making three of them, which traveled around, but the first one, the unveiling of it—it was amazing, the people's reaction. You see, you have to imagine there's no such thing as Asian American studies, Asian Americans; no one talked about the camps at all. We're talking about the late fifties, early sixties. So it was probably one of the first, at least in Southern California—well, I'm sure all over—of photos of camps. And I could really see how both Japanese Americans and other people were really moved by that.[16]

Nakamura and Visual Communications helped usher the Camp Cubes Photo Display to three other venues in the late 1960s and early 1970s, to all different chapters of the JACL, nationwide. It is apparent that from early on, the specificity of the public sphere is important to the work of VC. That VC's use of the camera image as the vehicle for breaking public silence around the internment speaks to the importance of reevaluating Asian American film history, not as a linear progression of technical competence, but one with specific ideological purpose at various points in time. Visual Communications' focus on the camera image privileged not necessarily the form of the still-versus-moving image but the importance of commemoration itself. It is this larger purpose of public memory and acknowledgment of racial injustice that contextualizes *Manzanar* and by extension, the prevalence of the historical documentary genre in early Asian American film and video.

## *Wong Sinsaang* (1971)

At roughly the same time that Nakamura was completing *Manzanar* at UCLA, his fellow VC founder Eddie Wong was finishing *Wong Sinsaang*,[17] a nonfiction essay film about the filmmaker's father, an aging Chinese man who runs a laundry in Hollywood, California. Shot in black and white with a soft jazz guitar score, the film promises a typical Chinatown tourists' view as

FIG. 3 Eddie Wong's father, Frank Wong, in his family's laundry business, from *Wong Sinsaang* (Eddie Wong, 1972). (Courtesy of Visual Communications.)

the opening shots reveal a large vertical street sign that reads "Chinese Laundry," followed by a shot of the subject sitting inside his laundry, smoking a cigarette and reading the paper, his back to the window, which reads "Frank Wong Laundry and Dry Cleaners." Then, the images change to shots of the machines that make up the work of the laundry itself, its monotony and the repetitive nature of the work followed by a sequence in which Frank Wong handles monetary transactions with various white customers.

*Wong Sinsaang*'s progressively disjointed use of sound and image belies the placid Chinatown tourists' view of its exposition. The film's overall reflexivity is expressed through this central contrast: documentary footage of the director's father working in a laundry, coupled with a soundtrack that includes Eddie's voice offering critiques of capitalism's collusion with racism. Later, the same looped, banally polite exchange between Wong and the customers, which at first appears to be synch sound, is played repeatedly over different shots, emphasizing the dulling effect of being a cog in a racist, capitalist culture. These sequences set up the film impressionistically, using the juxtaposition of image and sound to demonstrate the stultifying anonymity of trying to make a living in a capitalist economy that offers limited advantages to Asian Americans. Through the juxtaposition of footage of Wong running his business and voice-overs by the filmmaker and comments made by customers, the film offers a deconstruction of the stereotype of the Chinese laundryman. The film then contrasts this caricature with images of Wong's art, which include painting, poetry, and martial arts, revealing a dimension beyond his public life.

Upon closer examination, *Wong Sinsaang*'s visual/aural dialectic, which argues for the collusive relationship between racism and capitalism, belies the simplistic idea that VC documentaries were uninterested in form. However, it is specifically *Wong Sinsaang*'s critique of the content of racist imagery—that is, tourists' views of Chinatown that have historically "objectified and commodified the urban 'Other'"[18]—that roots the film in the tradition of ideological Asian American film and video. As in Nakamura's decrying of "art for art's sake," Eddie Wong's relatively experimental film is undeniably "not art," but a film that puts form in the service of its mission. For some, the formal parameters of the VC documentary were simply not enough to keep pace with global movements in experimental cinema. It is the quietness of *Wong Sinsaang*'s formal experimentation and its more overt ideological message that, in fact, detractors called "traditional and tentative."[19]

## Collective Authorship

Another important aspect of VC's social ideology of filmmaking was an emphasis on collective authorship and rejection of what Michel Foucault has termed the "author function," an illusory concept that obfuscates and mystifies the production of texts by a lone author. Though it is difficult to deny the technical authorship of *Manzanar* and *Wong Sinsaang* due to a number of factors, including that these films were both UCLA thesis projects, the earliest Asian American films were produced in a matrix of collectivity that eschewed the egoistic cult of the author encouraged by Hollywood and the burgeoning institution of academic film studies, which encouraged the bourgeois, capitalist notion of lone authorship. By contrast, VC's films represent what I call Asian American film's institutional authorship period, including several works that epitomized VC's anticapitalist, communal perspective: *Wataridori: Birds of Passage*, *Cruisin' J-Town*, and *City, City*.

Following *Manzanar* and *Wong Sinsaang*, Visual Communications production output in the mid seventies developed more fully the idea of collectivity through the realization of a model of communal filmmaking that purposefully replaced the function of the individual author with that of institutional authorship. As a full-fledged nonprofit film production company, Visual Communications was "community based," as Nakamura recalls. "We worked as a collective. That's why you won't see in a lot of the early films, you won't see credit lines except for people who weren't in VC. You won't see directed by or anything, so that was part of our collective thing."[20] Two aspects of what Nakamura expresses as a kind of gradual turning point for VC seem to illustrate the importance of the experimental period of institutional authorship.

One is the practice of leaving out directorial credit to an individual. In most films made during VC's collective authorship period, credit is given equally to everyone who worked on the film on a frame listing in no particular order the members of the collective, as in the credits for *Cruisin' J-Town*. In another example, in films such like *Wataridori*, VC's copyright trademark, which says simply, "A Visual Communications Production," appears at the end of the film. Therefore, the films themselves, as well as the way they were made, with the self-conscious intent at collectivity, became a core element of operations at Visual Communications. Later films like *City, City* also offer evidence of a much more focused formal preoccupation with the relationship between Asian American identity and multiculturalism, VC's role as media educator, and the relationship between race and labor.

In some ways, it is possible to see *Wataridori* as a corollary to *Manzanar* for its inverse relationship to the representation of the internment. Both are films about the Japanese American experience, yet they both have different attitudes about the role of the internment in Japanese American experience. This can be discerned mainly as a shift from that of an emphasis on a first-person narrative of the internment to that of a focus on the history of Japanese American laborers. This shift is significant in that it shows how institutional authorship, with its suggestion of collective memory and creation, had become important to the films being made at VC.

*Wataridori: Birds of Passage* (1974) documents aging Japanese American immigrant laborers who came to the West Coast of the United States to make better lives. The film's subjects are issei, or first-generation immigrants, who worked their entire lives in agriculture as sharecroppers and farmers or as commercial fishermen. One way in which *Wataridori* reflects a revision of *Manzanar* is in its rearrangement of the iconic status of the internment within the film. In *Manzanar*, the presence of the internment, the idea of imprisonment, of loss, permeates the entire film and fills every frame, while paradoxically this loss is unable to be fully represented. In *Wataridori*, reference to the internment appears toward the end of the film, as only an incidental yet key experience in the lives of the film's subjects. Specifically, the monument to the internment at Manzanar, a simple, white stone icon inscribed with Japanese script commemorating the events as well as those that died there, is the most striking and central image of the film. As *Manzanar*'s only reference point, besides the broken dishes and other remnants that survive the harsh landscape as a memorial to the internment, the monument is obsessively represented in the earlier film. In *Wataridori*, the same monument is shown, but only in the last segment of the film as a silent reminder of the internment, a mere symbol. This reference to the internment acts as the film's unconscious but it does not permeate the film in the way that it does in *Manzanar*. In the same way that the crisis of representation is a core issue of the internment documentary, the subtlety with which the monument to the internment appears toward the end of *Wataridori* allows it, paradoxically, to be represented because of the way it is rhetorically placed as the capstone to the narrative of struggle that precede it.

Another way in which *Wataridori* revises *Manzanar* is its shift in narrative perspective from that of an individual voice to a collective one. As *Manzanar* anchors its representation of the internment through the personal reflection of the filmmaker, *Wataridori* narrates the Japanese American experience as collective. Through its implicit focus on the history of labor, *Wataridori* reflects more of a literally socialist project on the part of VC, but it also reproduces the focus on collectivity and the representation of communities as vital to the project of Asian American communal film production. For example, the lives depicted in the documentary are explicitly shaped by their work. The opening shot of *Wataridori* presents one of the characters fishing in the ocean as a narrator talks of his life as a fisherman. The documentary takes place in the present, showing the lives of retired and semiretired Japanese Americans whose lives as agricultural laborers are presented to us in voice-over narration and aged photographs of various periods in their lives. The shift in tone, authorship, and ideological style from *Manzanar* to *Wataridori* reflects a different understanding about the relative importance of the Japanese American internment, the representation of which not only is difficult for material and psychological reasons but also facilitates more easily the kind of interiorized, personal reflection celebrated in the postmodern works of Tajiri, Tanaka, Yasui, and the like, or the sansei generation of filmmakers. The focus on labor history in *Wataridori* underscores the role of work as the significant theme that links the documentary's subjects and denotes a shift in priority in Visual Communications' oeuvre from that of the personal to the communal, both in subject matter and approach. The ideological shift from *Manzanar* to *Wataridori* reveals VC's understanding of the role of authorship as a political responsibility and the realization of collectivity as a necessary practice of social change documentary.

In the same way that *Wataridori* reflects on the history of labor as a function of its own self-consciousness about the communal work of filmmaking, *Cruisin' J-Town*, in particular, articulates a clear disavowal with the idea of individual authorship as a means of artistic expression. *Cruisin' J-Town* evinces a greater commitment toward communal authorship, particularly in the way it uses the collaborative metaphor of music, the role of the artist in community, and its ideological overtures toward the multicultural rather than an emphasis on national cultural identity.

Ostensibly a documentary about the Japanese American fusion jazz band Hiroshima, *Cruisin' J-Town* uses a rhetorical structure in order to underscore the radical social and political potential of art making. The film presents Hiroshima's music as a form that is essentially dialectical—the combination of East

Asian musical forms with the American idiom of jazz to create a utopian multicultural admixture that resonates with yet other ethnic groups. On the surface, the film is a short biographical sketch of Hiroshima, profiling each member and their views on their identities as musicians and Asian Americans. However, the documentary forwards an ideology of multiculturalism that reflects VC's growing commitment to institutional authorship. First, the idea of a musical group and its resistance to sole authorship is an obvious metaphor in the film. The film opens on the band in rehearsal and, like *Wataridori*, presents short interviews with each member of the group in a seemingly nonhierarchical fashion. Each interview uses the convention of straight interview, voice-over, and images of representative aspects of each interviewee, such as showing interior shots of the community bookstore run by one of Hiroshima's members as he talks about the importance of community involvement and heritage for ethnic identity. Although many have considered the conventional documentary techniques used by VC during this period as somewhat aesthetically banal, VC's purposefully didactic use of film as the propaganda for collectivity and community, particularly seen in context with prevailing mainstream exaltation of authorship, *Cruisin' J-Town*'s dialectical structure, collective authorship, and political message reveals its importance in the historical trajectory of Asian American film and video. The interviews, including the one in which the female member of the band, who plays the koto, a Japanese instrument, are extremely conventional, yet the ideas that are subtly interwoven throughout—that the members of the band create art out of a desire to use it as a political tool—as well as the film's representation of artists that work in a marginalized, experimental format—mirror VC's own narrative. The deliberate focus on the band's collectivity through scenes of building, rehearsing, and performing, and their portrayal as struggling artists who find their main method of survival through the sharing of resources, reflects Visual Communications own ideas about art and community and in particular, their experiment in collectivity and institutional authorship.

*Cruisin' J-Town* not only explores the collaborative nature of music and especially improvisation but also addresses the production of music and art in general as central to the revolutionary impulse of Visual Communications. In many ways, the subject of *Cruisin' J-Town* is a mirror image of Visual Communications as a group devoted to using the moving image for similar purposes. Like *Wataridori*, the idea of labor is once again brought up. The members of Hiroshima are represented as choosing a deliberately anticapitalist lifestyle in order to realize the progressive vision of collectivity.

Institutional, collective authorship as exemplified by Visual Communications is a historical phenomenon that has largely disappeared since the appearance of national venues like public television and the professionalization of independent film. The films made under the Emergency School Aid Act in

1975, a now discontinued grant that Visual Communications used to create educational videos and other media on multiculturalism, represent the acme of VC's commitment to institutional authorship that was evident in both content and form. For example, the abstract *City, City*, a film that can only be described as a psychedelic city film, represents the quotidian variety offered by Los Angeles through a kaleidoscopic series of shots of the city and its people at night and during the day. Nearly dialogueless but full of vibrant images that suggest, as a kind of contemporary urban worker's film, connectivity among all of LA's inhabitants, *City, City* articulates an even deeper commitment to communal authorship through its intimation of multicultural variety and harmony.[21]

As David James points out in "Popular Cinemas in Los Angeles," Visual Communications' period of collective filmmaking ended with an attempt to make a feature-length film narrating the parallel storylines of a slowly gentrifying contemporary Japanese American neighborhood, Little Tokyo, with the experiences of the first Japanese immigrant laborers at the turn of the century. Starring the Japanese character actor Mako, *Hito Hata: Raise the Banner* effectively bankrupted Visual Communications.[22] The experiment of institutional authorship ended with the production of *Hito Hata* due, ironically, to the organization's attempt at molding itself to mainstream notions of success—namely, feature filmmaking, a format that epitomizes Hollywood and commercial theatrical distribution.

## New York in the Seventies: Asian CineVision and Film Form

At the same time that Visual Communications was developing its ideology of social change cinema, New York's Asian CineVision (ACV) was also initiating similar programs to support and educate Asian American communities through media. Founded in 1976, ACV was an offshoot of Basement Workshop, a grassroots collective of artists and activists that was, much like Visual Communications, devoted to aiding the Asian American community through education, social services, and cultural production. In the same way that EthnoCommunications and the Japanese American Citizenship League provided the generative material in personnel and ideology for VC, Basement Workshop provided the initial framework for ACV. Sharing the pursuit of an anticapitalist, antiracist, and Third Worldist perspective of the Asian American movement, ACV began providing New York City Asian American communities with film and video services. The most important of these services was Chinatown Community Television (CCTV), which helped Chinatown residents address issues of discrimination through the nation's first

Chinese-language news programming on cable access television. In addition to community access television, ACV was crucial in the development of arts criticism through the publications *Bridge* (an Asian American arts journal that ACV took over in 1981) and *CineVue* (its quarterly journal), as well as in the creation of Asian American film culture through the Asian American International Film Festival (AAIFF), the first of its kind, in 1978.

In particular, the writings of the film critic and AAIFF programmer Daryl Chin distinguished ACV from VC in its focus on the importance of aesthetic and form over social change in cultural production. About the time that VC gained renown for its production of social change documentaries, ACV followed a completely different direction, questioning the very premise of the social change ideology in Asian American filmmaking. Chin recalls:

> At the time, I was one of the four regular film reviewers (the others being Jonas Mekas and Tom Allen, who were also the film editors, and Amy Taubin) for *The Soho Weekly News*. Obviously, I was the only Asian American in New York City who was employed as a writer on film. (Have there been any others since that time? There have been people who free-lance on occasion, but is there anyone who is employed regularly?) No, I did not write about Asian American films, or even Asian films: my "specialty" (such as it was) happened to be avantgarde and independent films.[23]

The importance of Chin's role as critic in early Asian American film and video was his voice of dissent, particularly against the ideological nature of many Asian American films that emerged in the 1970s and 1980s that he disparagingly called "noble and uplifting and boring as hell."[24] Chin's film festival program notes contain an impassioned plea to push the aesthetic boundaries of film, which was, importantly, coupled with a strong belief that social change filmmaking was a kind of death to the creative enterprise. Significantly, he asked not just what is a minority moving-image movement, but how could it be realized without recourse to the obligation of social change or as a kind of ideological exercise devoid of artistic inspiration.

Taking place over three days in February 1978 at the Henry Street Arts for Living Center on the Lower East Side of Manhattan, the first AAIFF was unique in its eclectic mix of international, local, avant-garde, documentary, and fiction short films. What is noticeable is that the films were programmed according to formal similarities rather than content. The first program, dubbed "Marathon Film Festival," showed over thirty films, mostly shorts, and lasted five and a half hours. The Marathon Film program showcased everything from Visual Communications' *Wong Sinsaang, Cruisin' J-Town,* and *I Told You So* to Japanese experimental filmmaker Taka Iimura's *Film Strips Number 2*. AAIFF's logic of eclecticism and formal diversity shows signs of an interest in inclusion of both ideological film and the avant-garde as important components of Asian American film and video.

Daryl Chin's first essay for the AAIFF contextualizes a widely disparate group of Asian American films, mostly documentaries and short subjects, with references to academic film criticism and history. While there are apparent disjunctures in this attempt, the overall goal seems to be an intention to maintain formal rigor as the festival's logic. Chin's opening remarks indicate a willingness for Asian American film and video to depart from the adamant belief that, according to Nakamura, "art wasn't very relevant to what we were about, what our communities were about." Chin notes: "In this, the first Asian-American Film Festival to be held on the East Coast, the attempt was to ascertain the perameters [sic] of that appellation. For the members of the committee, the questions involved in the creation of this festival included: what is meant by the Asian-American film? Is there a uniquely Asian-American expression? If so, what are the features of that expression?"[25]

Interestingly, Chin's answer to this question seems to lie not in issues of identity inherent to VC's position on Asian American film but in the importance of cinematic form, with a preference for East Asian and European avant-garde filmmaking. For example, Chin prefaces the films with an obvious preference and understanding of the rigor of formal cinema. He begins his overview of the films with reviews of three Japanese avant-garde films featured at the festival, Taka Iimura's *Film Strips, Number 2* (1969), in which news footage of the war in Vietnam "is subjected to effects of speeding up, slowing-down, flickering in order to test the footage at the very edge of perceptibility. The process of abstraction is a reminder of the potential of distortion in any image"; Nobuhiro Kawanaka's *Feedback* (1973), which "revels in a developmental consideration of the fact of cinematic projection"; and Toshi Matsumoto's *Atman* (1975), which "employs a staccato in-and-out zoom to create, to distort, and to negate the landscape in which sits a ritualized figure."

While the relationship of the international avant-garde and Asian American film and video is not immediately clear, Chin's discourse provides a wildly divergent view from prevailing historical thoughts on an Asian American cinema of social change. For example, Chin connects experimental Asian American films with larger tendencies in structural film, mentioning the important contributions of filmmakers such as Paul Sharits, Ernie Gehr, Hollis Frampton, and George Landow, and going so far as to mention their European counterparts, Werner Nekes and Klaus Wynborny, and British filmmakers Malcolm LeGrice and Peter Gidal. Chin's "East Coast" vision of Asian American film and video reveals a corrective to the notion that there was a united effort to create an Asian American film and video of social change. In fact, his perspective is the complete opposite of VC's opposition to "art . . . being a very Eurocentric part of a system of elitism and very irrelevant to community and to what we were."²⁶ Chin goes so far as to compare the work of Wayne Wang to the work of Jean-Luc Godard, Straub/Huillet, and Dusan Makavejev. Their films are described as "straddling the split between commercial narrative and independent abstraction [and they] . . . have provoked an awareness of illusionism through narrative means," in the same way that an early film by Wayne Wang, *New Relationships* (1977), does: "Wayne Wang attempts to consider the stereotypical nature of Asian-American identity in the minority status: how that identity is perceived 'out there,' how that perception oppresses selfimage. *New Relationships* attempts to correlate this consideration with a modernist narrative rhetoric."²⁷

Ultimately, Chin's goal in highlighting traces of formal rigor is, in many ways, prescriptive. Chin's exuberant exhortation of the vitality of form in any cinematic enterprise pushes Asian American film beyond the ideological task of "resisting negative images." In the same breath, Chin relegates Visual Communications' *Wong Sinsaang* to a somewhat lower status than Wang's "modernist narrative rhetoric," calling it a film that addresses the same issues as *New Relationships*, but in "a more traditional and tentative manner."²⁸ Chin's opinion of works that don't push the formal envelope is that they are missing something. For example, in summarizing a list of short films that "provoke a meditative consideration" of "stereotypes of Asian-American consciousness," he concludes, "what sets these films apart from, say, Iimura's work is their adherence to a sense of illusionist continuity." Chin's understanding of the line that separates the Japanese avant-garde films from Asian American films is limited by his insistence on strict adherence to an evaluation of form. His sense of "illusionist continuity" is interesting in that it is in the context of his adulation of structural cinema, which breaks down "illusion," and yet from VC's perspective, "illusion" would be the ideological problem of negative stereotypes and marginalization of Asian Americans in mainstream Hollywood cinema.

### *Fire Over Water*: The "Ur–*Chan Is Missing*"

Chin's palpable disappointment in the conservative direction of Asian American film and video can be summed up in a history-making event that began and ended at the AAIFF, one of the only exhibitions of Wayne Wang's highly experimental film *Fire Over Water*, better known as the precursor to *Chan Is Missing* (1982). Made during a time when feature independent filmmaking and the visibility of Asian American documentaries on PBS were on the rise, *Fire Over Water* strongly challenged this tendency, but not without confusing champions of the mainstream. The reception of *Fire Over Water* at the 1981 Asian American film festival reveals it to be nothing like the coherent narrative feature film that resulted—*Chan Is Missing*. The film is introduced with a sense of its unconventionality:

Wayne Wang's *Fire Over Water*, another Asian-America feature film from the West Coast, is an intensely personal work. It is remarkably ambitious: an attempt to create a narrative in a popular medium (in this case, a murder mystery) while simultaneously criticizing the codes and the conventions of the form. An unusual example of cinematic experimentation, *Fire Over Water* nevertheless retains elements which provide an intriguing narrative structure.[29]

Many Asian American film histories claim *Chan Is Missing* to have been an important move forward in the genre's teleological trajectory toward feature narrative filmmaking. However, the unconventional form of *Fire Over Water*, which no longer exists and which is known as the "director's cut" of *Chan Is Missing*, shows evidence of the important formative role of abstraction in early Asian American film and video. Members of the Asian American media community clearly recall the challenging nature of the earlier film:

> I met Wayne Wang who was trying to finish a film to be titled *Fire Over Water*. His height made an immediate impression, and his infectious laugh and sense of humor cemented it. He talked about the film as being a kind of informal deconstruction of Soviet-style montage theory with improvised dialogue with various Chinatown types. I didn't quite follow this, but I recall that the Chinese characters for "fire" and "water" played the role of thesis and antithesis that were to be resolved in new meaning.[30]

As it has been erased from history as far as we know, it is difficult to imagine what this film was really like, but unlike its descendent, *Chan Is Missing*, *Fire Over Water* was clearly attempting to use formal abstraction, not narrative continuity, as a strategy to express a politicized Asian American identity. In an interview in the 1981 AAIFF program, the film is described as being "divided into four sections" in which the first section contains still images; the second, "scenes with movement"; the third a synthesis of parts one and two; and the fourth section "which carries the bulk of the narrative, explores the relationship between image, ideas, and sound."[31] Clearly, it is a film that is strikingly abstract and Wang defends his first cut as such, saying, "Some people don't get the point. And others who have seen the film even think it's racist. So I really don't think we've succeeded in showing how film syntax can make you see things a certain way."[32] In the nascent art-house, independent feature film economy, the thought of a "dialectical," abstract cinema was an idea that had come too late. Consequently *Fire Over Water* was not well received or, at best, met with enthusiastic bewilderment.

*Chan Is Missing* was important to the Asian American community as well as to the burgeoning independent film scene in that it became a bridge between Asian American media arts and the larger critical and popular establishment of American cinema.[33] It could be said that Wang's choice to move forward in the direction of conventional narrative form was fundamental to the institutional impulse of Asian American film and video over the next decade to make more conventional narrative films. However, only in retrospect, after considering the film's commercial success and the launching of Wayne Wang's "non–Asian American" career in Hollywood does this make a seamless history.[34] The discourse of Asian American film and video before 1980 shows that what was sacrificed was the spirit of experimentation that arose in reaction to the prevailing dogma of social change in Asian American film and video.

The early 1980s saw a great shift in Asian American film and video with the release of *Chan Is Missing*, as well as Visual Communications' attempt at independent feature filmmaking, *Hito Hata: Raise the Banner*. An uncommercial, nonprofit narrative feature film, *Hito Hata* revisited many of the themes of VC's commitment to social change, telling a sweeping multigenerational saga of Japanese Americans victimized by abusive labor laws, illegal relocation, and the erosion of ethnic communities by gentrification.[35] In the ten-year anniversary program of the AAIFF, Chin discusses the difficulty and irreconcilability of Asian American film and video in its early years, comparing two, widely divergent films that would forever mark the character of the genre:

> In the 1981 festival, two Asian American features were programmed. One was *Hito Hata: Raise the Banner*, produced by the Visual Communications group in Los Angeles, and it's very much a "group" project: it's worthy and noble and uplifting and boring as hell. It doesn't have a whiff of "personality" or of genuine artistic vision. The other was Wayne Wang's *Fire Over Water*, which was to have been shown in a rough cut.... Some of us were (again) excited by the movie, but a lot of people involved with the festival hated it. We are talking pure hatred. Well, imagine their surprise when, the following year, Wayne Wang reedited the movie, made the structure far less complicated, toned down a lot of the "new talkie" audio-visual dissociation, synched it up and showed it straight and came out with *Chan Is Missing*.... Here, all along these Asian American media activists thought that something like *Hito Hata* was going to be the Asian American "breakthrough," and it wasn't, it was that damned quirky oddball personal experimental *Chan Is Missing*. Put that in your peace pipe and smoke it![36]

Chin clearly makes a distinction between two tendencies in Asian American film, the "noble and uplifting" text of social change, and the experimental, would-be sleeper hit. Not only was Chin disturbed by the prevalence of social change films in Asian American film and video, he understood how realistically problematic this formulaic attitude toward filmmaking could be. It is telling that the coincidence of *Fire Over Water* and VC's last film, *Hito Hata*, took place at the 1981 ACV film festival. Both films were feature-length Asian

American films that struggled with articulating knowledge about Asian American identity, but in totally different ways. Both films were as ambitious as they were flawed but in opposite ways.

*Fire Over Water*'s transformation from that of hated and misunderstood experimental film to that of successful art-house narrative feature marks a symbolic end to the wider use of formal experimentation in the debate over Asian American film and video. After the negative reception of *Fire*, Wong reedited the film to end up with *Chan Is Missing*, now a "comedy thriller," which screened at the 1982 AAIFF. Thus, the normative route to feature independent filmmaking soon became the goal of many Asian American independent filmmakers.

Although social change films were important in putting Asian American film and video on the map, the dogmatic and narrow adherence to this philosophy meant death to the art. That *Hito Hata* eventually "came close to destroying VC," reflected the problem of feature narrative filmmaking as social change enterprise. Furthermore, it is interesting that Chin compares *Hito Hata* and its double, *Chan Is Missing*, because as David James rightly claims, the latter film "marked the beginning of the shift in emphasis in Asian American filmmaking from community-based documentaries to crossover independent feature production."[37] But, as Chin's notes show, behind this well-documented linear shift from community to individual production style was a jettisoning of abstraction as the preferred mode of oppositionality in Asian American filmmaking. Importantly, the historical progression of communal social change filmmaking to commercial independent feature filmmaking heralded the disappearance of formal experimentation characterized by the exhibition of the highly experimental *Fire Over Water* and the avant-garde programming emphasis of the AAIFF and AAIVF in its early years. Chin's memoir and his role in shaping the unique New York perspective of Asian American film and video reveal another layer to its history in very instructive ways.

## Putting the "Video" in Asian American Film and Video

The distaste expressed by Daryl Chin's "noble and uplifting and boring as hell" quote about Asian American film and video resulted in the establishment of a separate video festival, the Asian American International Video Festival (AAIVF) in the early 1980s. The program of the first annual festival in 1982 seems to rectify Chin's barely concealed unease with the emergent Asian American film and video's almost exclusive penchant for the "positive image" to the exclusion of formal exploration. While including the mainstay of the straight documentary in the program, the AAIVF made sure to make connections between Asian American video artists and East Asian artists such as Nam June Paik and Taka Iimura. Chin's adulation of Paik and enthusiastic embrace of the most famous video artist in the world is reflected in an insert of the program entitled "Video Art Pioneers," where Chin exults, "few people realize the degree of impact that Asian artists have had on video as an art form." In some ways, the rise of portable video technology in the 1970s allowed for a new genre of "guerilla video," narrative documentary reportage; it also opened up a new field of artistic experimentation. Paik's notoriety as the "father of video art" and his Korean heritage made him, in the eyes of Chin, a natural boon for Asian American film and video, a fact that encouraged a return to rigorous modernist standards of form in the genre. In the early eighties, video art presented, on the one hand, "the problem of how to discuss the properties of video [that] is fundamentally tied to video's relationship to modernism, a relationship complicated by video's emergence in modernism's final stages."[38] Video's paradoxical stance as a medium intimately aligned with, as well as revolting against, the values of television, the ultimate postmodern medium, also complicated the notion of video as an "electronic language" based on its own specific formal properties. This is especially evident in examples from Asian American video art, itself a marginalized form.

The experimental video artists Bruce and Norman Yonemoto and Janice Tanaka were prominently represented in the AAIVF and epitomize ACV's interest in formal abstraction and experimentation against the dominance of the realism of social change filmmaking. Contemporaries of Wayne Wang, they operated in the shadow of the flourishing of Asian American documentary filmmaking via NAATA. The work of the Yonemotos and Tanaka, particularly their experimental work from the 1980s, has been marginalized in scholarship on Asian American film and video. Much of the omission of their earlier work is due to the privileging of documentary and narrative feature modes that have overshadowed historical conceptions of the genre in the 1980s. Although experimental video became much more prominent in the 1990s, Tanaka and the Yonemotos serve as the vanguard and model for a diverse Asian American film and video. Their work, particularly the selections showcased at ACV's video festival, is significant in its divergence from the social change documentary but also, specifically, in its emphasis on formal play, irony, pastiche, and other postmodern textual strategies that destabilized the problem of the "noble and uplifting" text of Asian American film and video. Tanaka and the Yonemotos epitomize the problem of form and the aesthetic in minority media movements because their work falls into the world of experimental media and also deals to some degree with the politics of race and identity. Because of the medium and formal specificity of their work, it has, on the one hand, been somewhat marginalized by Asian American film and video history but, on the other hand, been much more visible in the world of video art. Indeed, in the early eighties, it seemed that the legacy of experimental video, as it had been supported by public television stations like Boston's

WGBH or San Francisco's KQED, was a historical inclination to promote the divide between minority content and experimental form. For example, at WNET's TV Laboratory in New York, "Artists who were selected during the Lab's ten-year history formed a who's who of New York video artists of that decade."[39] However, "even though the roster included many documentary makers, it excluded artists airing minority viewpoints and others who didn't fit into the stylistic and conceptual framework demanded by the producers."[40] Out of this framework, Tanaka's and the Yonemotos' work emerged, dealing with Asian American topics (immigration, the internment) but treating them always from an abstract sensibility.

## Asian American Video Art in the Nuclear Age: The Work of Janice Tanaka and Bruce and Norman Yonemoto

Janice Tanaka exemplifies the artist who has straddled both the experimental media world and the Asian American film and video world. With a background in dance and music composition, Tanaka, whose biography mentions one of her accomplishments as building "an analog computer for processing of video imagery,"[41] comes from a position that is informed primarily by questions of aesthetics. She is most famous for *Memories from the Department of Amnesia* (1989) and *Who's Going to Pay for These Donuts, Anyway* (1992), her video meditations on family, history, and memory. Tanaka's work has been categorized as belonging to the tradition of Japanese American internment documentary. However, upon closer examination, her earlier work can be seen as a departure from overt Asian American subjects and as being more interested instead in questioning the video form as mode of expression. Her two video documentaries on the internment, for example, are important—not so much as a contribution to the archival and social change premise of Visual Communications, but in their more complex use of the immediacy and intimacy of video to serve as a countermemory against official versions of history. Tanaka's work understands "that the stakes in memory and history are ever present in electronic media (and postmodernism)—that despite its paradoxical relationship to the preservation of memory, television-video is a primary site of history and cultural memory, where memories, both individual and collective, are produced and claimed."[42]

Although she is most famous for her experimental documentaries about the Japanese American internment, Tanaka's video work in the early 1980s, which did not specifically deal with Asian American thematic issues, epitomizes the emphasis on form during this era of Asian American film and video. Tanaka's three short films that appear in ACV's First Annual Asian American International Video Festival—*Superhuman Flights of Submoronic Fancies* (1982), *Ontogenesis* (1981), and *Beaver Valley* (1980)—are notable, first, for the way that they are contextualized with films by Iimura and Paik in ACV's video festival. Like their work, Tanaka's films are concerned with the meaning of the electronic signal and the manipulation of the electronic image. Her films consist of mostly found footage of banal material such as television commercials, news footage, and iconic American images, which are distorted through the use of synthesizers and processing with computer programs. Thematically, the films are concerned with abstract critiques of mass-mediated ideas and imagery of American womanhood, nuclear holocaust, and religious fundamentalism. *Superhuman Flights of Submoronic Fancies*, for example, features repetitive loops of a highly processed and degraded electronic image of a television priest practicing a church ritual over which confessional monologues of transgressive experiences such as abandonment and incest are spoken. Definitions of guilt, lie, and fate read from the Doomsday Dictionary, which concludes in a story of a man being killed by his robot assistant coupled with a complexly diaphanous image of an orange nuclear explosion layered over a bleeding heart and news images of war.

Like *Superhuman Flights, Ontogenesis* (1981) and *Beaver Valley* (1980) deal with the problem of cultural repression in the nuclear age. *Ontogenesis*, the most abstract film of the trilogy, layers processed images of television newscasters, planes dropping bombs, the American flag, Uncle Sam, the Statue of Liberty, and contemporary American presidents from John F. Kennedy to Richard Nixon. A meditation on the price of patriotism in the nuclear age, the film offers ironic, electronic versions of the *William Tell* Overture as well as the ominous sounds of a telephone busy signal and the ticking of a bomb as a soundtrack. *The True Adventures of Beaver Valley* (1980) gives a similarly ironic take on the construction of femininity in commercial culture. Opening with a 1950s-style title frame that reads "This is one of a series of True-Life Adventures presenting strange facts about the world we live in. These films are photographed in their natural settings and are completely authentic, unstaged and unrehearsed," the film leads to a black-and-white video image of a baby doll being decapitated with a meat cleaver. A voiceover asks, "Wouldn't I make a good mother?" An unabashed and obvious deconstruction of postwar sexism, the film takes mediated mainstream femininity—Marilyn Monroe film clips, commercials for perfume and household items that pit women impossibly, as both sex object and obedient cog in postwar capitalist patriarchy—and splices them with her own processed images of "real" women inserting a diaphragm and another with prominent chest hair, putting into question cultural norms of gender and beauty. Viewed in hindsight, Tanaka's early video art is redolent of an ironic, 1980s countercultural sentiment as well as that era's penchant for processed video imagery. Tanaka's aesthetic is painterly, lingering over complexly layered images that make full use of analog video technology. Like Robert Nakamura's deceptively simple documentary *Manzanar*, the importance of Tanaka's work, though typical of thematic and formal concerns of this era, comes into high relief in historical context with other divergent works of Asian American film and video. For Nakamura's *Manzanar*, the context of the role of the photographic image and public commemoration of the Japanese American internment gives the film meaning in the extant histories of Asian American film and video, which began with this historical/commemorative impulse. Tanaka's experimental work, both her non–Asian American short videos and her two internment documentaries, show how their historical exclusion has helped form the dominant historical logic of Asian American film and video.

Like Tanaka, California-based artists and brothers Bruce and Norman Yonemoto are sansei artists who came of age in the Cold War nuclear age. Also, like Tanaka's work, theirs exists in the netherworld between Asian American film and video and experimental media. As they were children of the 1950s, their video soap operas reflect that era's repressed yet florid versions of domestic life and romance. Their videos, described as "the collective unconscious of the TV generation," effectively deconstruct and destabilize melodramatic notions of love and romance. On the other end of the abstraction spectrum from Janice Tanaka, the Yonemotos are more concerned with using video to deconstruct classical narrative cinema. In using the conventions and codes of realism found in Hollywood film and television, the Yonemotos' videos are loaded with references to Cold War pop culture like soap operas, the films of Douglas Sirk, and the discourse and politics of video art in the 1980s.

On the second night of the first annual video festival, ACV screened the Yonemotos' video soap opera, *Green Card: An American Romance* (1982). Produced in association with the NEA and Long Beach Museum of Art, *Green Card* is a video soap opera told in flashback by an old woman, Sumie, about her years in the early 1980s in Los Angeles, including her ambitions to become a working artist in the United States and her volatile relationship with Jay, her Huey Lewis–look-alike surfer/filmmaker lover. Although the film is "dedicated to Issei of all nationalities, past, present, and future," and deals with the theme of immigration, like many conventional Asian American films and videos, it is apparent how *Green Card*'s persistent irony, formal distance from its subject matter, and lack of a clear social change objective have alienated the Yonemotos' work in Asian American film and video.

As the theme song from Douglas Sirk's timeless 1950s classic, *Imitation of Life*, plays over the opening credits, it is evident that *Green Card* is an homage, not just to the form of the television soap opera, but to its own predecessor, the American film melodrama. Both an entertaining story of a woman's struggles for fulfillment à la Lora Meredith and a formal exercise in medium and genre, *Green Card* playfully deconstructs national constructs of womanhood via marriage and career and the representation of women in "mass media" by portraying a Japanese woman artist who discovers the sham of constructions of gender roles, especially through that of romance. The film's mixing of Hollywood film and video art composes the formal foundation of the film. For example, shots of Sumie made on location, such as in the desert and in the mountains, are edited with in-studio scenes of Jay and Sumie in front of a fake blue sky that turns red when they embrace. The wedding scene, which is shot on location outdoors, is then edited with close-ups of the wedding vows themselves, which are shot in front of a brilliant blue screen and later inserted. This jarring, humorous effect calls attention to the contingency of Hollywood's idea of romance to the problem of the realist text that is constructed of seamless, continuous space.

The subversive politics of Sirk are important as references in *Green Card*. Certainly, Sirk is present, not only the opening score, but in scenes where mirroring and doubling reveal other facets to the characters' moral and other dilemmas, such as the dichotomy of reality and art, nature and culture, technology and creativity. Nobi, a Japanese student whom Sumie spurns for her American lover, Jay, becomes the Annie to her Lora when he succumbs to a fatal disease. When he is dying in his hospital bed, Sumie comes running to be by his side—a scene very reminiscent of the death scene of Annie, the black maid, in *Imitation of Life*. Like the Annie character, Nobi represents the long-suffering racial and moral conscience of the main character. Another friend, Kyoko, who has a congenital disability and must walk on crutches, also provides a moral dimension to the film, attempting to dissolve the narcissism of the self-absorbed Sumie and Jay. These two characters serve as mirrors to reflect the "real," in contrast to the illusion of Hollywood life as epitomized by Jay and his morally corrupt friends. The main characters, who want to become stars—who are trapped in the imitation—"learn" from Nobi and Kyoko. The legacy of realism that is the soul of American film melodrama is important to *Green Card*, but also to the Yonemotos' understanding of art and representation. Therefore, although *Green Card*, like *Imitation of Life*, critiques the values of modern life including sexism and racism, it is ultimately a meditation on representation itself and the stakes of art making in a postmodern universe.

The work of the Yonemotos and Tanaka in the short-lived Asian American International Video Festival is important as correctives to the notion of a monolithic Asian American film and video and as a counterpoint to the dominance of the "noble and uplifting and boring as hell" aspects of the genre. Their inventive and ironic uses of video were, at one point, highly valued as examples of the genre's formal diversity and of its potential to go beyond expected institutional norms. Ultimately, the AAIVF expired as a separate festival in 1987, due in part to an understandable perception of the uphill battle to include form and aesthetics in the creation of a dynamic Asian American film and video. Daryl Chin notes:

> Three years ago, I stopped being involved with the selection committee for the film festival. I'd been doing it for seven years, and after the addition of the Asian American International Video Festival (the other people involved in the creation of that, if my memory serves correctly, were Renee Tajima, Nancy Tong, and Amy Chen), I'd had it. Every year, there were the same problems of trying to contact filmmakers, trying to make sure that representative films were included, trying to ensure that no faction of the Asian American film community was excluded or alienated in the process. But it always happened anyway, and those filmmakers working in more experimental modes were always being overlooked or penalized or neglected.[43]

The legacy of Daryl Chin and his discourse of dissent are important in presenting a different aspect of Asian American film and video that challenged prevailing notions of what a minority moving-image culture could be. The remaking of *Fire Over Water* as *Chan Is Missing* is also instructive of how minority cultural production alienates experimental art as a strategy to grow out of the margins of the world of nonprofit institutional film. The films of Tanaka and the Yonemotos show a preference for experimentation that has been forgotten: not only did *Fire Over Water* become *Chan Is Missing*, but Tanaka became widely known for her now classic experimental Japanese internment documentaries, and the Yonemotos have gone on to apply their postmodern, Sirkian sensibility to non–Asian American topics. However, their legacy and the prophetic discourse of Daryl Chin have lived on, not only in the work of queer experimental video artists that flourished in the later 1980s, 1990s, and beyond, but also in the promotion of Asian American film festivals since the early 1990s as the most important venues for the continued growth and diversity of experimental Asian American film and video.

# 2
# The Center for Asian American Media and the Televisual Public Sphere

The 1980s represent the decade of institutionalization of Asian American independent media. Nationally, Asian American film and video, as well as other minority film movements, consolidated through the establishment of the Minority Consortia, a funding body established by Congress in 1979 dedicated to supporting the diversity mission of public broadcasting. The Asian American contingent of the consortia named itself the National Asian American Telecommunications Association (NAATA), renamed the Center for Asian American Media (CAAM) in 2006.

The focus of this chapter is the impact of public television and the Minority Consortia on Asian American independent media. It is important, first, to establish the role of PBS, from its birth in the post–civil rights era reform of public institutions to its support of independent minority media in the 1980s and 1990s, as a *contemporary public sphere*, a space within modern capitalist democracy that Jürgen Habermas calls discursive spaces not controlled by the state and not beholden to commercial interests—an arena of "free" discourse.[1] This distinction of PBS as a contemporary, televisual public sphere is especially significant because I argue that though PBS has provided a necessary and welcome support matrix for Asian American independent media, its structural demands as a televisual public sphere has obligated Asian American media to uphold the problematic and limiting values of "injury" and ressentiment, thereby subjecting filmmakers to a proscribed, problematic, ideological agenda. As a structure, the public sphere offers specific capabilities as well as limitations that have directly shaped Asian American film and video as a genre. Specifically for Asian American independent media, an understanding of the rhetoric of what the political philosopher Wendy Brown has termed "injury" is important in pointing out the limitations of the national discourse of diversity in the public sphere and the necessity for counterpublics to make up for this lack.

## Diversity and Public Television

Key to understanding the dissemination of Asian American film and video is the history of racial diversity in public television. Public television was founded on the heels of President Lyndon B. Johnson's administration, which through its Great Society program implemented many social service programs in light of the civil rights movement of the 1960s. In 1967 Johnson signed the Public Broadcasting Act, which established a production and broadcast system that included a funding body (the Corporation for Public Broadcasting), a broadcaster (PBS), and local public television stations. Public television was developed in response to a study by the Carnegie Commission on Educational Television, which recommended that public television be "the clearest expression of American diversity, and of excellence within diversity."[2] Public television's role was to address the dearth of diverse content in commercial television, which was necessarily "incapable of serving the broader cultural, informational, and educational functions of a democratic mass communication system."[3] Although the commission stated its intention to broaden the "cultural function" of PBS, this did not result in an increase in representations of people of color on public television. In fact, many minority film and television producers throughout the 1970s protested this inequality until the problem was addressed in CPB's appointment in 1978 of an independent Task Force on Minorities in Public Broadcasting, made up of these producers and media activists, that sought to "determine how well that system . . . has met and is meeting the informational and educational needs and interests of Blacks, Asians, Latinos, and Native American citizens."[4] Its report, titled *A Formula for Change*, found that minorities were consistently underrepresented on public television as well as in the employment of local stations and at PBS and made recommendations to rectify the situation. Ultimately, beginning in the midseventies, minority independent producers and local public television stations began forming groups, calling themselves the Minority Consortia, to act as advocates and middlemen between minority filmmakers and PBS.[5]

By the early eighties, the National Latino Communications Consortium, Native American Public Television, National Black Programming Consortium, and NAATA formed the core of the Minority Consortia.[6]

The purpose of these consortia was to direct minority films toward public television and to create more funding opportunities for minority filmmakers. NAATA was one of the last consortia to be officially formed in 1981, after a three-day national conference on Asian American film and video in Berkeley, California, in 1980, "a gathering of tribes... that brought together Asian American producers and media activists from across the country from the VC (Visual Communications) contingent decked out in Hawaiian shirts to the worldly-wise and slightly cynical group from New York"[7] for the first time, to decide the fate of a centralized organization. NAATA was formed to acquire, package, and distribute independent Asian American films. The activities of the Task Force on Minorities in Public Broadcasting were followed by a decade of struggles between independent producers and the board of directors at CPB to increase appropriations directly toward programming rather than toward public television stations, resulting in the Public Telecommunications Act of 1988, which endowed the Independent Television Service (ITVS) and the Minority Consortia with increased funding to directly support independent films. While ITVS received a three-year contract for an annual endowment of $6 million, NAATA began to consolidate annual funding from CPB, beginning with about $135,000 in the 1980s to $350,000 in operations support and $636,363 in production support in 2003.[8] With the formation of the Minority Consortia and their fiscal relationship to CPB as a backdrop, Asian American film and video was finally given a formal conduit for national exposure and annual funding. Although it was a boost to the organization, this measure was often inadequate to the rising cost of film production.

The creation of NAATA has changed Asian American film and video in profound ways. Notably, it affects the way national audiences perceive Asian American identity by determining which films—based on subject matter, genre, and style—air on national PBS. Although NAATA is also beholden to programmers at PBS and the tastes of production executives at anthology programs such as *POV*, it became the gatekeeper of Asian American film and video beginning in the 1980s. In 1991, with assistance from CPB, NAATA was able to expand from an educational distribution service, formerly called Cross Currents, to a full-service media arts organization that offered production funding opportunities to filmmakers. Before major CPB funding came through with the Public Telecommunications Act of 1988, NAATA only had the power to acquire completed Asian American films as "NAATA Presents" programs to be picked up by individual PBS stations, such as its early anthology program, *Silk Screen*.[9] All films funded through NAATA bear the title "NAATA Presents," which is one of the first credits to roll before the beginning of each film that broadcasts on PBS and that make up its distribution collection.

## The Media Fund

It was not until 1990 that NAATA established the Media Fund, through which it could offer production and postproduction funding for independent Asian American films in amounts ranging from $20,000 to $50,000, with an average of $30,000.[10] This increased NAATA's influence over which films would be pushed to the national PBS schedule as well as giving it leverage to buy a film's broadcast rights for a limited time. Recipients of the Media Fund money are contractually obligated to appear in the San Francisco International Asian American Film Festival (SFIAAFF) or a similar exhibition venue. The filmmaker must also relinquish domestic broadcast rights to NAATA and public television for the first four years. Clearly, such a long-term contract presents a profound risk to independent filmmakers who decide to take the award. On the one hand, the Media Fund vastly improves the chances for independent Asian American producers to make their work and have it broadcast. However, this contract binds the films to institutional definitions of "Asian American film and video," reframing the meaning of the film and taking some of the representational power out of the hands of the filmmaker. Beyond NAATA's ownership of the film's broadcast rights for the first four years, the contract allows NAATA to decide whether the film would have its premiere on television or at its film festival, thereby influencing publicity and reviews.

Regardless of the constraints imposed by the Media Fund, its fiscal support remains a much-coveted award because of the slim chance that a funded film might air on national public television. According to NAATA's statistics for 1999–2001, 193 projects were submitted to the Media Fund, ranging from sixty to seventy-five per year within this period. NAATA selected twenty-seven of these projects for awards from the Media Fund, about 14 percent.[11] All of these films were aired on public television. Many, however, were aired during the month of May, which is Asian Pacific American month on PBS and represents the main period during which PBS broadcasts NAATA's films. Furthermore, each television station has the freedom to schedule these films at any hour, meaning that sometimes films may be aired at nonpeak viewing hours. In the end, of these twenty-seven films, only four were aired on a reliably national, high-profile, prime-time program, *POV: Rabbit in the Moon* (Omori, 1999) and *Of Civil Wrongs and Rights: The Fred Korematsu Story* (Fournier, 2001), both documentaries about the Japanese American internment; *Regret to Inform* (Sonnenborn, 2000), a film about the trauma suffered by women widowed by the war in Vietnam; and *First Person Plural* (Borshay-Liem, 2000), a personal documentary about transnational adoption. To be fair, three films—Ellen Bruno's *Sacrifice*, Spencer Nakasako's *Kelly Loves Tony*, and Arthur Dong's *Licensed to Kill*—were aired on *POV* in 1998, before these statistics were officially taken. *Mai's America* (Poras, 2002) aired on

*POV* in 2002, and *Daughter from Danang* (Dolgin and Franco, 2002) aired on another national program, *American Experience*. Both of these films were NAATA documentaries. These examples of recent films funded by NAATA demonstrate the cutthroat nature of the Media Fund and show that even being awarded money from this fund does not guarantee the kind of national broadcast exposure that most filmmakers desire. The Media Fund opens many doors for independent Asian American films, automatically winning a spot at the SFIAAFF and getting educational distribution and a shot at being broadcast on PBS. Yet contract stipulations dictate that once a film accepts funding from NAATA, it is beholden to the needs of a complex PBS broadcast scheduling process that may inhibit a film's wide exposure. The following example illustrates how filmmakers who accept the Media Fund must balance risk and benefit when dealing with NAATA.

When the filmmaker and veteran radio producer Amy Chen accepted funding from NAATA's Media Fund to finish her film *The Chinatown Files* (2001), a documentary about Chinese Americans jailed for suspected communist activity during the McCarthy era, she automatically relinquished the right to choose when and where her film would premiere, as stipulated in the contract. The film would premiere either on television or at NAATA's film festival. Although Chen agreed initially to have her film's premiere at the SFIAAFF, due to timing constraints NAATA offered it to the national PBS schedule, which did not end up picking it up. Since Minority Consortia policy demands that films that do not fit the national schedule must next be offered to individual local stations, the result was that Chen's film had very little wide-release publicity; hence, it lost much of the impact Chen hoped it would make. Chen attributes the problem to the lack of communication between local stations and the Minority Consortia as well as the lack of funding for marketing campaigns that would allow the filmmakers to increase audience potential for their films.[12] Therefore, public funding from the Minority Consortia carries with it a risk that an Asian American–identified film may not get enough attention—critical, popular, or otherwise—to register with the American public.

This situation points to the handicaps inherent in public funding for all ethnic-identified films that must compete with other films for general or commercial funding and furthermore be subsumed under the bureaucracy of PBS when they take Minority Consortia funding. As Chen's experience points out, the problem lies not only in the lack of production support but also in the lack of developed broadcasting outlets for minority independent films. This is particularly true regarding the precious few national public television outlets for the growing numbers of independent Minority Consortia–funded films that are made each year. However, a select number of films have found a measure of success on this path, largely through the anthology program *POV*, which, since the late eighties, has consistently aired nontraditional documentaries on national public television.[13]

In theory, the idea of a "public sphere" is useful for a discussion of public television in that PBS was instituted to be a "public alternative . . . a complementary supplement to the dominant commercial broadcasting system, not a fundamentally different way of organizing television culture."[14] The public sphere was a historical phenomenon that arose with salon culture in Europe during the seventeenth and eighteenth centuries:

> [It is] the space in which citizens deliberate about their common affairs, hence, an institutionalized arena of discursive interaction. This arena is conceptually distinct from the state; it is a site for the production and circulation of discourses that can in principle be critical of the state. The public sphere in Habermas's sense is also conceptually distinct from the official economy; it is not an arena of market relations but rather one of discursive relations, a theater for debating and deliberating rather than for buying and selling. Thus, this concept of the public sphere permits us to keep in view the distinctions between state apparatuses, economic markets, and democratic associations.[15]

Public television represents a contemporary public sphere in two senses: as a democratic space for the equal representation of all the citizenry's voices and as "a theater" for the noncommercial representation of these ideas. Moreover, Habermas's public sphere and public television are also crucially similar in that the idea behind them is, in essence, utopian. Because of the actual fragmentation of society by race, class, and gender, the idea of a sphere of free and equal parity for a unified public could not be realized fully as the ideal answer for democratic communication. In this way, PBS, with its utopian ideals of a televisual public sphere that would represent a pluralistic society's voices in all of its "diversity," would not live up to its name.

The story of Asian American film and video presents an important example of the impossibility of defining a single public sphere for a multitude of identities. As Patricia Aufderheide asks in a seminal article about public television reform in the late eighties, "Is the bygone public sphere of bourgeois males an expandable concept for a multicultural, multiclass, even multigender society?"[16] The creation of the Minority Consortia was one way of addressing this question of a public television for an actual, pluralistic public. In an effort to do this, the Minority Consortia attached itself to a larger movement for fiscal independence among independent film and video producers, resulting in the drafting of the Public Telecommunications Act of 1988, which began funding ITVS, an organization that would support independent films geared toward PBS, as well as annual operation and production funding to the five ethnically themed groups of the Minority

Consortia. By 1988, ITVS and the Minority Consortia had theoretically accomplished their goals in the program-funding arena of diversity in public television. On the broadcast front, the nationally broadcast personal documentary series (or programming strand, as it is called in public television) *POV* had emerged to address the representation of diverse "points of view" in public television.

## *POV* and the Politics of Ressentiment

*POV* demonstrates an ideal example of a "televisual public sphere" because its purpose is to present independent nonfiction films about controversial personal, social, and political issues while also engaging the audience's participation by creating a forum for viewer responses to its programs. One of the most important aspects of *POV* is its ongoing commitment to interactivity between the series, the audience, and the filmmakers through its "Talking Back" series of video letters and Internet message boards on *POV*'s accessory Web site, *POV Interactive*. Although the "video letters" that are aired on PBS are edited for content and style by *POV* staff, the "Talking Back" message boards on the Web site represent a more direct, unedited version of a "public sphere" where viewers are allowed to present their views more anonymously and communicate meaningfully with others about the films in the process.

Since its creation in 1988 by the independent media veteran Marc Weiss, *POV* has consistently aired a significant number of "NAATA Presents" films on national public television. *POV* presents a crucial case study for analyzing the national impact of Asian American film and video because its programs are "carried by most public television stations in the country and can potentially be seen in up to 96% of households nationwide.... Top programs in the series attract three to five million viewers."[17] Furthermore, as of this writing, there have been twenty "NAATA Presents" programs on *POV* since its initial 1988 season, the most films coming from a single member of the Minority Consortia.[18] Largely because of *POV*, Asian American films have been broadcast with some level of consistency to a national audience through this particular programming framework. Moreover, *POV* is crucial to independent Asian American film and video makers because of its independent marketing and publicity funds, which NAATA does not offer to its Media Fund recipients and which local public TV stations cannot match. *POV*'s marketing of independent films greatly affects the films in terms of the amount of attention they receive in the press.

What is revealing about *POV*'s identity as a contemporary, televisual public sphere, expanded "for a multicultural, multiclass, even multigender society," is how it frames Asian American film and video to reflect the national imagination/fantasy of the eternal divide between Asia (East) and America (West) rather than representing the innumerable inconsistencies and subcultures inherent in this double identity. In other words, the national fascination with Asian American identity still resides in the tensions caused by the various historical and imaginative rifts between Asia and America, which puts an unspoken burden of representation on Asian American film and video makers as well as on NAATA to reproduce these narratives for the demands of the very public sphere that purports to support their needs. Part of the problem here has always been the attempt to live up to the difficult, utopian ideals of a single public sphere. The Asian American films shown on *POV* have attempted to represent the Asian American viewpoint just as PBS attempts to be "the public arena in the singular."[19]

Asian American film and video has had a relatively successful history on public television, establishing itself particularly in the historical documentary area, yet problems arise in the conflicting institutional obligations of funding versus broadcasting. In other words, NAATA has made a commitment to fund a broad spectrum of films that "present stories that convey the richness and diversity of Asian Pacific American experience" as a way of supporting Asian American filmmakers and audiences. However, NAATA's institutional contract with PBS and CPB obligates it to present films on public television that "the Asian American community can embrace, but appeal to a larger mainstream audience, as well."[20] As the following examples illustrate, the space that NAATA has had to navigate between these two institutional obligations has split Asian American media's identity in important ways. This "institutional schizophrenia" has allowed for two versions of Asian American film and video. On the one hand, NAATA has struggled to provide a thriving backlog of independent films for its educational distribution catalog and to grant funding geared specifically for Asian American filmmakers. These efforts have encouraged the growth of a community of Asian American filmmakers and media activists from San Francisco to Los Angeles to New York. On the other hand, it has allowed an environment where many films are funded, only to be lost to the bureaucracy of PBS and never seen by wider audiences. Certain films do make it out of this limiting environment, and they are films that espouse a very narrow definition of Asian American experience, one that may seem universal (i.e., appeal to both the Asian American community and mainstream audiences).

However, the problem with *POV*'s particular selection of films is its consistent thematic concern with the politics of ressentiment.[21] Although *POV* has been important to Asian American film and video in that it has broadcast some of its most important films of the last twenty years, such as *Who Killed Vincent Chin?* (Tajima and Choy, 1988), *Days of Waiting: The Life and Art of Estelle Ishigo* (Okazaki, 1990), *Sa-I-Gu* (Kim-Gibson, 1992), *Who's Gonna Pay for These Donuts Anyway?* (Tanaka, 1992), *a.k.a. Don Bonus* (Nakasako, 1996), and *First Person Plural* (Borshay-Liem, 2000), *POV*'s selection has created a decidedly one-dimensional definition for Asian American film and video and excluded those films that complicate and expound on the complexities of Asian American identity.[22]

I classify *POV*'s Asian American films into two genres: the social-political documentary and the historical trauma film. This thematic dominance is what has colored the public's imagination about Asian American film and video as having the primary function of declaring various forms of injury. The award-winning documentary *Who Killed Vincent Chin?* which aired on POV in its first season, set the precedent for the place of Asian American political documentary on national public television.[23] The film documents the murder of a Chinese American by laid-off auto plant workers who mistook him for Japanese. It uses a *Rashomon*-style narrative that creates a "delirium" of images suggesting the complex series of events that led to the murder of Vincent Chin. The film handles its implied subject, white racism, in a way that avoids simplistic moral judgment. Bill Nichols calls *Who Killed Vincent Chin?* "the most important political documentary of the 1980s." In qualifying this statement, he cites that "it is so because it establishes a present moment of viewing in relation to what has already taken place in the film, such that we regard our own present as past, or, more conventionally, as prologue to a future outside the film which, through the very process of viewing, we may bring into being."[24]

It is this very quality of the film's call to social change that has made it a classic of political documentary. However, Nichols's phenomenological reading of the film as the ideal political film does not consider the "other politics" of the film. That is, it does not look beyond the political engagements of a theory of viewing and representational strategies to consider institutional politics that have enabled the film to come into existence in the public sphere. The institutional framework of *Who Killed Vincent Chin?* and other Asian American political documentaries suggests that there is an obligation on the part of Asian American film to claim an injury and to name the injurer. While I do not minimize the nuanced complexity and historical importance of *Who Killed Vincent Chin?* I think the film's critical success championed this approach of social change documentary over other forms and caused a deeper questioning as to what defined Asian American film and video as a genre. *Who Killed Vincent Chin?* showed audiences and critics the power of the political documentary to understand the complexities of Asian American identity. For Asian American filmmakers, it provided a model of funding and programming success. The film was a necessary step in establishing an Asian American media politics, but its success has made it the paradigm of "Asian American film and video" and of the structure that funds, distributes, exhibits, and broadcasts these films.

FIG. 4  Lily Chin speaks through an interpreter at a rally for her slain son, Vincent, from *Who Killed Vincent Chin?* (Renée Tajima-Peña, 1987). (Courtesy of Renée Tajima-Peña.)

Another prevalent trend among Asian American films on *POV* is the historical trauma film, which covers the gamut of subjects from the Japanese American internment to transcultural adoption. An example of the latter is Deann Borshay-Liem's *First Person Plural* (2000), a personal documentary about the director's adoption from a war-torn South Korean orphanage into a middle-class American family. The film is about both the trauma caused by the irreconcilability between history and memory and the politicization of Asian American identity. A "home movie within a home movie," *First Person Plural* begins as a camcorder video shot by Borshay-Liem that captures her search for her Korean birth mother and contains within it other home movies on Super 8 film shot by her American father. Borshay-Liem attempts to revise the sunny Super 8 footage of an idyllic, middle-class American childhood with her own interrogations of what this footage shows and omits. What she discovers is that her assimilation into American culture has meant sacrificing her Korean identity through an acceptance of history and the suppression of memory. As Borshay-Liem says, "The only memories I have are the images my father filmed while I was growing up. I relegated my real memories into the category of dreams." Through a reexamination of memories and dreams, Borshay-Liem relates what it is to understand the loss of cultural roots and the need to create an identity that is neither Korean nor American but Asian American.

*First Person Plural* is important to a politicized Asian American identity because it asks the common yet complex question about how Asians become Americans and examines the trauma of immigration common to many who experience it. The film is nominally about a Korean adoptee, yet it is philosophically concerned with a common theme of Asian American film: that of the process of becoming Asian American. Peter X Feng asserts that the representation of Asian American subjectivity "can be accomplished only by focusing on process rather than end result, on the act of 'becoming' rather than on the state of 'being.'"[25] Otherwise, a film like *First Person Plural* becomes merely a film about Korean adoption, even though it is actually a deconstruction of history and national identity that painstakingly arrives at an Asian American subjectivity. Earlier sequences in the film show home movies and photographs of Borshay-Liem's seamless transformation from Korean orphan to American teenager. Yet these identities are never integrated, as the language and memories of the past disappear until she deals with them in her adult life. *First Person Plural* is emblematic of the oeuvre of *POV*'s "NAATA Presents" documentaries in that it addresses the issue of personal trauma caused by the integration of memories with the turbulent history shared by America and Asia. This is the point of departure for exploring Asian American experience as it relates to a larger, more mythic relationship between the United States and Asia.

The Japanese American internment film offers an even more obvious event on which to project this notion of an identity embedded in national history. Four of *POV*'s "NAATA Presents" films have been about the relocation: *Days of Waiting: The Life and Art of Estelle Ishigo* (Okazaki, 1990), *Who's Gonna Pay for These Donuts Anyway?* (Tanaka, 1992), *Rabbit in the Moon* (Omori, 1999), and *Of Civil Wrongs and Rights: The Fred Korematsu Story* (Fournier, 2001). A subgenre of Asian American film and video in itself, the Japanese American internment film highlights "unacknowledged and yet deeply rooted family traumas, still-open wounds at the contradictory meeting ground of American racism and democratic promise."[26]

*Days of Waiting*, which won the 1991 Academy Award for best short documentary, introduced this genre of film to *POV* viewers and tells the life story of Estelle Ishigo, the Caucasian wife of Japanese American Arthur Ishigo, who followed her husband to the camps. Using photographs, Ishigo's own drawings that she completed during her relocation and that were later compiled for her book, *Lone Heart Mountain*, and an actor's voice-over to suggest Ishigo's, the documentary narrates a central event of Asian American history. This narrative is told from the perspective of a white woman who has been cast out by her own community and who "learns to take refuge in a socially transgressive 'outsider' identity within a community of color," a strategy that "avoids merely 'othering' Japanese American camp history and experience for a white audience."[27]

Importantly, *Days of Waiting* leaves the Japanese American internment open to a white, liberal, empathetic spectatorship through the representation of Ishigo's profound psychological awakening to white racism and her subsequent reawakening in a politically formed Japanese American subject position. This strategy helped the film become one of the first documentaries to show the internment as worthy of serious mainstream recognition. Although the film makes the internment palatable to a more general audience without resorting to the sort of melodramatic elision of politics of such Hollywood films as *Come See the Paradise* (Alan Parker, 1990), it does this at the expense of the more radical goals of minority media on public television, that is, realizing Asian American identity for Asian American audiences and filmmakers.

*Who's Gonna Pay for These Donuts Anyway?* is an experimental autobiographical documentary that relates a more abstract interpretation of the experience of the camps, describing the psychic fallout resulting from the violence and shame associated with internment. Janice Tanaka explores the Japanese internment through a search for her lost father, narrating his inability to come to terms with his incarceration in the camps, followed by his mental illness and social exclusion. The film intersperses voice-overs by the filmmaker, images of her estranged and now ailing father, Jack Koto Tanaka, interviews with her daughter and son, and photographs from the past.

*Donuts* differs from *Rabbit in the Moon* and *The Fred Korematsu Story*, which use a more straightforward documentary narrative style of talking heads and archival footage through which to unproblematically read a recuperation of Asian American history. Tanaka's film mixes sound, image, and text dialectically, expounding on the notion of a history lost and regained through reconstructed memories. Though its subject matter is an individual's recollection of the trauma of the Japanese American internment, and therefore makes a nod to the genre of documentary, Tanaka's film problematizes the very assumption of documentary and nonfiction film to represent so-called reality.[28]

One of the prevailing issues in this film is the distortion and misrecognition that camera images can sometimes create. Jack misrecognizes the people in a photo taken of him as a young man with his wife and his baby daughter, Janice. Jack does not recognize himself and misrecognizes his wife, thinking that it is his grown daughter instead. In a later scene, Janice's grown children remark that their own father, of Mexican origin, in fact strangely resembles their Japanese American grandfather, Jack. Photographic proof of this resemblance is revealed as Janice compares their striking physical similarity. Therefore, rather than the conventional documentary structure, *Donuts*' structuring principle is that of doubling, misrecognition, and misidentification.

All of these films have in common not only their subject matter but their exploration of a profoundly ambivalent Asian American identity and a difficult reconciliation of the toll that repression of injustice has taken on conceptions of family that is unique to the specificity of the internment. Because of its very clear civil rights violations, coupled with its erasure in history by dominant cultural representations of World War II, the Japanese American internment genre has filled in for lost histories. However, given its dominance in Asian American film and video, the internment genre has overshadowed attempts to overturn these politics, to recognize other modes and themes of Asian American film narrative.

This subject has generally received strong support from public funding bodies and appears as exemplary of the "politics of ressentiment," particularly in the context of multiculturalism on national public television. Giving considerable national airtime to Japanese American internment films, regardless of their artistic merits, perpetuates the notion of minority cinemas as simply "a turn toward law and other elements of the state for resolution of antidemocratic injury"[29] and minimizes the contribution of hundreds of other Asian American films supported by NAATA and independently produced each year that are rarely seen by a national public. Therefore, *POV*'s track record in airing "NAATA Presents" programs is tinged with an unwitting complicity with a politics of ressentiment that gives Asian American film a biased reputation, despite the variety of films being made against the grain of these implied notions.

## Alternatives to Ressentiment: Counterpublic Spheres

During the height of great changes in public broadcasting, such as the creation of ITVS and the early days of *POV*, a younger generation of Asian American filmmakers emerged from different areas of experience who have continued to work outside public funding systems in order to be free of its institutional obligations. Among them is Gregg Araki, an independent feature filmmaker, whose work (covered in depth in chapter 4 of this book) marks an important point in the construction of an "Asian American media identity," which has been based largely on the ideology of funding institutions that limit the range of subjects and definitions of other artists working in different modes. Making primarily low-budget features in the nineties, Araki has received some criticism for working outside the mainstream of Asian American film and video, his subject matter often dealing with issues of youth nihilism and not the historical ramifications of Asian American identity. However, his experience shows exactly how Asian American film and video has mostly and somewhat problematically been defined by institutional contexts, which have dictated the subject matter, mode, and ideology Asian American films should espouse. The critical success and exposure of Asian American film, then, has set up problems for other Asian American filmmakers who work in different modes, identify with different experiences, and speak of a different generation.

NAATA's definition of Asian American film and video and its criteria for deciding which films get funded is clearly driven, at least in some cases, by the demands of a public sphere that claims to be an alternative voice to a white mainstream audience. These examples of films aired on *POV* suggest that NAATA funds some projects with a necessary eye toward its probability of success for broadcast to national public television rather than trying to serve its diverse Asian American constituency. It also points to the problem faced by filmmakers who must decide if they are willing to risk giving up four years of broadcast rights to an institution that may find it necessary to push higher profile films onto the national schedule before their films, which may better fulfill NAATA's stated institutional objectives.[30] At the very least, this dual obligation to its Asian American constituency, which includes filmmakers, and to the demands of a "national audience" places opposing demands on NAATA that are emphasized by the unstable definition of Asian American film and video.

Clearly, the mission of large institutional frameworks such as the Public Broadcasting Service and the Corporation for Public Broadcasting have opened the door for Asian American film and video, yet they have also created a number of problems in assuming that there could be one public space to represent not only ethnic and gendered multiplicity but also a variety of self-representations. One way of intervening in this conceptualization of the public sphere is to look at alternatives that have been created by the same system that have engendered public television.

The idea of multiple public spheres is central to the discussion of multiculturalism and public television because originally PBS attempted to represent this "diversity" under the aegis of a single public sphere. Although this ideal collapsed, it was partially recuperated by years of trying to rectify the impossibility of representative parity in national public television by independent filmmakers. However, these attempts at rectification created the opportunity to consider alternative public spheres that the various Minority Consortia have developed since the creation of PBS. The San Francisco International Asian American Film Festival, started by NAATA in 1983, which has become the largest and most prestigious Asian American film festival in the United States, functions as such a "counterpublic sphere": "a local and oppositional space in which subaltern subjects may prepare to contest the hegemony of a dominant social order."[31]

NAATA's festival is counterdiscursive because it is an alternative to the "dominant social order" that is presented by the uniform public sphere of PBS. It is a festival that, on the one hand, has its roots in the local specificity of San Francisco independent film communities and, on the other, has connections to other local hubs of Asian American film and video activity, such as Los Angeles, New York, and Chicago. Not only are other points of view expressed at SFIAAFF, but other modes such as fictional narrative feature films and experimental films broaden the concept of the genre. Furthermore, the festival attempts to bring together "Asian American film" and films from East and South Asia and Asian diasporas in Canada and the United Kingdom. Films such as the Indian director Deepa Mehta's *Fire* (1996), which closed NAATA's fifteenth festival in 1997, and Iranian American films such as Ramin Serry's *Maryam* (2001 SFIAAFF) and Babak Shokrian's *America So Beautiful* (2002 SFIAAFF) represent a wide understanding of Asian American films that show a range of the Asian diaspora. The festival has also made efforts to connect contemporary Asian American film and video to the pioneers of cinema with rare archival programs that celebrate the careers of silent film stars such as Sessue Hayakawa and Ruan Ling Yu. SFIAAFF programmers linked the past with the present by commemorating this unusual fecundity of Asian American feature films with a special screening of two archival Hayakawa films, *The Cheat* (Cecil B. DeMille, 1915) and *J'ai Tué!* (*I Have Killed*, Roger Lion, 1924). This was a way of "reach[ing] back into Asian American film history."[32] What is more, the festival has engendered a discourse of the genre by imagining and constructing a spatial and temporal container for it that is much larger and more diverse than PBS and attends much more closely to the needs of an Asian American community of film fans, filmmakers, and activists.

The SFIAAFF allows one to consider the alternatives to an Asian American film and video envisioned and shaped by the national public sphere. Films that range in form from avant-garde to narrative-feature comedies offer themes about a variety of Asian American experiences and seem to better serve two constituencies that NAATA was originally set up to serve: Asian American media makers and audiences. Films that have been frequently featured include programs of experimental shorts and queer/gay/lesbian programs with films by veteran Asian American and Asian Canadian film and video artists such as Helen Lee, Richard Fung, Trinh T. Minh-ha, and Valerie Soe as well as younger media makers such as Nguyen Tan Hoang, Patty Chang, and Ming-Yuen S. Ma. Many of their films are committed to exploring the politics of gender, sexuality, race, and postcoloniality within the context of Asian American identity, yet it is doubtful they will ever be seen on PBS.

I am not suggesting that ethnic identity–based film festivals are the answer to the dissemination of minority media. In fact, they could be construed as a bona fide ghetto against other mainstream festivals such as the Sundance Film Festival and the Toronto International Festival. In addition, their local context and ephemeral nature make establishing wider audiences very difficult. However, SFIAAFF is an example of how institutions have tried to instill a genuine minority media culture that appeals to a greater part of its varied constituency of audiences, activists, and independent filmmakers. Over its twenty years of existence, NAATA's festival has become the largest of its kind and the only one of its kind among the other Minority Consortia. It has steadily grown to include not only films that would not fit PBS's broadcast schedule but premieres of privately funded, independent feature films like Justin Lin's *Better Luck Tomorrow* (2002), which eventually went on to win the audience award at Sundance and a distribution deal with MTV Films. Out of loyalty to the Asian American film and video community that had supported him in the past, Lin decided to premiere *Better Luck Tomorrow* at SFIAAFF.[33] This kind of loyalty within its filmmaker constituency shows a level of dedication between artists and NAATA that encourages the continued growth of the genre.

SFIAAFF has grown rapidly over the years and has become a world-class festival, not due to its institutional support but in spite of it, because of its progressive strategizing and a commitment to diversity on its own terms, that is, by including queer and feminist programs and showcasing feature films beyond the "Asia Pacific" paradigm such as selections from South Asia and the Middle East. Therefore, the counterpublic sphere of the SFIAAFF does offer an alternative to Asian American films shown on national PBS, and this split of the public and counterpublic is crucial to understanding how institutions intervene in how films make meaning.

The goal of this chapter has been to dismantle the notion of a monolithic Asian American film and video by looking at its various public spheres and the institutional obligations carried by the term "Asian American film and video." By clarifying the historical contingency of minority media in the United States and its relationship to public television, I have attempted to suggest a different way of understanding Asian American film and video as a genre in film and television scholarship. Overall, institutions have been crucial to the the genre's existence. Without NAATA and the tireless individuals involved in the formation of a community around Asian American film and video, there would simply not be as many films and opportunities for filmmakers as there are today. That being said, perhaps this success, however limited, signals the call for a new approach—one that will consider the need to change the established hierarchy in order to continue its growth.

# 3
## Pathology as Authenticity

ITVS, *Terminal USA*, and
the Televisual Struggle over
Positive/Negative Images

The arrival of the Independent Television Service (ITVS), a programming consortium for innovative content by way of the Public Broadcasting Act of 1988, transformed the discourse on race and representation in public media. What made ITVS different and experimental was that it was run by and for independent producers without the intervention of executives of the Corporation for Public Broadcasting. It represented a number of contradictions: a positive coup for independent producers who desired control, an ultimate fiscal failure, and of course, a chance for Asian American filmmakers to finally address the problem of the "positive image." This chapter considers how the creation of ITVS challenged PBS's diversity mandate (discussed at length in chapter 2) through a direct attack on the "positive image."

In its first years, ITVS nearly went bankrupt, and its critics blamed a lack of leadership as well as its decadent, too-esoteric content for its failure. Despite these critiques, I argue that ITVS's risk-taking endeavors, both aesthetically as well as operationally, created a window of opportunity to offer a more productive and culturally meaningful image of Asian Americans vis-à-vis the "negative image." In the context of Asian American film and video, the broadcast of Jon Moritsugu's short film *Terminal USA* on one of ITVS's first programs for PBS, *TV Families*, especially offered the possibility of a productive discourse on race and representation on television. By virtue of its incisive, sardonic critique of Asian American stereotypes, *Terminal USA* mobilized the "negative image" as a more authentic pathway toward an Asian American film and video aesthetics. In mining the positive/negative image debate in Asian American media, I contextualize *Terminal USA* with the broader history of representing race on television, specifically focusing on the first Asian American sitcom on network TV, *All-American Girl*—a semiautobiographical star vehicle for the comedian Margaret Cho about a Korean American family living in San Francisco. This juxtaposition allows me to examine the unique function of the negative image to forge an authentic televisual representation of Asian Americans that differentiated it from other represented racial groups. Crucially, this analysis includes the larger racial framework of television in the 1990s by comparing these shows to the quintessential black sitcom of "enlightened racism," *The Cosby Show*. This complex web of comparative raced texts reveals the unique contribution of Jon Moritsugu and ITVS and their attempt at challenging the positive/negative image divide at a crucial moment in public media, race, and television.

As several scholars have pointed out, a "positive" image is just as insidious as a "negative" image. It is not "simply the matter of proffering the moral inverse of the negative image: the inverse of Fu Manchu (evil mastermind bent on world domination) is Charlie Chan (deferential public servant), but Charlie Chan is hardly a positive image."[1] Despite the problems inherent to the positive/negative structure, television and the civil rights movement seemed to intensify the illusion of the "positive image" as a way to counteract the negative ones, particularly for African Americans.[2] Yet for the image of Asian Americans, the opposite was true, especially with the neologism "model minority," coined in a *New York Times Magazine* article by the sociologist William Petersen and published on January 9, 1966, "Success Story: Japanese American Style," in which he extols the hard work by Japanese Americans as the recipe for their success. A year later, *US News and World Report* published a similar article about the success of Chinese Americans.[3] Much of this discourse was a direct reflection of the 1965 immigration act, which reversed years of discriminatory policies regarding quotas of immigrants coming from Asian nations.

The model-minority myth was promulgated in an effort to combat the notion of institutionalized racism. In other words, if Asian Americans can be model citizens, the myth argues, it shows that all minorities have the potential to succeed according the capitalist, democratic, Horatio Alger model, regardless of race, religion, or creed; therefore, racism does not truly exist. Yet, the problem with the model-minority myth stems from the glorification of the American dream, in which hard work brings economic gains. Indeed, the myth created even more divisiveness among racial groups, resulting in hate crimes against Asian Americans for their purported success and a backlash against other "problem minorities" whose subordination in society was thusly justified.⁴ Since the wide acceptance of the model-minority myth, Asian Americans have taken the "positive" position in the racial paradigm.⁵ Because Asian Americans were already pegged as "positive" examples of minority behavior against the "negative" example of other minorities, the myth had itself become a burden and, ironically, a negative stereotype, particularly in the wake of racial hate crimes against Asians due to their perception as an economic threat.⁶ As a reaction, Asian American performers and filmmakers explored the necessity of the "negative image" as part of a dialectics of representation toward authenticity. In other words, the struggle for authenticity in Asian American self-representation meant, in the broadest sense, the establishment of a "negative image."

Several scholars have theorized notions of a productive "negative image" in Asian American media. Eve Oishi has used the term "Bad Asian" to describe Asian American media makers who reject minority media status:

> There is a white-supremacist fiction that Asian Americans are overwhelmingly interested in something called "saving face" and therefore will not do anything to call undue attention to themselves or their communities. Therefore, any Asian American who makes noise, acts nasty, or in any way flouts the expectations of racist stereotype is a Bad Asian. Bad as in "badass." Bad as in anyone who does not covet white patriarchal approval; anyone who challenges racism, class oppression, sexism, homophobia; anyone who talks candidly about sex and desire.⁷

While Oishi uses "Bad Asian" specifically to describe lesbian, gay, transgendered, queer, and bisexual Asian Americans making independent experimental film and video, the concept applies directly to the idea that "badness" or "negativity" is a uniquely Asian American aesthetic position. In the same vein, Moritsugu's *Terminal USA*, which aired in 1993 on PBS, was symptomatic of the productiveness of the negative image in representations of Asian Americans as model minorities. Full of campy, scatological imagery and abject humor, Moritsugu's extreme send-up of an Asian American TV family serves an ideological counterpoint to ABC's *All-American Girl*. In contextualizing the function and significance of ITVS and Jon Moritsugu's *Terminal USA*, it is necessary first to understand the broader patterns happening vis-à-vis the representation of Asian Americans on the small screen.

## The Enlightened Racism of African American and Asian American Sitcoms

Network television was a powerful force in shaping the discourse of the model minority as well as in pushing the positive-image agenda for all minorities. *The Cosby Show* was the prevailing model for the ethnic sitcom of the 1980s—an image of positive, but inauthentic, "enlightened racism." Though the Asian American sitcom followed suit with *All-American Girl*, the logic of post–civil rights racial harmony, which helped compose the powerful fantasy of watching the Huxtables, did not successfully graft itself onto the Asian American narrative, a failure that revealed the deep flaws of the Manichaeism of negative and positive racial representations.

For decades, network television largely avoided any representations of Asian Americans, except in marginal, supporting roles. By the late 1980s and early 1990s, there was a gradually growing mainstream visibility of Asian Americans in starring roles in bigger-budget Hollywood motion pictures such as Wayne Wang's *Joy Luck Club*. On television, there had been a few short-lived shows featuring Asian Americans in lead roles, notably *The Courtship of Eddie's Father* (1969–1972), which starred Bill Bixby as a widowed father and Miyoshi Umeki as his Japanese housekeeper; its conceptual opposite, *Mr. T. and Tina* (1976), about a Japanese inventor (Pat Morita) and his nutty American housekeeper (Susan Blanchard); *Gung Ho* (1986–1987), an adaptation of the feature film of the same name about a US auto plant taken over by a Japanese firm, starring Scott Bakula and Gedde Watanabe; and *Ohara* (1987–1988), with Morita as a Los Angeles cop. Despite these brief appearances, there had never been a sitcom featuring an Asian American family. Then, in 1994, *All-American Girl* appeared on ABC's prime-time lineup to rectify this lack. The show was touted as "based on the stand-up comedy of Margaret Cho," which was in turn based on biographical details of Cho's life growing up in an immigrant Korean American household in San Francisco. Though Cho's show may have been ideal for positioning of the "negative image" for Asian Americans, audiences were not yet ready for it, as its reception history shows.

In the early 1990s, Cho was a rising star in the world of stand-up comedy, having started in the business at the age of sixteen and winning a series of competitions, including one in which the first prize was opening for Jerry Seinfeld. Cho's extreme popularity in the college stand-up comedy circuit, for which she was nominated for Campus Comedian of the Year, expedited her quick rise to fame. Soon, Hollywood came calling with the offer of a starring role and executive producer credit to do *All-American Girl*. As she infamously explains in her award-winning concert film, *I'm the One That I Want* (Lionel Coleman, 2000), Cho's experience on *All-American Girl* was a nightmare during which network producers brutally criticized her physical appearance, which subsequently resulted in the development of anxiety, depression, and an eating disorder that resulted in liver failure and hospitalization.

Despite the personal costs to Cho, *All-American Girl* did provide Asian American audiences with a moment of recognition. Although other ethnic sitcoms, especially *The Cosby Show*, had paved the way for nonwhite TV families, Asian Americans had never had their own sitcom. The fact that *All-American*

*Girl* had found a place similar to that of *The Cosby Show*, on a prime-time network spot in the most popular TV genre of the 1980s and 1990s, meant that Asian Americans had arrived. Thus, *All-American Girl* represented the ultimate sign that multiculturalism had normalized with a hard-won "Asian American turn" in US television. However, the eventual failure of *All-American Girl* to reach a vaunted *Cosby Show* status or even to survive beyond one season on network television contributed to the eventual failure of that turn. One of the reasons for *All-American Girl*'s failure was the botched attempt to fit the unique representational circumstances of Asian Americans—that of the "model-minority myth"—into the ideological function of the ethnic sitcom's "American dream" exemplified by *The Cosby Show*.

For African Americans, the "positive image" connoted alignment with white, hegemonic virtues of bourgeois upward mobility. The television situation comedy provided the most obvious space in which the relationships between socioeconomic upward mobility, race, and representation were worked out against the backdrop of white, hegemonic values. As Herman Gray points out, "in black-oriented situation comedies of the late 1970s and early 1980s, especially the long-running *The Jeffersons*, as well as *Benson*, *Webster*, *Diff'rent Strokes*, and *Gimme a Break*, black upward social mobility and middle-class affluence replaced black urban poverty as both setting and theme."[8] What was key to these shows as precursors to *The Cosby Show* was that despite showing a trajectory of upward mobility that got closer and closer to hegemonic white privilege, they maintained the racial order. As Gray again emphasizes, "because they continued to construct and privilege white middle-class viewers and subject positions, in the end they were often as benign and contained as shows from earlier decades."[9]

*The Cosby Show* was a perfect example of how network television engaged in "enlightened racism" through the promotion of the "positive image" for African Americans. Especially since *The Cosby Show* became the text to which all other ethnic sitcoms were measured because of its success with a mainstream audience, it is necessary to understand it as the model, in many ways, for *All-American Girl*. Many television scholars uphold their ambivalence about *The Cosby Show* and its opening up of "a space of production" for black representation in television.[10] Praised for its representation of black cultural diversity and holding up an idealized vision of the black upper-middle class, *The Cosby Show* improved on many of the one-sided representations of African Americans as "surrogate managers, nurturers, and objects of white fascination."[11] Yet, much of the impetus for *The Cosby Show* was to correct the consistent string of "negative images" that have haunted televisual representations of African Americans since *Amos 'n' Andy*, that infamous and first TV comedy that invited audiences to laugh at the misfortune and incompetence of black caricatures. As Gray argues,

Positioning *The Cosby Show* in relation to the previous history of programs about blacks helps explain its upper-middle-class focus. More significantly, the show's discursive relationship to television's historical treatment of African Americans and contemporary social and cultural debates (about the black underclass, the black family, and black moral character) helps to explain its insistent recuperation of African American social equality (and competence), especially through the trope of the stable and unified black middle-class family.[12]

*The Cosby Show*'s historical and narrative and stylistic logic, then, was to correct for television's "historical treatment of African Americans," which tended to be about the problems and foibles of the black underclass and its inability to be socioeconomically mobile.

What was even more insidious about the success of *The Cosby Show* was its agreement with what white audiences wanted to see, which was the disappearance of the acknowledgment of institutional racism as the cause of black economic struggle. As Christine Acham explains in *Revolution Televised: Prime Time and the Struggle for Black Power*, black sitcoms provided a site of resistance during the years of the Black Revolution in the 1970s. However, by the 1980s, the success of *The Cosby Show* showed that "among white people, the admission of black characters to television's upwardly mobile world gives credence to the idea that racial divisions . . . do not exist. Most white people are extremely receptive to such an image."[13] The idea that "affirmative action was not needed" was a powerful message exuded by *The Cosby Show*. As reported by Jhally and Lewis, one American viewer summed up many of the positive feelings about the show saying, "I like this show because it depicts black people in a positive way, I think he's [Cosby] good. It's good to see that blacks can be professionals."[14]

While "the blackness represented on the show was subdued and dignified, and came across in such things as blues and R&B music, African American portraiture art that hung on the living room walls, references to civil rights and anti-apartheid leaders, and the 'Abolish Apartheid' sticker on son Theo's bedroom door," it tacitly avoided the history of struggle, specifically economic struggle, that was not only a part of African American history but part of the history of black sitcoms that had come before it.[15] *The Cosby Show* was nonetheless one of the most popular shows on television in the 1980s and 1990s and the longest-running sitcom in history (until *The Simpsons* surpassed it), airing from fall of 1985 to 1995.[16] Its popularity rests on the projection of a fantasy of unproblematic upward mobility that both "leaves white audiences with the impression that all economic barriers for African Americans have been removed through affirmative action, while it placates black audiences by portraying a respectable, non-stereotyped African American family."[17] Despite this huge flaw in the representation of the history of African American struggle on *The Cosby Show*, it remained and remains one of the most watched shows on television. Therefore, its popularity in spite of the glaring misrepresentations reveals the logic of the positive image as a powerful and necessary fantasy, particularly for African American viewers.

The black middle-class family fantasy, as epitomized by *The Cosby Show*, operated similarly to the Asian American model-minority myth in that it justified the argument that there was no such thing as institutional racism. Although they were mostly invisible in television in the 1980s, representations of Asian Americans were already burdened by notions of bourgeois upward mobility that designated them as the "model minority." As argued by David Palumbo-Liu, by the end of the 1960s, in quasi-sociological articles spearheaded by the *New York Times Magazine*, the model-minority myth directly pitted supposed "high educational achievement levels, high median family incomes, low crime rates, and the absence of juvenile delinquency rates and mental health problems among Asian Americans, and juxtaposed this against the 'failure' of blacks in America."[18] Therefore, the legacy of "the model-minority myth" had already embedded the representation of Asian Americans as "positive," that is, adhering to middle-class, white ideals. Accordingly, the task of television in the post–civil rights era, as exemplified by and culminated in *The Cosby Show*, was not relevant to Asian Americans.

Although negative representations of Asian Americans had clearly been defined in old Hollywood films as embodiments of evil in simplistic Orientalist narratives (Fu Man Chu and the Dragon Lady), the rise of postwar capitalism had redefined "negative" not as being morally bad but as being economically unviable, as Palumbo-Liu's study of the journalistic origins of the model-minority myth shows. Whereas in the pre-1950 "yellow peril" discourse, which chiefly "helped Christians to understand why they are not pagans, Americans to understand why they are not Europeans nor Native Americans, and whites to understand why they are unlike people of color,"[19] the post-1960s understanding of racial difference pitted Asians against blacks by using the socioeconomic logic of ideal citizenship. Thus, while both African Americans and Asian Americans were struggling for authenticity in representation, Asian American activists at the forefront of the ethnic studies debates sought to remove themselves from the racist logic of the positive image via the model-minority myth, and consequently a few Asian American filmmakers and performers found the answer in "pathology as authenticity."

*All-American Girl* still remains the standard for commercial television's failure to authentically represent Asian Americans. Infamously deconstructed and eviscerated in Cho's subsequent concert film, *I'm the One That I Want* (2000) for sanitizing the centrality of her identity as a "slut," the sitcom's biggest problem was, as Rachel Lee puts it, "bowing to white civility."[20] A lack of "authenticity" was one of the most telling contextual discourses about *All-American Girl*, which revealed themselves in the common critiques it received.

Critiques of *All-American Girl* ranged from its being unfunny to its being inauthentic as it pertained to representing Korean American culture. One example of such a critique was that *All-American Girl* was not nearly as funny compared with the "authentic" hilarity of Cho's standup show. Another critique was that Cho was often funnier than the show.[21] Furthermore, the show held the problematic distinction of dividing audiences in the opinion of whether it was "groundbreaking" or "stereotypical" as it pertained to representation of Asian Americans. In other words, audiences were either grateful for a "positive" portrayal of Asian Americans or they hated the show's kowtowing to white stereotypes of Asians.[22]

Many stand-up comics who rose to the top in the 1980s and 1990s, like Jerry Seinfeld, Roseanne Barr, and Ellen DeGeneres, won network contracts and developed successful sitcoms, and Cho followed suit. Yet, the resulting product, which featured storylines loosely based on her stand-up act, was, as many critics suggested, "not big yucks."[23] Despite the racist bias of television criticism in itself, what the critical reception shows is that inauthenticity, whether in its portrayal of Korean-ness or in its forced jokes, bogged the show down. What is most telling is Cho's reflection that network straitjacketed her into a "positive image" role—that of funny yet good girl—when in reality, Cho was a foul-mouthed, self-proclaimed slut. In other words, the inauthenticity that saturated the show reveals the inauthenticity of the upwardly mobile, positive image narrative for Asian Americans as an effective fantasy. This is a fantasy that worked for African Americans because it corrected for historical inequality. However, for Asian Americans, the image that could potentially correct for the stymieing model-minority myth would be negativity itself. The reason why Cho became a stand-up star was because she figured out that the formula for authenticity, as an Asian American, was to be bad.

Although all model-family sitcoms from *The Donna Reed Show* to *The Cosby Show* involve desired fantasies of ideal upper-middle-class life, because of the specific placement of Asian Americans in the racial paradigm as already "model," an "Asian American sitcom" misses the ideological purpose that *The Cosby Show* served. On the one hand, the first episodes of *All-American Girl* show some potential for an Asian American–specific narrative logic of resisting the model-minority stereotype. The show presented Margaret Cho's character, "Margaret" as a Generation X twenty-something who lives in her family's home in San Francisco and whose main conflicts included her failure to rise to the rigid, old-world expectations of her Korean business-owner parents and to keep pace with her high-achieving brother, played by the Tony award–winning actor B. D. Wong.

Though *All-American Girl* ultimately failed as both a mainstream success and as an authentic Asian American text, the first episodes demonstrate a glimmer of hope in the potential for dismantling the model-minority myth as the narrative of becoming unique to Asian Americans. For example, the first episodes establish Margaret's rebellious character through negotiations of her American values with her mother's Korean values, thus becoming the *All-American Girl* of the title. Indeed, their overarching narrative logic is one of resistance to model-minority status through the disciplining of Margaret, as exemplified by an adversarial conflict with her mother over interracial and interclass dating as well as career decisions.

In the show's pilot, "Mom, Dad, This Is Kyle," Margaret and her mother come to blows over Margaret's choice of boyfriend: a white auto mechanic named Kyle. Especially telling in this episode is that the nature of the adversarial sparring between Margaret and her mother is anchored to the signifiers "white" and "American." While Margaret accuses her mother of not wanting her to date a white man, her mother retorts that it is because he is American. Though upward mobility through intermarriage is in itself complex and "marrying white" has controversially meant marrying up in America for other ethnic groups, this episode bizarrely pits the conflict as one about Margaret wanting to assimilate to American culture versus her mother's wishes that she maintain her Koreanness. And yet the conflict also reads as one overtly about class—the model-minority, upwardly mobile Asian Americans versus the working-class whites. Though a heteronormative marriage to either a Korean or a white man is deeply problematic to the notion of resistance and queerness as exemplified through Cho's stand-up identity, the episode seems to weakly suggest that Margaret's desire to marry a working-class white man expresses her resistance to model-minority status. The episode is resolved when Margaret decides eventually not to move in with Kyle, thus successfully being disciplined.

Likewise, in the second episode, "Submission Impossible," Margaret agrees to be set up by her mother with a Korean doctor played by Garret Wong. This storyline is resolved when Margaret reveals that she is not able to fit into the criteria of a submissive Asian woman. These episodes, while entirely formulaic, potentially dismantle an aspect of model-minority status through the dissenting character of Margaret as both Asian and woman. By (ineffectively) resisting society and her family's wish for her to move up socioeconomically by marrying a Korean doctor, Margaret suggests that capitulations to capitalism are irrelevant to her identity. However, her consistent choice of white males as ideal suitors undermines and further weakens Margaret's resolve to mobilize a politics of "negativity," and thus one of authenticity.

Although the first two episodes show Margaret to be somewhat dissenting from her role as a "submissive" daughter and a model minority, this logic quickly dissolves as the dating conflicts suddenly disappear from the show's plots. Later episodes, such as "Educating Margaret," "Loveless in San Francisco," "Notes from Underground," and "Pulp Sitcom," do not problematize the fact that Margaret dates unsuitable, socioeconomically marginal, white men over suitable, upper-middle-class Korean men; they simply show her dating different white men of a variety of socioeconomic backgrounds. In "Educating Margaret," Margaret dates her British film professor; in "Loveless in San Francisco," she has a dating dry spell and finds a date with a white doctor at the end of the episode; in "Notes from Underground," she dates a handyman who fixes up the basement into which she has recently moved. In "Pulp Sitcom," Margaret dates a struggling filmmaker played by director Quentin Tarantino. None of these later episodes contain an adversarial relationship between Margaret and her mother over interracial and interclass dating. Thus, the fact that the majority of the later episodes were criticized as having lost focus is crucial to the show's lack of an ideological anchor on which to hang the narrative logic of overcoming that *The Cosby Show*, with its strongly implicit purpose—to show African Americans in a constantly positive light—promoted. While the first episodes contained an inkling of Margaret's resistance to being a socially and culturally acceptable "positive image" and veering toward a more meaningful enactment of a "negative image," the show's swift normalization of Margaret as unproblematically assimilated into the white dating pool seemed to lose its motivation. Whereas both black and white audiences basked in the fantasy of the Huxtables as an ideal, upper-middle-class black family, there seemed to be a lack of a similar purpose in tuning in to *All-American Girl*.

*All-American Girl* was literally a failure in that it was cancelled at the end of the first season. Ultimately, the episodes' lack of focus as well as a fundamental misunderstanding of the function of the ethnic sitcom in the 1990s—that is, to project a joyous fantasy of upward mobility—led it to completely misfire. *All-American Girl*'s premise—a young Asian American woman defying the conventions of model-minority status—seemed not to fit into what "white civility" would ever want to see in minority behavior. Since, according to Herman Gray, the function of ethnic sitcoms, by virtue of the African American example, is to adhere to white hegemony, *All-American Girl*'s premise of defiance did not meet those standards. Then, as the show changed narrative course, having accepted Margaret's behavior as not particularly defiant, but in line with normative capitulations to capitalism, the show seemed to lose a sense of purpose. If the fantasy of *The Cosby Show* occurred in its unproblematic display of black upward mobility as an escape from black stereotypes, the fantasy of *All-American Girl* would have been more effective if it had articulated a narrative of escape from stereotypes about Asian Americans, that is, "model minority" status.

What is unique about the Asian American turn in US television is not only its failure but also how it expressed a dialectical moment in the history of Asian American film and television. At around the same time, ITVS's televising of *Terminal USA*, Jon Moritsugu's acerbic satire on the racial politics of sitcoms, provides an effective counterpoint to ABC's *All-American Girl* through strategies of parody, camp, and abjection and shows the necessity of the articulation of a "negative image" of Asian Americans. Moreover, despite ITVS's controversial failure to achieve the paradigm shift in innovative content envisioned by its founders, *Terminal USA*'s effective and truthful take on the politics of Asian American identity demonstrates the uniqueness of its struggle in televisual representation.

## ITVS and the Problem of the Positive Image in Public Television

While network television was busy negotiating the positive-image problem through the vehicle of the family sitcom, public television was going through its own upheaval in positive-image management. In pinpointing the transformation of the positive image in Asian American film and video, it is necessary to emphasize the institutional discourse of minority media that helped inform the creation of ITVS in the 1980s. One of the ongoing criticisms of public broadcasting during this time was PBS's failure to fulfill its diversity mandate. The object of particular scrutiny by independent producers was PBS's simplistic use of the "positive image" of racial minorities as a way of placating diversity-minded media activists. As pointed out in chapter 1, public television's mission was to be "the clearest expression of American diversity, and of excellence through diversity." Since that time, advocacy groups attempted to hold PBS to its word, and the 1989 development of ITVS, a programming consortium funded by CPB and independently controlled by the National Coalition of Independent Public Broadcasting Producers, was the latest in a series of attempts to authentically engage so-called diversity. The appearance of ITVS and its production of Jon Moritsugu's *Terminal USA* was the result of a years long struggle of independent producers to break down the negative/positive image debate and to open up public television to representational authenticity.

A decade after the establishment of the Minority Consortia and the Program Fund, a solution to the problem of the positive image arrived in the form of "innovative programming" that sought to complicate simplistic notions of positive-image multiculturalism. Headquartered in Minneapolis, ITVS was developed in the late 1980s as a result of the revision of the Public Broadcasting Act by the US Congress in 1988. Much contentious discourse in the world of independent public media had taken place since the previous Public Broadcasting Act of 1979, which launched the Program Fund. The Program Fund was created to give funding to independent producers for the creation of public media content, but its coffers were controlled by nonartists, or the "suits" at PBS. This, according to independent media activists, presented the biggest challenge to the funding pipeline between filmmakers and broadcasters.

Unlike the Program Fund, ITVS was completely controlled by independent producers. The terms of the Public Broadcasting Act of 1988 held that the funder, the Corporation for Public Broadcasting, directly consult with the National Coalition of Independent Public Broadcasting Producers to produce programs through ITVS. As in the Minority Consortia, ITVS would initially receive a budget of $6 million from CPB without creative/editorial input or interference from them or PBS. Leaders of the ITVS initiative believed that the key to reshaping PBS so it would truly live up to the Carnegie Commission's original directive to provide "excellence in diversity" was to take the money and decision-making out of the CPB bureaucracy and into the hands of independent producers. The leaders in the development of producer-friendly programming initiatives, the "three Larrys"—Lawrence Sapadin, Laurence Hall, and Lawrence Daressa—spearheaded the project of solving the lack of programming diversity. Daressa, a longtime member of the nonprofit media center Newsreel, believed that the "solution and answer" was to give the opportunity to independent producers to come up with programming "independently of the priorities of the stations."[24] Daressa combined forces with Hall, a theoretical physicist turned media activist, and Sapadin, who was at the time the executive director of the Association of Independent Video and Filmmakers, in order to lobby Congress during a critical time in the 1980s: under the Reagan administration's PBS budget cuts, when the promise of a televisual public sphere free from commercial or private interests was being endangered.

Independent producers working in public media hoped that ITVS would ideally become a national media center for artistically daring and politically challenging work. The reality was quite different. By 1990, conflict had arisen between ITVS and CPB about the deal that was cut in allowing for the unique noninterference clause: though ITVS could develop programs independently of CPB or PBS, there was no guarantee that PBS would broadcast the resulting programs. This resulted in complaints on both sides—ITVS begrudging the lack of funding left for production after paying for overhead costs and CPB defending its realistic position on budgets.

Although the establishment of ITVS seemed to be a landslide victory for independent producers working in public television, its initial years and continued existence were fraught with problems. John Caldwell has commented that ITVS's problems continued to stem from its inability to cater to a national audience and from its reproduction of a central bureaucracy, ironically the very problem it was trying to solve by eliminating the CPB as middle man.[25] Likewise, Laurie Ouellete criticizes ITVS primarily because it "reinforces social and cultural hierarchies—and invites authoritarian-populist accusations of elitism—by equating progressive television with unconventional documentaries and avant-garde artistry only."[26] Citing award-winning fiction and nonfiction programming like Marlon Riggs's *Black Is, Black Ain't* and *TV Families*, which featured Jon Moritsugu's *Terminal USA*, both Caldwell and Ouellette point to the disconnect between the elite taste culture of independent filmmakers and the needs of working-class audiences. They suggest that ITVS completely missed the mark for enabling the true function of a democratic, televisual public sphere.

Although these criticisms against ITVS are valid in an assessment of its ultimate failure to change the face of public television, from the perspective of independent filmmakers and producers, another picture appears. Specifically, what has not been adequately explored is not necessarily why ITVS failed, but what forces demanded ITVS to go in the direction of formal and narrative innovation. I would argue that by pushing the envelope on the difficult issues of race, gender, and sexuality, public television was the only place that held the possibility to shift and challenge racist stereotypes in the "wasteland" of television. If not on public television, where would Americans be able to see "unconventional documentaries" and "avant-garde artistry"? Though Riggs had already courted controversy in public television for the 1991 airing on *POV* of his film about black men and AIDS, *Tongues Untied*, his association with ITVS, which funded his next film, was both a badge of honor and a target for critics of PBS. In the case of the highly publicized *Black Is, Black Ain't*, its aesthetic and subject matter, an examination of racism and sexism in the gay community and homophobia in the black community, do not just represent "elite taste culture" but exemplify the complexity of the positive/negative debates argued in the world of independent media for a decade. Therefore, although Riggs's last film became a poster child for aesthetic excess according to critics of ITVS, its accomplishment in unmooring simplistic representations of race, gender, sexuality, and class remains a coup in the history of race and representation in television. The attempt to conflate race, sexuality, and "innovation" seemed to be at once ITVS's intention to innovate and also the root of its problems. As pointed out previously, public television was set up according to rigid, superficial standards of diversity, namely, the nominal representation of minorities. ITVS desired to complicate this notion of diversity within a televisual public sphere that ultimately could not support it.

Another significant issue that ITVS addressed was its courting of audiences of color and other underrepresented viewers. Ultimately, who is to say what is and isn't elite taste culture? The critique that ITVS was "too avant-garde" for the average viewer brings up the question of who the average viewer is. The rhetoric of this critique dismisses the possibility of a complex audience that is not only capable but also welcoming of new perspectives that challenge existent stereotypes. As in commercial television, public media audiences are not static, nor the equivalent of what Stuart Hall had termed, "cultural dupes," that is, merely able to enjoy the programs aimed at them, but quite possibly capable of discernment, critique, and sophistication in their viewership.[27] Furthermore, though ITVS is highly criticized for being out of touch with the average working-class white viewer's interests, what about working-class and middle-class black, gay, and Asian American audiences? Not only did its programs address a diverse audience, ITVS provided the possibility to challenge the "positive image" problem in minority media. Programs like *Black Is, Black Ain't* and the *TV Families* series completely dismantled the lie of the positive/negative image, which not only affected what independent producers of color were allowed to produce but also addressed the problem of underrepresented viewers. Particularly in the age of *The Cosby Show* fantasy and its Asian American counterpart, *All-American Girl*, ITVS attempted to overcome the "enlightened racism" of these network shows. What the ITVS experiment illustrates again is the need for more complex narratives by and for minorities, which ITVS did indeed accomplish during its otherwise uneven and highly criticized beginnings. Though it is ultimately impossible to say exactly what led to the problems that ITVS faced, the innovations and the envelope-pushing by filmmakers most certainly had the potential to diversify public television in interesting ways.

For makers of Asian American film and video, ITVS provided another caveat-laden opportunity to compete for funding, although due to the funding squeeze, the odds were low. Although its utopian high-art TV gambit made its programming less appealing to a mass audience, this same gambit allowed for a possible break from the seriousness of the ideological project for Asian American film and video. One of ITVS's first and most anti-"wasteland" endeavors was *TV Families*, a program that satirized network television sitcoms and dramas and "serialized family diversity as an antidote to network television's one dimensional paradigm."[28] Tellingly, *TV Families* signed on Jon Moritsugu, who was quite familiar with fringe underground film festivals and ultra-low budgets, to make his apocalyptic vision of the ultimate cultural repression, that is the American television family, and, through it, a critique of Asian American film and video. As exemplary of ITVS's failure to fulfill the difficult task of carrying both innovation and racial diversity to public television broadcast, the following analysis will look at *Terminal USA* as an example of the persistent incompatibility of race and innovation in the televisual public sphere.

## *Terminal USA* (1994)

Jon Moritsugu's *Terminal USA* represents a significant break in the tradition of injury, history, and memory in Asian American film and video made for public television. Through the formal play of pastiche, irony, and satire, *Terminal USA* parodies the politics of injury in Asian American film and video. That *Terminal USA* is a product of both the Minority Consortia and ITVS shows even more strongly the difficulty public television faces in successfully marrying formal innovation with the nominal representation of ethnic diversity. While *Terminal USA* is a successful combination of ideological content and personal style, the overall failure of ITVS to follow through on its ideals within the larger logic of PBS drives home the persistent idea that the rigid ideological imperatives of the public sphere have made Asian American films incompatible with formal experimentation.

Because of the unique circumstances of ITVS, which during its initial years gave filmmakers a wide range of freedom as artists, Moritsugu produced what could only be described as the answer to the problem of the positive image of Asian Americans: a scatological satire of race and television. In 1992, Jon Moritsugu, along with Todd Haynes, was among twenty independent filmmakers given $9,000 by ITVS to develop scripts for *TV Families*, a high-concept, ironic series take on the family sitcom.[29] Moritsugu's resultant script for *Terminal USA*, an acerbic, black satire about a Japanese American family on the verge of post-apocalyptic meltdown, passed the grant competition gauntlet to be awarded a $360,000 production budget. The film had a highly mixed reception, winning awards on the festival circuit in 1993, including from the Toronto and Rotterdam Film Festivals. Yet when it aired on PBS in 1994–95, *Terminal USA* was rejected by a number of local public television stations and aired in only 150 out of about 210 markets nationwide.[30] *Terminal USA* cleverly turned the mirror onto Asian American film and video as well as on network sitcom/drama formulas featuring white families, questioning the possibility of a genuine, televisual representation of Asian Americans.

As a kind of photographic negative to *All-American Girl*, *Terminal USA* presents ways to think about the purpose of public television's mission of diversity, as well as the problems associated with representing Asian Americans on television. *Terminal USA* exemplifies the paradoxical, historical, and importunate entanglement of Asian American identity politics with independent film and public television. At the same time that ITVS was trying to radicalize public television with queer takes on TV families, the Asian American family itself was an object of crisis in the early 1990s, specifically through the airing of ABC's *All-American Girl*. In many ways, *Terminal USA* is a corrective to the failure of the multicultural "enlightened racism" of network TV as well as to the failure of mainstream media to authentically represent Asian

Americans. Although the Asian American turn in television failed, it is in many ways recuperated by the efforts of independent Asian American film and video. *Terminal USA*'s appropriation of the "negative image" through the use of an aesthetic of abjection fulfills much of what was repressed in *All-American Girl*. In the same way that *The Cosby Show* provides a fantasy of upward mobility that satisfied a need to correct much of the history of the negative representations of African Americans, *Terminal USA* corrects the problem of Asian American model-minority status. Its aesthetic completes the circle of many of the "positive/negative" debates of the previous decade.

## The Abject as Resistance

*Terminal USA*'s engagement with notions of the abject (including the form of the scatological) suggests an important aesthetic alternative to the limiting politics of injury that underlie the ideological principle of Asian American film and video. *Terminal USA* enters into a crucial dialogue with its double, ABC's *All-American Girl*, which appeared in the same year on television. Abject imagery in *Terminal USA* parallels Cho's own scatologically informed critique of her sitcom in her popular stand-up comedy concert film, *I'm the One That I Want*, which Rachel Lee describes as significant in its use of the abject to critique "white civility."[31] In that show, Cho discusses the ribaldry, intimacy, and travesty of the sexual, digestive, and excretory processes of her body. Both Moritsugu and Cho, by using strategies of the abject in their work, provide an effective window into expressions that have hitherto been disallowed—in network TV, public television, or other legitimate space. As "failures," then, both Moritsugu and Cho successfully saw through to the inevitable trajectory of Asian American expression on stage and screen.

Moritsugu is an example of an American filmmaker of Asian descent who has clearly differentiated himself from the norms of independent Asian American film and video production. Because he doesn't make documentaries about historical trauma and political injustice, which are the requirements of the televisual public sphere (as discussed in chapter 1), his work represents ambivalence about institutional expectations for the genre. In an interview, Moritsugu says:

> I don't think there's any problem in my mind with the reality of my not making Asian American–themed films, or whatever you call them. But within the community itself, both my films, Gregg [Araki]'s films, and the [films of] a few other filmmakers such as Rodney Bogawa, are seen as rebellious youthful punk-rock products.... We're looked upon in a hostile way by a lot of people in the Asian American community because they feel we've forsaken our heritage, our roots. I think that's just really stupid.[32]

But more than this, Moritsugu had bypassed both Hollywood and the professional PBS documentary route by making super-low-budget films that have rendered him free to work outside of these systems. Moritsugu, who has resided in Hawaii, Seattle, and Santa Fe, had worked for many years in San Francisco, making a kind of "underground cinema" that found fringe prominence in the late 1980s and early 1990s in film festivals such as the New York Underground Film Festival and the Chicago Underground Film Festival.

Educated at Brown University where he majored in semiotics, Moritsugu was predictably influenced by the irreverent nihilism of the films and theories of Jean-Luc Godard and Guy Debord. By 1991, Moritsugu had already made a name as an "underground" filmmaker, showing his rudimentarily made 8mm short films at the now defunct New York Underground Film Festival. His early short films, like *Mommy Mommy Where's My Brain* (1986), were first claimed institutionally and critically as part of the Cinema of Transgression movement, whose 1985 manifesto recommends "that all film schools be blown up and all boring films never be made again" and proposes "to go beyond all limits set or prescribed by taste, morality or any other traditional value system shackling the minds of men."[33]

*Mommy Mommy Where's My Brain* is a black-and-white collage film "dedicated to AC/DC and Jacques Derrida" that combines images, text, and music to form a kind of music video critique/celebration of popular culture, a theme that Moritsugu revisits again and again. The film illustrates the kind of quick, associational montage style pioneered by classic avant-garde films like Bruce Conner's *A Movie* (1958), Stan Brakhage's emulsion scratched films (1954–1964), and even the abstraction of Fernand Léger's *Ballet Mecanique* (1924). Bookended by scenes in which several punks demolish a car by hand and one in which an announcer called Johnny Public dances in a grimacing mask, pointing to a "Wheel of Fortune"–like device. Regardless of his "natural" affinity and affiliation to Cinema of Transgression, and the lack of any reference to an Asian American identity politics, *Mommy Mommy Where's My Brain* was featured in the Center for Asian American Media's San Francisco International Asian American Film Festival in 2002 as part of its Japanese and Japanese American Films program. Despite its lack of identity issues or ethnic or cultural content, *Mommy Mommy Where's My Brain* exemplifies how a filmmaker like Moritsugu is hailed by the institutional structure that dictates the parameters of Asian American media. Although Moritsugu's work is included in a program called *First Steps, Experimentally Speaking*, his career reveals how insufficiency of the category of Asian American film and video to easily include a rationale for experimental and avant-garde work.

Connected by a DIY, lo-fi aesthetic, Moritsugu's films riff on variations of the mod teen film genre, full of disaffected youth, lengthy punk rock music performances, luridly meandering exploitation plots and subplots, and special effects more reminiscent of Russ Myer than of Wayne Wang. For example, his 1994 independent feature, *Mod Fuck Explosion*, described as "blonde teenage posturing, Japanese biker freak-out, backstabbing mods, pretty poseurs, pills, petty crimes, leather jackets, and more" is a low-fi, low-budget riff on the teen film whose loose narrative revolves around a lonely teenage girl's search for a leather jacket while a turf war between mods and bikers looms. His other features *My Degeneration*, which was made for $5,000, and *Hippy Porn*, which enjoyed a yearlong run in an independent theater in France in 1993, are similar DIY takes on punk rock, mod kids, and existentialism. With the exception of *Mod Fuck Explosion*, Moritsugu's short films are light sketches that are mere preambles to the more fully realized feature narratives that are the arena in which Moritsugu's talent for provocation, irony, and camp aesthetics find their strongest application.

## Putting the Camp in Camp

*Terminal USA*'s engagement with tactics of the abject suggests an important aesthetic alternative to the limiting politics of injury that underlie the national subject formation project of Asian American film and video. Unlike the serious historical documentaries that form the basis for the genre, *Terminal USA* delves in abject imagery and parody in order to emphasize the absurdity of the "positive image."

*Terminal USA*'s use of abject imagery is a way out of "white civility," the boundaries beyond which most Asian American films made for PBS have not ventured. Forced into the preexisting ideological framework of Asian American film and video on public television, *Terminal USA* critiques the concept of recognition through injury in interesting ways. Julia Kristeva defines the abject as "simply a frontier, a repulsive gift that the Other, having become alter ego, drops so that 'I' does not disappear in it but finds, in that sublime alienation, a forfeited existence."[34] In psychoanalytic discourse, the abject represents that which was once a part of you but is no longer, and which cannot be gotten rid of; it is treated first and foremost with profound alienation and disgust. Exemplified by body waste, and severed body parts, the abject is also a metaphor for the bodies of racial others in white society. In *Terminal USA*, the abject is elicited as a reaction to the film's representation of urine, dismembered organs, blood, and references to defecation and seminal ejaculation, which are important motifs that implicate the complacency and rigidity of Asian American film and video as a grave (as dead, in fact), aesthetic problem and also signifies Moritsugu's own alienation as an Asian American who makes non–Asian American films.

*Terminal USA* centers on a Japanese American family on the verge of neurotic, violent, and sexual implosion. Stylistically a mixture of lurid soap opera,

1960s teen films, and family sitcom, *Terminal USA* deconstructs all three genres by way of high camp. *Terminal USA*'s TV family is headed by a father who reacts to racist slurs at his job in an industrial plant by harboring increasingly paranoid and violent fantasies about Armageddon. His nymphomaniac wife plots with her corrupt lawyer to kill her bedridden father-in-law in order to benefit from a life insurance scam. Meanwhile, she helps herself to his pain medication, which she injects into her arm. The three children further the irony of the perfect American family by leading secret lives of clichéd taboo beneath their respectable, equally clichéd roles of gender, race, and class. The twins, both played by Moritsugu, live split lives. Kazumi, whom his father calls the "blooming idiot," is a drug-dealing teen who has dyes his hair blond, wears makeup, listens to hardcore punk music, and has only managed to get into his "dream community college." Marvin is Kazumi's nerdy, sexually repressed doppelgänger, "a virtuous teen guy" who gets straight As and studies all the time while harboring fantasies of S/M-style gay sex with men in uniform, which he hopes to live out as a student at West Point. Lastly, Holly, the youngest, is a popular cheerleader who discovers she is pregnant, becomes the victim of a vicious plot by her cheerleader colleagues to publicly screen a sex tape she made with her boyfriend, and is tricked into a prostitution ring through an unwitting dalliance with the family attorney. Each character, in high melodramatic style, is involved in a plot that leads to an explosive denouement, replete with a burning cross on the front lawn, skinheads, and a Peckinpah-style living room massacre.

Moritsugu's expressionist, stagelike mise-en-scène places emblems of a materialist, hypermasculine American milieu into high relief and also into the service of irony. There is extended use of cowboy motifs to these ends—from the giant horse mural in Marvin's bedroom and the hobby horse he uses to stimulate himself while looking at gay porn to Holly's white fringed cowgirl costume that she wears on her unwitting path to sex slavery and to the father's own donning of a cowboy hat and pistol to enact his end-of-the-world scenario. Rather than denoting the West and the Western's inevitably racist, violent domination, the cowboys, horses, guns, and spurs serve to connote kinky and kitschy sexuality, from S/M role-play fantasy to bestiality, which the characters gleefully play out to delirious effect.

*Terminal USA* cleverly and humorously attacks the typical problems of Asian American identity politics, particularly the model-minority myth, which is played out by way of the dual characterization of Kazumi and Marvin. Whereas "serious" Asian American films would have a typical "positive image" approach to a dismantling of the model-minority myth, *Terminal USA* presents an alternative "negative image," as that of total dissipation and a flouting of both the model minority and its politically conscious, serious "Asian American film and video" opposite. Kazumi, the drug-dealing punk, exemplifies the fringes of society, while his twin Marvin assumes all of the surface attributes of the myth, while secretly harboring sadomasochistic homoerotic desires that go against the grain of the heteronormative, patriarchal, military-industrial complex. In one scene, Marvin takes some white powdered substance given to him by Kazumi and, released from his sexual repression, goes berserk and subsequently makes an ill-advised sexual pass at a skinhead. Gratuitous sex and drug use are offered as sensible alternatives to model behavior. But more importantly, *Terminal USA*'s energetic allusions to exploitation cinema, such as the 1970s drug cinema of Roger Corman and Russ Meyer, offer an even more rational alternative to the model behavior of the Asian American film and video artist. While the 1970s saw the emergence of "positive image" documentaries like *Manzanar* and *Wong Sinsaang*, Moritsugu's cinema references the countercultural ethos of the same era, itself marginalized by both Hollywood and "straight" funding and distribution systems like PBS. In this way, Moritsugu's films share the oppositional spirit of grassroots Asian American film and video while espousing a completely different aesthetic derived not from ethnic studies and postcolonial theory but from trashy TV shows, punk, and camp.

Beyond the usual attacks on capitalist, sexist, racist mainstream culture that is the mainstay of the white TV family sitcom, *Terminal USA* is careful to also critique Asian American film and video itself, particularly the notion of an aesthetics based on ideology. In the film's most important joke, at one point, the father comes home to complain of racism at the car plant where he works, to which he complains to his wife, "I can't believe they still think I'm a Chink! I'm a Jap! We are not Chinks—we're Japs!" This joke, which seems the antithesis of serious Asian American film and video, articulates the way identity politics, particularly in independent film, have missed the point entirely, in trying to develop a space in which Asian American filmmakers can work freely. In focusing on the difference between Chink and Jap, in making sure that the American public is aware of different ways to label racism and oppression, Asian American film and video has created an institution built solely on the correct recognition of difference and the representation of injury as the sole end to its project. It is this crucial myopia at which Moritsugu directs his critique.

More than this, in trying to identify with American identity through the logic of the TV sitcom, each character's struggles with the split between a nominal Asian American identity read as model behavior—the high-achieving worker, mother, student, and cheerleader—and another set of undesirable hidden behaviors that narratively constitutes the character's "real" repressed identity. For example, the mother's Asian Americanness is her duality as both model minority and larcenous, homicidal drug addict. These undesirable behaviors and characteristics, such as sexual perversion, insanity, and

FIG. 5  Mom and Dad, from *Terminal USA* (Jon Moritsugu, 1993). (Courtesy of Apathy Productions.)

narcomania, are what should be jettisoned as examples of the abject, according to the narrative logic of the TV family sitcom, but they make the characters who they are. This is the predicament in which Moritsugu seemingly finds himself as an Asian American filmmaker who harbors undesirable compulsions in filmmaking.

As examples of the abject, blood and urine are also reminders of the ultimate alienation, not only of minority identity but of the "non–Asian American" filmmaker. One pivotal interaction takes place in a mall public restroom, where Kazumi and his white girlfriend, Eightball (who turns out to be an alien from outer space), go to sell drugs, and where they meet an unscrupulous drug dealer, Fag Toast. After admitting to having taken a "satisfying dump," Fag Toast shoots Kazumi in the leg. Back in Kazumi's bedroom, where he and Eightball plan retaliation, Kazumi's wound becomes infected, and as he goes into shock, we are shown various inserted close-ups of his bleeding wound. As the wound gets progressively worse, Kazumi inexplicably vomits blood in explosive fashion. The incoherent buckets of blood that appear in this scene and later in the Peckinpah-style shoot-out in the last scene, are, like the other strategic scenes of dismemberment, an attempt at representing all that is undesirable to the raced national subject formation project of Asian American film and video.

Another scene in which the abject comes into high relief is when Fag Toast is attacked by Eightball, resulting in his eye being gouged out. Again, a

FIG. 6  Kazumi and Eightball, from *Terminal USA* (Jon Moritsugu, 1993). (Courtesy of Apathy Productions.)

close-up of the eye, which falls on the carpet, is followed by Eightball's platform boot crushing it like a grape. In an homage to the eye-slicing scene in the avant-garde classic *Un Chien Andalou*, this last abject image is not only of a dismembered organ but of an important one in visual culture—the eye. When Luis Buñuel slices the eye in *Un Chien*, an involuntary shudder goes through the audience; it is an instinctive, immediate reaction felt in the body. By punctuating *Terminal USA* with strategic inserts of this and other images, Moritsugu elicits the abject in the viewer; he wants to awaken audiences to a more viable, vital, and vivid understanding of identity formation, Asian American and otherwise.

The scene that exemplifies Moritsugu's strongest stance against public television's project of Asian American national subject formation is when Eightball urinates in a jar. The close-up insert of the jar of urine was, importantly, deleted for the broadcast version, which signals the most obvious way in which notions of the physical abject are directly linked to Moritsugu's alienation as an Asian American filmmaker. Rather than using injury as a path to recognition, as that which seeks to be looked at, *Terminal USA* uses the physical abject as a way of challenging a kind of filmmaking that requires recognition as a prerequisite. By pushing the envelope in this way, *Terminal USA* raises many of the critical issues of his stance as a non–Asian American filmmaker. In this way, the value of *Terminal USA*, and thus ITVS's investment in innovative content, can be linked productively to a politics of resistance against the positive/negative conundrum of racial representation in television.

Despite *Terminal USA*'s problemetizing of Asian American subject formation, it is the existence of the physical abject that provides the best example of Moritsugu's challenge of conventional strategies of self-representation in Asian American film and video. For example, in one scene, we are shown a close-up of Kazumi's mother injecting morphine, stolen from her dying father-in-law, into her arm. The close-up insert shows a badly constructed papier-mâché arm into which a giant needle injects liquid and from which syrupy blood pools up. This scene announces the first of Moritsugu's betrayal of the Asian American film and video formula—that which seeks recognition for injury. Rather than announcing pain as the means and the ends of the genre, the mother in *Terminal USA* saucily helps herself to stolen painkillers, illegally relieving her own psychic pain, getting high, and illicitly enjoying the pleasure of the act. Rather than taking anything seriously or making a noble and boring film, the characters in his film enjoy their symptoms as the world goes to hell. Then, Moritsugu delivers the ultimate in abjection, Kazumi's corpse, which arrives at the end of the film, after much bodily shuddering and blood spilling from limb and mouth. The coup de grace in Moritsugu's aesthetic of abjection is formally realized in a specifically Asian American abjection and comes full circle from Kazumi's violent victimization by skinheads as a "Jap" in the opening scene. Therefore, it is through these over-the-top images of blood, guts, and gore that *Terminal USA* finds a path to a more authentic realization of Asian American identity.

Moritsugu's rejection of institutional obligations as an Asian American filmmaker is important in revealing the consistent problem of the historical formation of Asian American media. That is, because the revolutionary media activists and filmmakers of Visual Communications in the 1970s brought to life a politicized film movement, there was a strong need and purpose in making Asian American films. By the 1980s, as filmmakers like Moritsugu came of age, a different need arose, the need for artistic freedom, which for Asian American filmmakers was, to a certain extent, freedom from the obligation to make Asian American films about "heritage, our roots." While Bob Nakamura and Eddie Wong made films in the early 1970s to tell histories that had never been told because of institutionalized racism in commercial media, later Asian American filmmakers felt a double need—to be emancipated from both the "sell-out" culture of commercial Hollywood cinema and the ideologically driven films of Asian American media.

Moritsugu's experience with ITVS and PBS provides an important turning point in his career, one that reveals the complex impact of institutional support on independent filmmakers. On the one hand, *Terminal USA*, in conventional terms, represents Moritsugu's "big break," giving him his largest budget as well as the widest exposure to audiences through broadcast television. On the other hand, the experience did not propel Moritsugu toward bigger budgets and audiences but ensured his return to independent, artisanal filmmaking. Unlike the then little-known Todd Haynes—whose short film *Dottie Gets Spanked* (1993), which was also commissioned by ITVS to air on *TV Families*, launched his Hollywood career—Moritsugu retreated to make low-budget features over which he would have sole artistic control.[35]

Moritsugu's ITVS experience also importantly reveals the profound influence of the historical institutional mandate to produce an identity politics based on the positive image. It is significant that *Terminal USA*, Moritsugu's most widely accessible and "successful" film, not only pursued conventional plot and story structure but also the subject of Asian American identity because it shows the viability of a clearly marked Asian American identity politics for the public media market. One of the markers of institutionality includes the assumption that Asian American media consists of the narrow scope of autobiography, history, and critiques of identity construction. Moritsugu turns this assumption on its head, and *Terminal USA* offers a productive alternative to it.

In order to adequately discuss the complexity of the failed televisual Asian American turn, it is necessary to weave together the discourses that treat the problem of race and representation, including the development of ITVS, network TV sitcoms, and independent filmmaking. As a campy, body genre artifact, *Terminal USA* realizes aesthetic alternatives in Asian American film and video and the complexities of US ethnic media production. The film's context as both a product of and a rebellion against the Asian American media institution allows reflection on the importance of institutional history in the emergence of minority media movements of the 1970s and 1980s and the reactions against them in the 1990s and beyond.

# 4

# Dismembered from History

Racial Ambivalence in
the Films of Gregg Araki

> The films of Jon Moritsugu and Gregg
> Araki participate in a kind of counter-
> nostalgia that truncates Asian American
> media from history.
> —Michael Bronski, "Reel Politick"

As discussed in this book's introduction, the question of definition has been the timeless dilemma of Asian American film and video. Indeed, independent filmmakers of Asian American descent who refuse to participate within the genre's institutional bounds have exacerbated the problem of defining it. Enter Gregg Araki. As Peter X Feng puts it, "this problem was so familiar to everyone concerned that I used shorthand to refer to it—I called it "The Gregg Araki question"—and everyone knew that I was asking, 'If an Asian American filmmaker makes a movie which doesn't engage with Asian American issues, would you include it in your definition of Asian American Cinema?'"[1] Gregg Araki's films are, on the surface, so blatantly non–Asian American that they have been used as the example against which all self-proclaimed Asian American films, and even the Asian American film movement itself, have been defined.

If *Chan Is Missing* represents a kind of modernist moment in the short history of Asian American media, then the cinema of Gregg Araki has produced its inevitable postmodern counterpart. One of the original figures of the New Queer Cinema movement, Araki made his name making films that were as far removed from Asian American film and video as could be. Instead, his films are libidinally driven, postmodern fantasy riffs on noir, sci-fi, and the road picture, focusing on alienated youth with a commitment to a punk aesthetic and an obsession with the apocalypse. And they mostly feature white actors as leads, avoiding an overtly racial discourse.

Araki's iconoclasm emerged chiefly through his stance that regardless of his ethnicity and support of the Asian American independent film community, he "doesn't make Asian American films." Despite this, Araki has paradoxically held a central place in the discourse of Asian American film and video. From the 1990s, when he began showing short films in both underground and Asian American film festivals, the filmmaker has, along with compatriots Jon Moritsugu and Roddy Bogawa, held court at discussion panels sponsored by the very institutions that have produced the concept of Asian American media that he so adamantly resists.[2] Araki's outsider status, therefore, is something that the institution of Asian American media cultivates knowingly, with the implicit understanding of the limitations of the concept and application of "Asian American media." Therefore, his work and its place in the history of Asian American media are crucial to understanding the fraught relationship between Asian American film and video and institutional history.

This chapter analyzes the paradoxical position of Araki as simultaneously included in and excluded by the Asian American media institution, and how his films as well as his public rejection of Asian American media are important to its very constitution.[3] I want first to examine the institutional discourse of the "outsider" that has been produced both by and around Araki and how it has ironically shaped mature notions of Asian American media. In examining discursive print contexts, this chapter will reveal how he has produced an Asian American media politics that resists both the usual suspects of Hollywood and commercial production and also the restrictive ideological demands of the independent public media establishment. Moreover, by exploring relations to other global film movements, popular culture, and American avant-garde and underground cinema, Araki's oeuvre attempts to carve out an Asian American film aesthetic that, importantly, diverts from preconceived ideas about its purpose. Specifically, his films explicitly utilize the aesthetic strategies of punk as a way to express resistance to dominant cultural forms. Punk emphasizes a highly attuned attention to style and form, which necessarily avoids the ideological content that defines much of Asian American media. Yet, despite the lack of Asian American issues in his films, the aesthetic of both queerness and punk aligns with the underlying principle of resistance in Asian

American media practice. And upon closer inspection, despite his seemingly vigilant avoidance of the discourses of race, Araki's narratives deploy subversive strategies to create what amounts to an incisive critique of racism. Therefore, paradoxically, although Araki is known as the filmmaker who most challenges the going definition of Asian American film and video, he plays a key discursive role in Asian American film. Specifically, the covert race politics in his films demonstrate the persistent traces of institutionality in his work to reveal an engaged Asian American film and video that has not easily been recognized as such.

## The Discourse of Inclusion/Exclusion

Araki poses an interesting counterpoint to the young filmmakers who established Asian American media as a fledgling film movement in the early 1970s. A sansei, or third-generation Japanese American, Araki is in some ways an heir of the Los Angeles filmmakers Robert Nakamura and Eddie Wong, who established Visual Communications decades before Araki came of age. In some ways, his approach to filmmaking as resistant to established, industrial practices—both commercial and institutional—resonates with the first Asian American films ever made. The initial burst of the "critical alternative" aesthetic in the rudimentary student films *Manzanar* and *Wong Sinsaang* ushered in a uniquely Asian American worldview of resistance. Soon that worldview had been lost to the structured compromise of the PBS-supported Asian American film of "injury" and "ressentiment." Araki intervenes in the history of Asian American media, not only through an aesthetics/economics of alternative independent cinema, but also through his own discursive reconceptualization of Asian American film and video history. Yet, as someone born and raised in the upper-middle-class white suburbs of Santa Barbara, Araki's relatively privileged class position and generationally attained cultural assimilation have estranged him from the social change perspectives of Visual Communications and old-school Asian American filmmakers such as Nakamura and Wong. With the rise of film programs at elite universities, many filmmakers had the advantage of formal education in film, a path that Wong and Nakamura, in fact, had paved for minority filmmakers.

What makes Araki's filmmaking unique is not only his anti–Asian American media stance but also his notoriously fastidious and efficient production style. His ability to make commercially viable independent feature films with very small budgets has enabled him to completely eschew the institutions of Asian American media as well as of Hollywood. Araki received his training in the MFA program in filmmaking from the University of Southern California, the bastion of commercial Hollywood cinema. Arriving at the peak of the New American independent cinema, he made his first two features for

$5,000.[4] Moreover, Araki worked alone. Not only did he act as the writer, director, and producer, he was the cameraman, sound recordist, and editor for these two films.[5]

One of the ways that Araki has shaped his paradoxical position as both inside and outside the institution of Asian American media is through the production of a contextual discourse in the press that is very similar to the critical role that Daryl Chin played in the early years. Over two decades, Araki's films, but mostly the discourse contained in his interviews and public panel discussions, hold to an unwavering belief in the problem of the category of Asian American film and video. Since 1991, when Araki began to appear at Asian American film festivals to announce his lack of allegiance to so-called Asian American media, he and his lesser known but equally disgruntled compatriots, Jon Moritsugu and Roddy Bogawa, raised the question of Asian American media as an existential dilemma—asking what it means to be an Asian American filmmaker and whether attachment to it is equal to the kind of "selling out" associated with Hollywood. When asked the same question regarding his affinity to the institution of Asian American media, Araki says:

> My feeling about both the gay issue and the Asian issue is that I don't let anybody tell me how to make my films. I'm certainly not going to let some Asian American media group say I should make a film about the relocation camps. My parents were interned like everybody else's, but I feel that if they want to make a film about that, that's their experience. Being thirty-one, I was never in those camps, that's not part of my experience. I personally think that's a little bit exploitative of the pain that your own parents went through. That's where I stand on that. On the other hand, I do absorb criticism and feedback on my own work and there are certain things that influence me. One thing that does bug me about my first two movies is that they're very white movies.[6]

Too young to have experienced the political events that formed Asian American political consciousness, such as the Japanese American internment or civil rights demonstrations in the 1960s, Araki nonetheless shares an ambivalent realization of his relationship to the Asian American media community. Though understandably removing his films from the compromise of Asian American media, Araki's unease about the "whiteness" of his films points to the question of race in his films. Though many, including Araki, assert the absence of a critical race discourse in his films, I argue that it is present in subversive forms, particularly through the representation of racial ambiguity via sexual ambiguity and romantic triangulation.

Having come into renown with his feature film, *The Living End* (1992), Araki had originally been known as a leading figure of the New Queer Cinema. *The Living End* is a queer revisionist road film, a familiar trope in the

Araki oeuvre. *The Living End* features gay, white male characters who go on an aimless road trip during which one of them, Jon, finds out that he is HIV positive and the other, Luke, a hitchhiking drifter, decides to be infected when he willingly has sex with Jon. The attitude of nihilism and black-humored despair of the film critiques both the revolution that marked the heyday of sexual liberation and the political conservatism of a post-HIV "safe sex" world. Not only was it a film with a queer aesthetic, what put *The Living End* on the map was its self-conscious and clever mixture of contemporaneous issues (gay male identity and HIV-AIDS), Godardian self-reflexivity, and allusions to classical Hollywood genres like film noir and the road picture, which brought the film into wider renown. Consequently, this film was the prime example used by the *Village Voice* critic B. Ruby Rich in her coining of the term New Queer Cinema.[7]

Even before his anointment as one of the originators of New Queer Cinema with *The Living End*, Araki had been initially considered a definitively nonethnic alternative filmmaker. Araki's earlier, more rudimentary features and shorts explored polyamory and queerness crossed with meditations on film theory and genre. In the late eighties, Araki showed his second feature film, *The Long Weekend (o'despair)* at the American Film Institute's film festival. The film, dubbed "a minimalistic gay/bisexual postpunk antithesis to the smug complacency of regressive Hollywood tripe like *The Big Chill*,"[8] was Araki's calling card, which led to the airing of his first feature, *Three Bewildered People in the Night*, on PBS, as well as his winning the Bronze Leopard at the Locarno Film Festival in 1987. Like many of his films, *Three Bewildered People in the Night* is concerned with a threesome—two men and a woman—and the philosophical inquiry into sexual ambiguity coupled with the analysis of romantic or sexual consummation as narrative closure.

Though claiming to be a self-professed "card-carrying member of two oppressed subcultural groups," Araki's career has nevertheless been affected by the race question.[9] As much as Araki belongs to a cadre of "gay filmmakers experimenting with narrative" that includes Todd Haynes, Jack Walsh, Su Friedrich, Peggy Ahwesh, and Gus Van Sant, he is also "an Asian American filmmaker working with nontraditional subject matter" with affinities to Roddy Bogawa, Trinh T. Minh-ha, and Jon Moritsugu.[10] The idea that his films complicate sexuality without complicating race is an ongoing critique by critics. For example, his first three feature films—*The Long Weekend (o'despair)* (1989), *Three Bewildered People in the Night* (1987), and his breakthrough film, *The Living End* (1992)—unproblematically feature white actors in situations that are otherwise critiques of establishment attitudes and roles.

In addition to his queer aesthetic, it is important to see the work of Araki through the theoretical lens of "punk cinema" because of its resistance to capitalist forms of production, and its penchant for loosely constructed and open-seamed visual and narrative style. Punk, as an ideology, stands in opposition to the requirements of institutional attachment. Araki's aesthetics and economics of punk—expressed through music, philosophy, and working methods—show the limitations of the Asian American media institution as creatively limiting. Araki defines his work thus:

> We were part of this punk rock generation. I was in high school when the Sex Pistols came out and that whole idea of D.I.Y. and being able to be [a] garage band and make things outside of the conglomerate corporate world[;] it was a very exciting time. So there was this point of feeling, "Why not?" It was very much like, "This is what I do." At that point in my life, films were all that mattered to me. So it was sort of like, "I'll do this movie or I'll die trying."[11]

Asian American institutional filmmaking was, at least on the surface, at odds with punk. The institutional requirements of Asian American media that are directly tied to funding are anathema to a punk aesthetic philosophy. Stacy Thompson defines punk cinema as that which must be reflected in both aesthetic and economic terms; "those films made without any support—in terms of production, distribution, or exhibition—from the eight major studios that dominate the film industry today (Columbia/Tri-Star, Warner Bros., Paramount, Universal, MGM, Twentieth Century Fox, New Line Cinema, and Disney)."[12] Despite the fact that Asian American film shares its marginalization from the studios with punk cinema, what differentiates the two is Asian American film's institutionalization and industrialization through state support. Therefore, Araki's allegiance to a punk aesthetic is in itself a resistance to any kind of relationship with an organized support system. Yet, there is a strong correlation between Araki's approach and that of the preinstitutional Asian American filmmakers, Bob Nakamura and Eddie Wong, particularly in their resistance to capitalist forms of art. Looked at from this perspective, ultimately, Araki's resistant stance affirms Asian American film and video's original purpose.

Although the origins of punk belong to another art form—music—the underlying philosophy of punk is one that is easily and visibly taken on by the moving image. Like punk music, punk cinema is that in which there is a material continuity between the economics of production and aesthetics. Thompson points out that "when punk passes into film, it demands of film that it offer up material traces of its production, that it open itself up to its audience as an 'open' text by pointing out how it came to be, rather than reifying its means of production and thereby folding in on itself as a 'closed' text."[13] Certainly, many Asian American films and videos can attest to this notion. Yet, what is illuminating is the fact that Araki's films, which are definitively punk, and Asian American films made before national institutionalization by PBS have a lot in common in their disregard for perfection and their offering up of their "material traces," as Thompson puts it.[14] What Araki's films do, in fact, is to acknowledge the limitations of the institutionalization of Asian American film and video by being completely untethered—narratively, aesthetically, and industrially—from the demands, requirements, and expectations of the institution.

Nevertheless, one problematic aspect that continues in Araki's work is the dominant place of whiteness as an invisible unproblematic yet central presence in his films, despite punk's otherwise liberal ethos. Certainly one of punk's most salient characteristics is its critique of classism and capitalism, particularly in its original context of deep class stratification in late-twentieth-century Britain. Regardless of its resolutely resistant and outsider status, however, like many vanguard movements, punk has not fully succeeded in working out the problem of inequality regarding race. An unchallenged racial politics becomes a glaring issue in Araki's films precisely because of his undeniable punk politics/aesthetics. Hence, Araki's status as a filmmaker of color as well as of punk serves as a unique challenge to the study of race, representation, and aesthetics. In punk, racial difference is a murky idea that is difficult to assimilate. Therefore, embracing an ideology that leaves out the problem of racism in the critique of capitalism remains a problem for the otherwise radical stance that Araki takes on. On the surface, the films of Araki are white—they use mostly white leads. On the other hand, upon deeper analysis, many of his films negotiate the problem of racial difference in myriad ways that are often subtle and are always steeped in the aesthetics of punk. Since punk must offer itself up as an open text,[15] the legibility of race is often a complex endeavor. Unlike the texts of the political documentaries produced by the Center for Asian American Media and Visual Communications, which often lead viewers to powerful and inevitable conclusions about racial prejudice and racial identity, the films of Araki demand other things from viewers, specifically through the postmodern strategy of meta-representation—in other words, representing what it means to be representing race. This often self-aware, detached, and ironic handling of race and representation shows an important development in the evolution of Asian American media.

## James Duval—Racial Ambiguity in the Teen Apocalypse Trilogy

Despite their seeming avoidance of race issues, upon closer inspection, Araki's films are uniquely concerned with the ambiguity of identity, both sexual and racial. Especially in Araki's "Teen Apocalypse Trilogy," *Totally Fucked Up* (1994), *Doom Generation* (1995), and *Nowhere* (1997), the continuum between race and sex is uniquely present. Araki's postmodern milieu problematizes the notion of the indexical relationship between race and identity, which critiques the very principle of the ideology of Asian American film and video. By unmooring identity from fixed racial and sexual labels, Araki's films necessarily stand outside of conventional representational practices in Asian American film and video, but they also enable the possibility of a more engaged aesthetics that goes beyond rigid national, racial, ethnic definitions. Particularly in his use of the biracial actor James Duval, who stars in all three films, Araki manages to articulate a subtle visual and narrative intervention into the problematic dominance of whiteness in discourses about sexuality.

Specific and central to Araki's concept of racial and sexual identity is the confluence of biracial and bisexual identity. Araki's Teen Apocalypse Trilogy cemented his specific brand of the indie "queersploitation" teen movie through its explicit yet sardonic worldview of fluid sexualities through the narrativization of gay, lesbian, and bisexual relationships. Although sometimes played by a multiracial cast, including Latino, black, and hapa (racially mixed Asian) actors, his "out and proud" characters never make the discourse of race explicit in the narrative. Araki's characters also speak from a uniform white Southern Californian "Valley speak" register, which problematizes neither culture nor class. Peculiarly, race is seen explicitly on the surface and never heard. On the other hand, the overt multiracial casting speaks to the fact of race and representation and how it plays out in the overt sexual economy of his tales. Specifically, the pivotal character in these films, as played by the biracial Duval, complicates the relationship between sexuality and race in ways that register an engaged politics of Asian American identity that takes sexuality into consideration.

> I say it half jokingly but Jimmy was the lead in three of my movies, the trilogy I did in the mid-'90s. . . . Jimmy is half Vietnamese, quarter Vietnamese, and also French and Indian, he's a melting-pot kid. It's interesting because he's not viewed as Asian enough to be considered Asian American even though he was called a chink or whatever when he was growing up . . . and I think that's in a way kind of explanatory of the Asian American representation in my movies. My experience, growing up in a largely White neighborhood in Santa Barbara, which didn't have an Asian American subculture that a lot of larger cities have, I was always very assimilated in more mainstream White culture. I never really viewed myself as different. That's kind of an explanation of how race in general is viewed in my movies. The differences are not as important as the similarities.[16]

Reading Duval's characters as biracial, and more specifically as hapa, opens up the repressed racial dimension of Araki's trilogy and its effect on his cinematic aesthetic. Duval's characterizations as narrative problem, motivation, and resolution reveal the subtle, multidimensional meanings that arise from the confluence of biracial and bisexual identities. Biracial actors have been used in Hollywood cinema to represent both the utopian and dystopian aspects of hybridity in globalization. The presence of the hapa actor Keanu Reeves in dystopian narratives like *Johnny Mnemonic* (1995) and *The Matrix* (1999, 2003) series has generated discussions of the intrinsic role of multiculturalism and multiracialism as a key visual element of postmodern, postcolonial, and globalized media.[17] I argue that, unlike the solution offered by Reeves's unproblematized "face of globalization"[18] in Hollywood cinema, Duval signifies its opposite: a recalcitrant racial and sexual other whose fluidity needs to be destroyed to create resolution in the narrative.

*Totally Fucked Up* is the first of Araki's Teen Apocalypse Trilogy. Ostensibly an episodic narrative about a group of six gay teens, with its multiracial characters (Steven is Latino, Deric is black, and Andy is Asian), *Totally Fucked Up* is as much about the alienation of teens of color as it is about queer youth. Steven, a videographer, makes grainy, Hi-8 video interviews of the cast, which are interspersed within the narrative. The group includes Tommy, a happy-go-lucky promiscuous teen whose conservative parents kick him out when they find his gay porn magazines, and a happy lesbian couple, Michele and Patricia, who attempt to have a child together by taking contributions of semen from their gay male friends, who participate by collectively ejaculating into a turkey baster.

In his book about the history of avant-garde filmmaking in Southern California, *The Most Typical Avant-Garde: History and Geography of Minor Cinemas in Los Angeles*, David E. James categorizes *Totally Fucked Up* as an example of a geographically specific, spatially informed, minor cinema that uses the backdrop of Los Angeles to work out meditations on the capitalist, consumerist landscape that surrounds its existentialist characters. The natural and artificial environment of Los Angeles is key to James's analysis of the film, which is made distinct by "thematics that are elaborated, not through depth, or nuances in characterization, which is broadly schematic and cartoonlike, but through photography and mise-en-scène."[19] James argues for a historical through-line that connects Araki to Josef von Sternberg and Jon Jost, whose films were equally fascinated by the overdetermined mass mediation on Los Angeles. In many ways, *Totally Fucked Up* is, as James suggests, a film in which the most significant and pervasive aspect is that "the boundary between the architectural fabric of the city and the mass media dissolves." The most striking thing about the film is "the "visual clamor" of Araki's mise-en-scène, filled with the neon-lit storefronts, mini-malls, parking lots, and billboards. However significant this reading of the film's dominant spatial aesthetic is, the seemingly superficial narrative—its banal, predictable love triangles—is just as important to the characters' alienation from the "text" of Los Angeles. James goes on further to say "fully queer and fully postmodern, Araki's aesthetic can

FIG. 7  James Duval in *Totally Fucked Up* (Gregg Araki, 1994).

only endorse nothing except a negative: an opposition to homophobia that links with nothing else, not even a celebration of homosexuality."²⁰ I would like to extend this idea of "an opposition to homophobia that links with nothing else." Particularly in thinking about the alienation of queer youth that ties the Teen Apocalypse Trilogy together, I argue that racial difference problematizes the supposed queer acceptance of white homosexuality. As buried as it is underneath Araki's postmodern nihilism, racial difference, exemplified by Duval's screen image, contributes to the unease of Araki's alienated, queer universe.

Although the film, like all of Araki's films, never explicitly points out the racial difference of its characters with backstory, it is important that the three male leads all experience the subtle alienation of gay male culture's preference for whiteness.²¹ On one of many walks through the parking lots that dominate the Los Angeles landscape, the conversation leads to the topic of which movie stars the characters masturbate to. As one of the characters offers Matt Dillon, an intertitle flashes that reads, "Tom Cruise: Rock Hudson for the 90s" and "Mel Gibson: Homophobe A-hole." This commentary on the rampant repression and homophobia of Hollywood crossed with the libidinal energy it inspires is reminiscent of a queer cinematic lexicon that dates back to the experimental films of Kenneth Anger. Anger's invention of the language of queer cinematic sensibility in *Scorpio Rising* (1963) arises from both a direct critique and celebration of Hollywood's hyperheterosexuality and, importantly, the false dichotomy of these opposite impulses. This avant-garde classic uses an elaborate montage structure to create a new vocabulary about the seemingly incongruous marriage of homophobia and homophilia, violence and sexuality, and the libidinal energy contained ironically therein. Anger's reframing of screen idols and emblems of unbridled white male masculinity, Marlon Brando and James Dean, put them in a new light as powerfully ambiguous, pan-sexual sex symbols. Yet, for Araki, his contemporaries Gibson and Cruise seem somehow bereft of this power. Hidden in the subtext of this discussion of sexual desire and movie stars is the obstacle of whiteness. The discussion among the multiracial teens about their sexual desire for white movie stars in homophobic Hollywood reveals the subtext of the self-hatred implicated in the institutionalized racism that constructs and binds Hollywood and, by extension, Los Angeles.

One main narrative around which the film revolves deals with the rocky relationship between Steve and Deric, the film's "happy" gay male couple. While they are initially seen as a loyal couple, they begin to suffer when Steve begins to seek sex outside of the relationship with a white lover, Brendan. Likewise, the other main narrative begins in sexual ambiguity. Initially Andy declares his bisexuality, adding, "Sex is just a hassle." When he meets Ian, a white UCLA student, they embark on an affair. When Ian eventually rejects Andy, Andy impulsively kills himself by drinking a cocktail of cleaning agents and drowning in a swimming pool.

The two narrative problems in the film have to do with nonwhite gay teens being rejected sexually by or in favor of white men, showing that racial rejection is implicated in Araki's problematics of queerness. Although this is an ensemble film whose ambling, loose, and flat narrative stands in contrast to the vivid, evocative, alienating mise-en-scène that is late twentieth-century Los Angeles, in shifting our understanding of racial masquerade, racial performance, and the notion of the biracial in the figure of James Duval, *Totally Fucked Up* can also be seen as an ironic twist on the tragic mulatta/o narrative. When Andy offs himself on such an impossibly sunny, typically bright Los Angeles day by falling, unconscious and poisoned, into a clear, blue pool, it's not only an allusion to the suffocation and subsuming of characters by the sterile, beautiful surroundings but a contemporary M. Butterfly tale set in Encino, California. *Totally Fucked Up* is not just a film about society's intolerance to queer teens, it is also about white preference in gay male culture and hence a film implicitly about race, which is a classic and significant topic of Asian American film and video. The film's episodic structure allows several examples of how the hegemony of whiteness in gay male culture produces self-hatred and self-destruction. Through these visual and narrative subtexts, Araki subtly but emphatically plants a discourse of the problem of race, which is central to the institutionality of Asian American film and video.

The second film in Araki's trilogy, *Doom Generation*, also starring Duval, continues with a preoccupation with racial subtext seething just beneath the surface. *Doom Generation* is a road film, similar in theme to *The Living End*, in which a teen couple, Jordan White (Duval) and Amy Blue (Rose McGowan) pick up an older, bisexual hitchhiker named Xavier Red (Johnathon Schaech). Within this Arakian threesome, representing the colors of the American flag, no less, Duval's character, Jordan, serves as third wheel and sacrificial lamb. Again, although Duval's biraciality is never made explicit, he represents excessive difference that must be annihilated in order to allow for narrative resolution. Among the three main characters that compose the ménage a trois, Jordan is the only nonwhite one. Jordan's racial difference signifies an obstacle in the film's economy of heteronormative desire.

Ironically named Jordan White, Duval's character's Asianness is expressed as socioeconomic and psychological difference as well in the positioning of his sexuality. As a sacrificial lamb, Jordan is the Jesus-like figure who forgives the sins of others. When Xavier and Amy have sex behind his back, he forgives them. Not only this, Jordan is the only one among the three who comes from a bourgeois upbringing. When the three end up together in their first hotel room on the lam, they reveal their respective family backgrounds and set up the characters' propensity for violence. Amy Blue's mother is a former heroin addict turned Scientologist, and Xavier Red's mother shot his father before killing herself when he was twelve. Jordan reveals that his parents "live in Encino," a placid middle-class yet bland enclave in the San Fernando Valley of Los Angeles County.

Jordan is not only racially different; as the well-adjusted, bourgeois, sexually passive, Jesus figure, he represents the film's model minority. Sexually, Jordan is always on the bottom. When they first attempt to have sex, Jordan is afraid of contracting AIDS, and Amy reminds him that they are both virgins. Amy is always the aggressor and always on top. In contrast, Amy and Xavier are seen from the beginning as the film's star-crossed, film noir–inspired sexual soulmates. Although the dialogue indicates their hatred for each other, their matched, aggressive sexual appetites and instinct for survival are what allow them to remain alive at the end of the film. Like the antiheroes and femmes fatales of *Double Indemnity* (Billy Wilder, 1944), *Out of the Past* (Jacques Tourneur, 1947), and *Gun Crazy* (Joseph H. Lewis, 1950), Xavier and Amy are bound by sexual and moral compatibility, which are the only things that are of value in this violent postmodern landscape. Jordan must die in order to resolve the problem of socially unacceptable polyamory as well as his unstable bisexuality, which restores classical heterosexual union at the end of the film. Furthermore, being the film's only nonwhite character only adds to Jordan's extraneousness in the racially homogeneous, heteronormative economy of the genre picture. Although the plot would seem to follow a classic Hollywood moral structure, in Araki's film, it is clearly an indictment of homophobia and racism. Moreover, Jordan's status as the film's only middle-class character adds to the film's critique of class. The survivors, Amy and Xavier come from so-called white trash backgrounds, which allow them to survive. Jordan, who is from "Encino," must suffer the consequences of being middle class. More than this, again, James Duval dies in the end as a kind of sacrificial, tragic mixed-race character, neither gay nor straight and, more importantly, neither white nor Asian.

Whereas *Totally Fucked Up* and *Doom Generation* contest the sexual and racial status quo through subtle and not-so-subtle means, *Nowhere* remains Araki's most questionable film in regard to a politics, and a poetics, of resistance. Mixing his postmodern style with ideologically problematic images of race and gender, the film is indicative of a negotiation between underground sensibility and the higher budgets and requirements of mainstream cinema. Predictably, although Araki's earlier films embraced a low-budget, punk cinema style, his later films began to edge closer to a consumerist, mainstream approach as he became better known and his budgets rose.

Like the two previous films in Araki's Teen Apocalypse Trilogy, *Nowhere* marries ironic, countercultural images and icons to a bare-bones narrative structure. The last of the trilogy, *Nowhere* structures a TV drama–like ensemble cast of teenagers who experience a spectrum of traumatizing effects of their out-of-control libidos on the way to a big party, which coincides with

FIG. 8  James Duval in *Nowhere* (Gregg Araki, 1995).

Armageddon. Added to this is a side story of a reptilian alien who comes to earth to parasitize teen bodies à la James Cameron's *Aliens*. As David James has said of *Totally Fucked Up*, Araki's strength is his shot composition and mise-en-scène, both of which comment most viscerally about and against dominant cultural forms and attitudes about gender, sexuality, and art. And it also follows that the film is peopled by cardboard-cutout characters who do little more than provide elements of this mise-en-scène. It is especially true of *Nowhere*, which is notorious for being a who's who of young Hollywood stars who have gone on to mainstream stardom. However, without totally throwing narrative and character complexity out the window, it is important again to note how the film problematizes mixed-race identity by delineating its protagonist as racially and sexually unstable. James Duval, making his final appearance as the narrative linchpin of Araki's troubled teen universe, again plays a tenderhearted love victim, vulnerable to the aggressions of both male and female characters. In *Nowhere*, the problem of Dark's (Duval's character) bisexuality motivates and enables the narrative.

*Nowhere*'s exposition sets out the problematics of the film's narrative development. A high crane shot moves down through a miasma of white steam to land on a medium shot of a naked, dark-haired man masturbating in a shower. Dark is introduced as the film's protagonist. Three daydream sequences are cut in with this exposition to reveal the relationship between Dark's sexual frustration, that is, inability to ejaculate, and the sheer variety of his sexual fantasies. In one, Dark has straight, missionary position sex with his black, alpha female girlfriend, Mel (Rachel True). In the next, he is whipped into submission by two female dominatrices, Kriss (Chiara Mastroiani) and Kozy (Debi Mazar). Lastly, Dark fantasizes about a new boy in school, the strawberry blond, blue-eyed Montgomery, and of getting it on with him in the boy's locker room at high school. The sheer number of these fantasies and their competing levels of titillation distract and confuse Dark to the point of preventing sexual climax. Before he is able to finish, his mother (played in green face-mask drag by Beverly d'Angelo) knocks on the door to get out and stop "flogging his puppy" in a rancorous, campy, fish-eye lens close-up that functions to interrupt and cut off pleasure. Interestingly, this scene references a similar one in George Kuchar's avant-garde classic, *Hold Me While I'm Naked* (1966). In that film, a sexually frustrated filmmaker (Kuchar) fantasizes about an erotic encounter while dejectedly taking a shower wearing a feminizing shower cap, and he is also interrupted by his meddlesome mother nagging, yelling, and threatening at the door. Araki's homage to Kuchar in his opening scene reminds us of his roots in underground, avant-garde film, yet this is ultimately contradicted by the requirements of conventional, narrative storytelling.

Dark's inability to reach the logical conclusion of sexual fulfillment in the film's exposition serves as a microcosm of the film itself. On one level, the film's narrative structure mimics the path to pleasure's fulfillment, which is presented as either sexual, chemical, or otherwise. In one scene, three high school girls scarf down a dessert only to consider bulimic purging to get rid of it immediately. In the same way that Dark is defined through a frustrated attempt to get off, each of the film's supporting characters is paired off and attempts, to varying degrees of success, to attain sexual fulfillment. This structure serves to define the film as ironic commentary on legitimate media narratives of high schoolers, especially popular 1990s television shows like *Beverly Hills 90210* and the high school films of John Hughes. Rather than the sanitized narrative problems presented in those mainstream movies and TV shows, *Nowhere* shows its teens steeped in graphic yet comic depictions of violent suicidal deaths, bloody sadomasochistic sex, and aggressive drug use. Araki's teens are not only motivated by their most base desires, they perform them with an inordinately ardent and campy vigor.

In *Nowhere*, Duval is the linchpin in two love triangles that suggest his chameleon-like ability to be both masculine and feminine. In the first triangle, which is presented in the first part of the film, Duval's character, Dark, competes aggressively for the attention of his sexually omnivorous and voracious girlfriend, Mel, with Mel's best girlfriend, Lucifer. Physically affectionate and playful, Mel and Lucifer are presented as often kissing and groping each other. The first scene in which we see them, they dress and groom each other in Mel's bathroom and kiss each other on the lips, which mixes overt cultural signs of feminine masquerade with the possibility of it spilling into homoeroticism. On witnessing this extreme public show of physical affection, Dark cringes, often hurling misogynistic insults at Lucifer. To be certain, Mel plays off this triangular sexual energy and juices it for the power it gives her as a phallic woman. With the exception of the protracted, polysexual exposition montage sequence, Dark's heterosexuality is emphasized in contrast to the quasi-lesbian coupling of Mel and Lucifer. In vying with a lesbian for the affections of Mel, Dark becomes conventionally straight in his sexual proclivities, even asking at one point if he could shoot Mel topless for the film he is making. In a classic reference to male visual pleasure, Dark gets off on seeing Mel's breasts, which are never shown to the audience as the shot of Mel abruptly cuts away to Dark receiving a jarring phone call, yet another agent of the constant coitus interruptus from which Dark (and by extension, the audience) suffers. At first, Dark positions himself as relatively white in the film's racial and sexual triangulation of Mel, Dark, and Lucifer. Especially in the first act of the film, Dark is portrayed as a classic white male protagonist, a situation that shifts as other triangles threaten to disrupt the status quo.

Things shift in the economies of both sexuality and race, as sexual appetites shift in the narrative. During the climax of the film, another triangle develops between Mel, Dark, and Montgomery, the white, gay boy who appeared first in the exposition in Dark's sexual fantasy. During the turning point in Dark and Mel's relationship, Mel proclaims once and for all her status as sexually liberated alpha female and utters to Dark, "isn't sex the best tension release there is?—it's like a really good, sweaty game of racquetball only you get to come at the end." To this, Dark recalibrates his position in the sexual economy of the film by responding, "I adore you... will you marry me?" In other words, this postcoital exchange shifts Dark's sexual identity from white, straight male with a movie camera to feminized, racialized, romantic victim. Again, as in the previous films of the Teen Apocalypse Trilogy, shades of Duval's M. Butterfly persona come out as the film shifts perspective. Subsequently, at the party, which is the de facto narrative destination, Mel decides to have a ménage à trois with twin blond surfer boys and thus effectively breaks up with Dark. It is notable that the twins are exaggeratedly white, with fair skin and blond hair, which by contrast, brings Dark's racial "darkness" into high relief. Dark's inability to perform fully as a white, straight male is also precipitated by his attraction to Montgomery, who earlier joined them in a game of hide-and-seek but got lost. Montgomery was presumably abducted by a reptilian alien, who earlier showed up at a bus stop to vaporize a trio of valley girls with a laser gun, a bizarre act of horror that Dark witnesses. After the party, Dark goes home in defeat without Mel, but seems to get another chance at love when Montgomery unexpectedly shows up naked at Dark's bedroom window. Dark invites him to sleep over and each declares his attraction to the other. However, as they are about to consummate their relationship, Montgomery explodes and from his body, an insect alien emerges, which has hatched inside his body, à la Ridley Scott's *Alien*. As in the exposition, Dark is left unfulfilled both sexually and existentially.

*Nowhere*'s narrative world is dependent on the insatiable horniness of its constellation of teen couples, particularly in its display of variety in sexual tastes, which functions as the film's ironic organizational logic in spoofing straight TV teen melodrama. Instead of race, class, gender, hair color, costume, and personality type, each teen is seemingly identified through their unique flavor of sexual perversity, whether that be masochism, sadism, promiscuity, or bisexuality. For example, in one minor storyline, a white, heterosexual couple, Shad and Lilith (played by Ryan Phillippe and Heather Graham), are constantly copulating, displaying a penchant for sex play in which they appear to be killing each other through overenthusiastic intercourse while spouting existential quips about sex and death.

Despite *Nowhere*'s progressive interracial and nonheteronormative sexual politics, the film does unfortunately rely on shopworn racist stereotyping, especially in its depiction of black men and women. Shad's twin sister, Alyssa (played by Jordan Ladd), is involved in a sadomasochistic sexual relationship with Elvis, a "macho" black man of few words who not only gyrates overtly and displays an uncommon sexual voraciousness but is ironically, a masochist, who requires a spanking to get off. When Alyssa and Elvis have sex, it involves spanking and a montage of close-ups of his Calvin Klein underwear, a reproduction Greek statue, and a paperback copy of Nietzsche's philosophy. This mixture of high and low signifiers connotes the film's correlation of pleasure and pain as a postmodern recombination of nihilism, youth as physical perfection, and capitalism.[22] Although at first glance, Elvis's exaggerated sexual appetite does not stand out particularly from that of some of the white characters, the film clearly articulates the special, racialized difference of his particular sexual prowess and association with the myth of black male hypersexuality. For example, when Elvis first shows up on his motorcycle to pick up Alyssa, one character asks what Alyssa sees in Elvis, to which she replies a wordless hand gesture referring to his outsize penis, yet another tired racist stereotype of black men, which seems peculiar in the otherwise progressive outlook of Araki's universe.

Another character who is saddled with an even more unfortunate racist stereotype is the film's leading lady, Mel, played by Rachel True. The film is unable to avoid the cliché of the hypersexual black woman, whom the film portrays as both sexually aggressive and insatiable. On the one hand, as one of the main characters of the film and as a black woman playing the girlfriend of a hapa man, the character of Mel is somewhat progressive. Black women coupled with Asian men generate the most problematic representations in mainstream media, and to have a positive coupling in any film is a coup.[23] However, in much the same way that Dark is associated with weakness and tragedy, Mel is burdened with the hackneyed hypersexuality of women of color. On the other hand, Mel is a strong character who dominates her male paramour. This prototype has been established in other similar characters in the Araki oeuvre, specifically in the excessively sexual Amy White (Rose McGowan) in *Doom Generation*. However, by bestowing hypersexuality on a black woman character, the signifier of race changes all meanings completely, which is one of the most problematic aspects of Araki's refusal to engage in a discourse of race. The disingenuousness of this stance, not to mention the impossibility of engaging in a discourse of race while peopling his mise-en-scène with nonwhite characters is palpable, especially in *Nowhere*. While sexuality dominates in *Nowhere*, as it does in all of Araki's films, the sheer range of interracial couplings and the prominent representation of a superficially politically correct, multicultural cast, opens up the film to multiple critical readings that result in ambiguous, sometimes racist meanings. Regardless of Araki's official denial of a race politics in his films, his seemingly PC-friendly casting profoundly implicates race and especially the interconnectedness between race and sexuality.

Gregg Araki has occupied an ambiguous place in Asian American film history. His mainstream success as an independent filmmaker seems to rest on the fact that he avoids affiliation with the institution of Asian American media. Yet, ironically, he has become an important part of its institutional discourse, and upon closer examination, his films do engage in the politics of race and representation, even as he is known as a figure of New Queer Cinema rather than one of Asian American film and video. What is surprising is how important the discourse of race becomes in his explorations of teen sexuality in his most important films, the Teen Apocalypse Trilogy. Araki's consistent use of the biracial actor James Duval and the problematization of whiteness in mainstream representations of gay sexuality are profoundly in line with an engaged Asian American identity politics. And yet, as a filmmaker, Araki had made his desire to stand outside of the institution of Asian American film and video very clear.

The question that ultimately arises from the range of racialized problematics that emerge in the Teen Apocalypse Trilogy is, What are the racial politics of Araki's films? Although he explicitly tries to avoid being categorized as an Asian American filmmaker—and by extension, having a concern about race, representation, and politics of identity—his trilogy, upon closer viewing, reveals a different story. Ultimately, in Araki's trilogy, the trauma of racial difference is both hidden and ambivalent. Contextualizing the films with Asian American film and video history suggests that the films' frequent focus on the biracial actor Duval's sexual ambivalence also shows a racial ambivalence—and quite possibly the ambivalence of desiring whiteness while being nonwhite. Specifically, Duval's ambivalent main character reveals layers of conflicted meaning that have as much to do with race as they do with sexuality. Although Duval's character does not always become the sacrificial lamb/tragic mixed-race character of *Totally Fucked Up* and *Doom Generation* (in *Nowhere*, he gets to live), his biraciality functions as a covert signifier of problematic Asian American masculinity.

Despite his reluctance to be included in the milieu of Asian American film and video, Araki's Teen Apocalypse Trilogy has not only established his reputation, it foregrounds race in some fashion, however invisible this may seem to mainstream audiences. Araki's humorous and clever conflation of sexuality and race, coupled with the boldness and frankness of his approach, has definitely contributed to his triumph. And yet, at times, the obfuscation of racial discourse in favor of a sexual one in these films also suggests that race is still the last taboo, the last barrier to recognition in American cinema, and that its concealment continues this disturbing tradition.

# 5

## *Better Luck Tomorrow* and the Transnational Reframing of Asian American Film and Video

> "Not all of us became Justin Lin. Even Justin Lin didn't become the Justin Lin most of you know until much later. This is almost funny to say, but in 1997, I think we all had a glimmer of hope. Asian American film as a genre? A future film deal? The next Spike Lee? Distribution? Anything? I felt like we were actually the center of the universe—and in Asian American land, we were. Being part of it was a curse for sure, but also a blessing.
> —Eric Nakamura, "Class of '97"

*Better Luck Tomorrow* (Justin Lin, 2002) occupies an exceptional place in the history of Asian American film and video in that it achieved mainstream, popular acceptance, a rarity within the genre. By entering into the mainstream, Lin's film addressed an ongoing theme of the genre's history, which is ambivalence toward "selling out" to Hollywood. How could Asian American film and video engage in the institutional racism of dominant media without sacrificing its social change ethos? *Better Luck Tomorrow*, for all intents and purposes, seemed to solve this conundrum by blending a seemingly contradictory mixture of Hollywood genre cinema, Hong Kong action film, and crucially, a socially conscious message about race and representation. A high school crime drama based on a true story, *Better Luck Tomorrow* tells the tale of a coterie of high-achieving Asian American high school students who cleverly take advantage of their role as model minorities in order to cover up larceny, drug trafficking, and eventually murder. The film tackles head-on the double-edged sword of the model-minority myth. From an institutional standpoint, the film engages in representational strategies of the "Bad Asian" and of the negative image (discussed in chapter 3) as a way to subvert the sanctimoniousness of institutional Asian American film and video. Key to *Better Luck Tomorrow*'s success was its ability, in the eyes of critics and scholars, to be that rare Asian American film that achieves the best of both worlds, that is, a film that entertains while also maintaining its political credibility. Roger Ebert praised it, saying: "*Better Luck Tomorrow* is a coming-of-age film for Asian-Americans in American cinema. Like African-American films that take race for granted and get on with the characters and the story, Lin is making a movie in which race is not the point but simply the given."[1]

Ebert's quote highlights the virtues of *Better Luck Tomorrow* from the mainstream perspective, that it was fresh and entertaining, and not bogged down by somber messages about race, a fact that had alienated many viewers to Asian American films. Margaret Hillenbrand has argued that *Better Luck Tomorrow*'s "parody and metacinema . . . may be one answer to an Asian American film industry that both aspires to the big time and is loath to surrender its oppositional edge."[2] By 2002, *Better Luck Tomorrow* seemed to represent what many believed to be the formula for success: the postracial Asian American film. All in all, *Better Luck Tomorrow* was indeed Asian American media's "great yellow hope" and proved that in 2002, Asian American media had arrived.

And yet, as much as the critics have praised the narrative and stylistic virtues of *Better Luck Tomorrow*, they do not explore how or why this particular film at this point in time managed to grasp Hollywood's brass ring. Although, like Ebert, many enjoy the film's lack of focus on race, this problematizes Lin's film in terms of the pressure that Asian American filmmakers are under to "represent." Indeed, what is at stake in the strategic redefinition of the genre in an increasingly postracial media environment? For Asian American film and video, the struggle to banish the notion of foreignness and alienness has been central. Yet, by the 1990s, this foremost issue came up against a cinematic culture that grew more and more globalized and diasporic. Particularly in the 1990s, art house and genre cinemas from Hong Kong, Taiwan, Japan, China, and elsewhere in Asia became an important aspect of Asian American film festivals. For younger Asian American filmmakers like Justin Lin, there was a great incentive to jump on the bandwagon of Asian films that were getting the international attention that Asian American films never had before. Certainly there is a fiscal incentive in marketing Asian American films as belonging to a more exotic, foreign Asian cinema platform. Does the marketability of foreignness serve as a step backward in the progressive aims of Asian American media? Or does the awareness of the transnational and diasporic nature of Asian American identity itself find new meaning in films that highlight cultural otherness rather than cultural assimilation? Ultimately, I argue that *Better Luck Tomorrow* and Lin's steadily meteoric rise in Hollywood depended on his deployment of a self-consciously superficial transnational aesthetic that simulated the aesthetic of Hong Kong new wave cinema while deemphasizing the social-change ethos on which Asian American film and video was built.

This chapter aims to explore these questions through an analysis of the institutional and historical underpinnings of *Better Luck Tomorrow*'s success. It is important to reiterate here that my emphasis on *Better Luck Tomorrow* amid many other Asian American feature films during this same period is based primarily on institutional history and economic prominence. Justin Lin's "sophomore effort" feature film (following his well-received *Shopping for Fangs*, codirected with Quentin Lee) broke into the mainstream after serial attempts by microbudget Asian American feature films to do the same, a phenomenon that the discourse of the SFIAAFF calls "the Class of 1997." Though many other independent Asian American feature films appeared in the 1990s, including those by South/Southeast Asian Americans and immigrant/transnational directors such as Ang Lee, Evans Chan, Tony Bui, and Mira Nair, these films have not been materially crucial to the shaping of the institution of Asian American film and video in the same way as *Better Luck Tomorrow*. The main reason for this is the way the institution itself tells its story as one of gradual and progressive "success" in the mainstream through the adoption of stylistic gestures that attempt to skim the surface of transnationality without engaging deeply with its narratives. This presents precisely one of the essential problems of Asian American film and video as one of *recognition*, not primarily through injury and ressentiment but through *capital*. In other words, the story of Asian American feature films that I tell in this chapter looks at how the CPB-funded San Francisco International Asian American Film Festival, the one officially sanctioned by PBS, has shaped the history of Asian American feature filmmaking as a paradigm of center to periphery favoring the Hollywood/MTV mainstream. In fact, the way that the SFIAAFF has shaped this history raises interesting questions about the gerrymandering of Asian American film and video through the lens of marketability and mainstream success, which ironically runs counter to the impulse of grassroots filmmaking of the past inaugurated by Visual Communication in the 1970s.

This narrow institutional history demonstrates that success didn't arrive in a vacuum, that in fact, the film belongs to a historical trajectory of Asian American independent feature films that began in the 1990s, which self-consciously erased the boundary between Asian and Asian American in an outward awareness of the changing global cinema market. Though it is true that Asian American film festivals and showcases throughout history have blended Asian art house and popular genre films with Asian American films in their programs, this is mostly because there weren't enough Asian American films available to screen. The micro-budget independent feature film phenomenon of the 1990s addresses a completely different issue, and that is aspiration toward the mainstream. I contextualize the proliferation of Asian American feature films in the 1990s against a larger phenomenon of global cinephilia, which transformed the binary of foreign/American into a constellation of possibilities for Asian American film and video. One crucial context in this trajectory is the San Francisco International Asian American Film Festival, which not only championed *Better Luck Tomorrow* but, years earlier, had promoted Lin's first feature film, *Shopping for Fangs*, and other low-budget independent feature films emerging in the 1990s. The emergence of the contemporary Asian American feature film coincided with both global cinephilia and the transformation of Asian American film festivals into hybrid Asian American/global Asian art cinema enterprises that blurred the line between their original social change mission and the future of transnational cinema. This shift signals the ambivalent path of the Asian American feature film between the film of social change and the film of the transnational aesthetic in the drive to mainstream exposure.

## SFIAAFF and Global Cinephilia

Before engaging in an analysis of the film texts that form the core of this chapter, I would like to give it ample context by discussing the reincarnation of one of the most visible Asian American film festivals, the San Francisco International Asian American Film Festival, as well the larger historical circumstances of global cinephilia that changed the face of cinema and of Asian American independent film and video and paved the way for the success of *Better Luck Tomorrow*.[3]

In the 1990s, Asian American film and video emerged from the margins to meet with global cinephilia. The shift toward cinephilia that was especially taken up by the SFIAAFF has been an overlooked agent of transformation that influenced *Better Luck Tomorrow* as well as the genre as a whole. Schooled in international cinematic traditions, younger, emerging Asian American filmmakers, some of whom were themselves born in Asian nations, worked within an increasingly transnational framework. The feature films that I will examine in the context of global cinephilia in the 1990s are *Yellow* (Chris Chan Lee,

1998), *Strawberry Fields* (Rea Tajiri, 1997), and *Shopping for Fangs* (Justin Lin and Quentin Lee, 1997), films that appeared in the 1997 SFIAAFF and represent the peak of the Asian American independent feature filmmaking period of the 1990s.[4] I focus on these three films to delimit the discussion of Asian American feature to its most significant year, 1997, during which an unprecedented number of feature films appeared at film festivals.

The filmmakers involved with this mini-movement of independent feature filmmaking were grouped together and labeled "GenerAsian X" as the new generation of filmmakers who would break through Hollywood's so-called yellow ceiling. Although these films were featured widely at Asian American film festivals, none of them, unlike *Better Luck Tomorrow*, won a major national distribution deal. I think about these four low-budget feature films as a testing ground for *Better Luck Tomorrow*'s ultimate success. As these examples show, Asian American feature films have taken either of two tactics: the narrative of social change or the narrative of global cinephilia. As I will argue, the success of global cinephilia against the equal impulse to engage the classic rhetoric of social change was key to the advancement of Asian American film and video toward a larger recognition and relevance within an increasingly globalized cinematic marketplace.

Given the history of Asian American media laid out in the previous chapters, it would seem that cinephilia, or the apolitical love of cinema, would be diametrically opposed to its aims. Cinephilia is an idea that arises from the culturally and historically specific notion of "photogénie," in which, according to Marijke de Valck, "the cinephilic moment is located in the personal relationship of the viewer to the screen, when he/she discovers extra information—a gesture, body position, look, mise-en-scène, etc., that was or was not choreographed for the spectator to see—that touches his or her subjectivity."[5] The indispensible fact of "the personal" in cinephilic discourse belies the underlining structure of "the public" that has supported Asian American film and video for decades. Film festivals began in postwar Europe and coincided with the cinephilia associated with the French new wave, auteur theory, and contemporary film criticism in *Cahiers du cinéma* and *Positif*. By contrast, Asian American media's roots lay in recovering the institutionalized racism of dominant film industries. So how could Asian American media practitioners, in clear conscience, follow a philosophy so radically opposed to their aims?

Around the time of cinema's centennial, the discourse of cinephilia became very relevant to Asian American media and other marginalized cinemas when its simultaneous "death" and its rebirth emerged through globalization. In a 1996 *New York Times* op-ed, Susan Sontag infamously opined that "perhaps it is not cinema that has ended but only cinephilia—the name of the very specific kind of love that cinema inspired," but also that this death portended "the birth of a new kind of cine-love."[6] In her study of film festivals, de Valck outlines the various elegiac arguments in the 1990s over the death of cinema and of cinephilia in the face of TV and other new technologies. These arguments launched by Sontag, Paul Willemen, and Thomas Elsaesser are ultimately refuted by de Valck, who argues that "the most crucial characteristics of contemporary cinephilia are its truly global nature and reach, and its popularization in terms of practice." Indeed the "new kind of cine-love" implicated, of course, a turn away from the old-school, established art cinemas of the world toward low-budget, ethnic, queer, independent cinemas that were burgeoning everywhere. Whereas cinephilia was a phenomenon that was born of European postwar art cinema, a renewed global interest in film festivals from Asia, South America, and Africa resurrected it as a decisively non-Eurocentric concept.

It is significant too, that during the "death of cinema" period of the mid 1990s, the SFIAAFF emerged as an important festival that bridged Asian American media to the global. In fact, it is cinephilia's death as a narrow concept historically aligned with European and, by extension, Hollywood-linked film festivals that enabled its resurrection as "global cinephilia." In other words, the same technologies—the Internet, television, cable, and so on—that threatened classic notions of cinema and cinephilia, allowed it to be reborn as a globally networked phenomenon based on diversity and not as much on exclusivity. Therefore, the death of Eurocentric, white, geopolitically limited cinephilia in the 1990s allowed "other" kinds of cinephilia to be born.

Asian American film and video's merger with cinephilia came in the reincarnation of the SFIAAFF, then the largest Asian American film festival in the United States, in the mid-1990s. Whereas Asian CineVision in New York City effectively began an Asian American film festival in the late seventies, the advent of NAATA, which supports the SFIAAFF, gradually created a shift from East Coast to West Coast, resulting in the SFIAAFF becoming the most significant Asian American film festival in the nation by surpassing one hundred films in 1994.[7] As mentioned in chapter 1, NAATA's earliest years supported a much more scaled-down version of the global film festival that the SFIAAFF eventually became. The SFIAAFF's original incarnation was the Bay Area stop for a small traveling showcase of Asian American films that was grassroots in nature. From 1982 to 1989, Asian American film and video output was very small; therefore, the festival consisted of a handful of Asian American films supplemented with feature films from Asia, a fact that anticipates the transnationality of the global film festival that it would later become. During the first half of the 1990s, NAATA stabilized a yearly festival, responding to the proliferation in Asian American films, whose representation more than doubled during this period. NAATA then hired its first full-time festival director, Bob Uyeki, who, with succeeding director, Paul Mayeda Berges, helped usher in the rapid growth and diversification of Asian American film and video culture, along with "previously underrepresented communities such as Pacific Islanders, South Asians, queers, and hapas."[8]

The years 1995 and 1996 were pivotal years for Asian American film festivals. The biggest change in the SFIAAFF arrived in the form of its new festival codirectors, Paul Yi and Corey Tong. Both under forty, Yi and Tong brought a youthful, contemporary, and global perspective to the shift in Asian American media. Tong has been a San Francisco–based independent producer in addition to working for the SFIAAFF. Yi has also been an independent producer as well as a key player in Asian film markets, having been one of the founding advisers of the Pusan International Film Festival. Their understanding of Asian American feature filmmaking as coterminous with contemporary new wave cinemas in Hong Kong, Taiwan, and Vietnam was crucial in lifting Asian American feature films on a global platform. Previous festivals had made a distinction and separation between Asian films and their Asian American counterparts, but Tong and Yi stretched the definition of the transnational to create an inclusive global cinephilic environment that transformed the SFIAAFF, and hence Asian American film and video, in the 1990s.

One way of tracing the shifts in identification between Asian American film and video and Asian cinema is through naming. Thus, an important signifier of this transnational shift in NAATA's film festival came in its strategic renaming in 1995. That year, the film festival, which had seemingly changed its name practically every year since its inception in the early 1980s, went through its final name change to San Francisco International Asian American Film Festival. As the festival program explains, the festival in its current and final incarnation "commemorate[s] the centennial anniversary of the birth of cinema by assembling a program (the largest yet) celebrating 'A Century of the Asian Diaspora in Motion.' In arguably the most ambitious program to date, films from throughout Asia and the diaspora, both new and old, explore the ways in which Asian identity has evolved."[9] The prominent use of the term "diaspora" strongly emphasizes an international element that had only been assumed in previous years' festivals.

Originally, when the film festival began in 1982, it was called the Asian American International Film Festival. Subsequently, the name was changed in 1986 to Bay Area Asian American International Film Festival for two years. In 1987, the festival was briefly replaced by the New Chinese Film Series, which was devoted to highlighting the emergent Fifth-Generation Chinese filmmakers such as Zhang Yimou and Chen Kaige. Thereafter, the film festival was called Bay Area Asian American International Film and Video Showcase, which reflected a brief dalliance with video as a separate medium. In 1990, the film festival was renamed Asian American International Film Showcase/World Series of Asian Films; and in 1991, it reverted to Asian American International Film Showcase until 1994, when it was again renamed to San Francisco Asian

American International Film Festival. Then, in 1995, the festival went through its longest-lasting title, which was simply a switching of the signifiers "International" and "Asian American" to San Francisco International Asian American Film Festival.

The history of the SFIAAFF's name changes is significant because it clearly signals a wish to appeal to a larger audience by fitting into the model of all other international film festivals. Particularly the festival's last renaming, which changed from the SFAAIFF to the SFIAAFF, indicates a subtle yet profound shift toward global cinephilia and away from its roots in the social change–oriented Asian American film and video. In addition to the privileging of "international" over "Asian American," the previous year's festival, in 1994, had for the first time made the city's name, San Francisco, more prominent than the national/cultural label, Asian American, and speaks to a specific strategy of highlighting Asian American media's link to globalization through the model of the international film festival. Although this festival has always included foreign films and included the word "international" in its title, the reordering of the terms privileges both the signifier "international" to precede Asian American, and to highlight the international character of the location, San Francisco. Whereas before, the festival at times emphasized its location (Bay Area) or focus (Asian American), this new incarnation finally began to follow the model of all other significant international film festivals: Locarno, Cannes, Toronto, Pusan, Telluride, Berlin, Venice. The replacement of "Bay Area" with "San Francisco," especially, suggests a favoring of the global over the local—whereas "Bay Area" is inclusive of the city's outlying suburbs and connotes the acceptance of local outsiders, and possibly of class and ethnic diversity, "San Francisco" highlights the urban exclusiveness that typifies a modernist European fetishization of cities and a connection of cinema with the urban. In fact, San Francisco is one of three "global city regions" in the United States, which "owe their successes in becoming dominant global city regions less to interaction and flows within their home countries, than to their articulation into the global (cultural) economy; an economy embedded in networked global city regions that are dispersed across the globe."[10]

Another way to look at this shuffling of signifiers is to see the last term of the series of words as the one losing the most efficacy: American. By splitting Asian and American, thereby bypassing the unspoken hyphen between them, one is left with a series of strategically placed signifiers in order of significance: San Francisco, International, Asian, and American, with American being the least significant. From this perspective, it appears that in losing its allegiance to US forms of production, distribution, and exhibition, Asian American media may be productively unmooring itself from its ties to the United States. Particularly when some independent Asian American filmmakers as well as the famous and successful Taiwanese American director Ang Lee have found many of their resources outside of the United States, this unmooring is appealing to aspiring Asian American filmmakers. Not only is there ample evidence to suggest this, as I will soon point out, but there are many interesting implications arising from this notion of breaking away from the Asian American media model. The linking of globalization with cinephilia has also had the effect of problematizing the definition of Asian American film and video and thus, gradually making institutionality invisible. What was once a movement emphasizing a distinctly American identity was, in the cinephilic moment of the 1990s, moving toward a more transnational notion of Asian American identity.

## "GenerAsian X" and the Class of 1997

An important part of recontextualizing and redefining Asian American film and video was the appearance of the term "GenerAsian X," which was briefly promulgated by journalists and critics in the 1990s. In 1998, a *New York Times* article titled "A Film Festival Focuses on 'Gener-Asian X'" noted that "for the first time in its 21-year history, the monthlong festival, the oldest of its kind in the country, is screening more features made in the United States by directors of Asian descent than films from overseas."[11] That the mainstream press had picked up on the trend showed how crucial a medium the feature-length film was to the relevancy of Asian American film and video.

In reality, many medium-budget Asian American feature films had been made after *Chan Is Missing* and before 1997, including such groundbreaking ones such as Ang Lee's *Pushing Hands* (1992) and *The Wedding Banquet* (1993); Mira Nair's *Mississippi Masala*; Wayne Wang's *Eat a Bowl of Tea*, Peter Wang's *A Great Wall* (1986), and Kayo Hatta's *Picture Bride* (1995). However, the crucial difference between a film like *The Wedding Banquet* and any of the films of the Class of 1997 was in the extremely divergent comparative budgets. Ang Lee's feature film *Pushing Hands* had a budget of $480,000 and his subsequent hit *The Wedding Banquet* had one of $750,000. In addition, Lee had backing from a Taiwanese government contest that he won, and *The Wedding Banquet* had the production support of a legitimate independent production company, Good Machine in New York City. Kayo Hatta patiently stitched together a combination of state and private funds to fulfill her $1 million budget.[12]

By contrast, Justin Lin and Quentin Lee's first feature, *Shopping for Fangs*, had an estimated budget of $100,000 and no support from the Taiwan government, though Lee's Canadian citizenship did grant him access to funding from the Canadian Council.[13] The films made by the Class of 1997, therefore, were ruthlessly independent in the model of Robert Rodriguez's $7,000 film, *El Mariachi* (1992). As these numerical comparisons clearly show, the Class of

1997 was a new class of brave, if not foolhardy, filmmakers hell-bent on making a narrative feature film despite lacking finances. The films of Lin and his compatriots are unique in their extreme microbudgets and for daring to go beyond the radar of the legitimate Sundance Film Festival circuit/independent film world of Ang Lee, Mira Nair, Wayne Wang, and Kayo Hatta. It was in this spirit, in fact, that that Lin's *Better Luck Tomorrow* was eventually made.

The concept of "GenerAsian X" presented both opportunity and instability for Asian American filmmakers. GenerAsian X denoted young Asian and Asian American filmmakers coming of age in the 1990s. But it represented more than this because the group included both Asian Americans and those born in Asia, allowing for fluidities, which also included gender and sexuality. Gina Marchetti notes:

> The hybridity of transnational culture has enabled the dismantling of stable categories and has created the potential for the reformulation of increasingly fluid notions of race and gender. Examining the intersection of race and gender within GenerAsian X provides simply one entry into this global transformation of the imagination of identity. Postcolonial and postmodern, the combination of "Asian" with "Generation X" recognizes a separation based on racism and the legacy of colonialism, while embracing the hybridity the condensation implies. On the move around the world, this is a polyglot generation in which English as a Second Language dominates much of the popular imagination. It is a generation marked by its class and class aspirations, defined by consumption and its ability to consume, forging an identity out of commodities.[14]

Significantly, in her definition of GenerAsian X, Marchetti collapses those born and raised in Asia with Asian Americans. These two definitions of GenerAsian X blurs the line between Asian Americans and Asians even further and establishes the role of the transnational as a key part of this movement of independent feature filmmakers. Most importantly, Marchetti includes the crucial element of class aspirations and the important role of consumption in the concept of GenerAsian X, which is anathema to the old-school, Third Worldist, Marxist worldview of Asian American identity politics. One of the exemplars of the new class aspirations of GenerAsian X filmmakers is their ambition to make narrative feature-length films, a format that is most assuredly and necessarily commercial and bourgeois.

Despite the enthusiasm of GenerAsian X and the new wave of Asian American feature films in the 1990s, Asian American scholars warned about the increasing collapse of the boundaries between Asian American identity and the mythic homeland of Asian nations. The literary theorist Sau-ling C. Wong cautioned against "too celebratory a stance" toward a "relaxation between what is Asian American and Asian" precisely because transnational identities have "the potential to glamorize a noncommittal stance in one's land of principal residence."[15] Wong cautions: "To Asian Americans, the term 'roots' could evoke contradictory meanings: either 'origin,' where one or one's family hails from in Asia, or else commitment to the place where one resides. The second meaning, on which Asian American Studies was founded, is what today's Asian Americans must not lose sight of amidst the enthusiastic call for denationalization."[16] Wong's urgent emphasis on Asian American roots is, in a way, a direct response to Marchetti's celebration of GenerAsian X and its postcolonial, postmodern, and global identity. On the one hand, Marchetti minimizes the history of Asian America in favor of a celebratory postmodern, boundless identity. On the other, Wong's warning against "denationalization" problematizes the newer generation of Asian Americans who have more recently immigrated to the United States and who do not lay claim to Asian American historical "roots." This conundrum also reflects the two impulses of the emerging Asian American feature film of the 1990s: the film of "roots" and the film of global cinephilia.

Designating *Better Luck Tomorrow* as a historic marker for Asian American film and video makes it clear that the aesthetic of the transnational has had the commercial edge over those films that are overtly of Asian American "roots." Here I compare the two tendencies of the nascent Asian American independent feature films as important precursors of *Better Luck Tomorrow*. I read Chris Chan Lee's *Yellow* and Rea Tajiri's *Strawberry Fields* as films falling into the social change mode of the genre, not in the "noble and boring" sense ascribed to the first Asian American documentaries in chapter 1, but in view of their commitment to the same political principles of resistance through remembering and recognizing the grievances of the past and the continued structural inequalities of the present. Justin Lin and Quentin Lee's *Shopping for Fangs*, by contrast, enters into the language of global cinephilia, specifically in its homages to the Hong Kong new wave, which differentiates it from the efforts of the past. One of the intractable issues of Asian American film and video, as I have argued throughout this book, has been the stalemate that exists between the political obligation to address social change and the desire to become more visible in the mainstream, commercial cinema. This deep ambivalence about the "selling out" of Asian American identity politics in favor of global cinephilia is readily apparent in *Shopping for Fangs*, and Lin's follow-up, *Better Luck Tomorrow*.

What is clear in the emergence of the microbudget Asian American independent feature film of the 1990s is a struggle between two dominant aesthetic strategies: countermemory and the transnational. Countermemory is a strategy by which works by marginalized artists revise history through the lens of the local. Memory, as opposed to history as metanarrative, is especially important to countermemory. George Lipsitz has located the unique space between the "oppressions of History" and the "lie of myth" that marginalized groups such as Asian American filmmakers must occupy. He argues that although myth and folklore are indispensable for those people made invisible in history, they offer only a temporary respite from the onslaught of abuses that history has wrought.[17]

Asian American feature films raise the complex and rather ironic problem of fulfilling both noncommercial and commercial needs. Theoretically, countermemory negotiates a middle ground between the commercial, racist Hollywood cinema and the austere, politically correct pedagogy of the Asian American documentary film. For example, both *Yellow* and *Strawberry Fields* engage in references to history as it collides with myth to emerge with truths about the Asian American condition. The way that they weave fictional narratives around references to the Rodney King riots and the Japanese American internment is a way in which these films specifically invoke the ethos of Asian American film and video.

## *Yellow* (1998)

Born and raised in San Francisco, Chris Chan Lee wrote and directed *Yellow*, his thesis film at the University of Southern California School of Cinema/Television, for $150,000. *Yellow* showed at more than a dozen film festivals, was picked up for distribution by Phaedra Cinema, and was released theatrically in 1998. *Yellow* relates the misadventures of graduation night for a close-knit group of eight Korean American high school friends. Appearing during the period of reconstruction of Koreatown after the 1992 riots in Los Angeles following the Rodney King verdict, the film comments directly on one of the most controversial topics of the riots: black-Korean relations. Though the film identifies superficially within the teen film genre, its narrative backdrop of the racial tensions between blacks and Koreans in Los Angeles crucially suggests a more deeply engaged film of ressentiment as defined in chapter 2. Indeed, in many ways, *Yellow* is a narrative fictional treatment of the same topic that was explored in the award-winning documentary *Sa-I-Gu* (Dai-sil Kim-Gibson, 1996), a film that explored the Rodney King riots from the Korean perspective. Part coming-of-age comedy and part race parable about late-twentieth-century Los Angeles, the film brims with issues and stylistic flourishes typical of first features as well as of the postmodern cinema of the 1990s. Yet, the driving force of its narrative is the relationship between a father and son, which pivots on a lie that is held up by the assumptions of racism. Los Angeles as a contested site becomes central to *Yellow*'s commitment to the chosen place of residence among Asian Americans and Asian immigrants.

The narrative centers on high school senior Sin (Michael Chung), who faces a grim future of working in his father's Koreatown convenience store

FIG. 9 Ensemble cast in *Yellow* (Chris Chan Lee, 1998). (Courtesy of Chris Chan Lee.)

unless he finds a way to cover the costs of college. His father, a stern, exceedingly frugal disciplinarian, refuses to allow him to attend college unless he receives a scholarship. One night, Sin is robbed of several thousand dollars while working at the store. The film's narrative unfolds as his close-knit group of school friends tries to raise the money to replace what was lost in the robbery. The film's denouement reveals that the robbery was a ruse to cover up Sin's inability to face up to his father.

On the one hand, *Yellow* could be categorized as belonging squarely to the milieu of American independent cinema with its cobbling together of different genres and epitomizing the principle of "allusionism," on which 1990s cinema rests.[18] The 1990s "death of cinema" discourse accompanied the sheer exhaustion of stories and formulas and genres that had sustained cinema for a hundred years. In this way, the 1990s were poised for the heavy recycling and nostalgia associated with independent cinema of that decade. Called by one reviewer as an "Asian American Graffiti,"[19] generically, *Yellow* borrows from the teen films popularized in the 1980s. *Yellow*'s smart yet mischievous suburban middle-class high school characters seem to be lifted straight from John Hughes's *Sixteen Candles* (1984) or *Ferris Bueller's Day Off* (1986) and the film's characterization of each member of its motley teen crew as embodying a particular social type (the jock, the princess, the weirdo, the nerd, etc.) riffs on the iconic 1980s teen film *The Breakfast Club* (John Hughes, 1985).

In thinking about the evolution of the Asian American feature film, *Yellow* shares many of the aspects of the "breakthrough" Asian American film, *Better Luck Tomorrow*, including its alienated Southern California setting, clearly marked allusions to other films, and its high school characters. Too, *Yellow* emulates narratives of a certain kind of ethnic, American male protagonist, namely the gangster film and the films of Spike Lee, drawing its example of an economically frustrated, working-class young man of color mixed with violence from the classic gangster films *The Public Enemy* (William A. Wellman, 1931) and *Scarface* (Howard Hawks, Richard Rossen, 1932) to the oppositional politics of Spike Lee's classic film of racial conflict and social change, *Do the Right Thing* (1989). In many ways, *Yellow*'s milieu is more akin to the critique of *Better Luck Tomorrow* as a film of postmodern mimicry of Hollywood genres. Yet, whereas *Better Luck Tomorrow* is a fantasy dependent on homage to Hong Kong action films, *Yellow* is more embedded in the genres of American cinema in order to tell the tale of ethnic struggle.

*Yellow*'s commitment to narrativizing racial conflict makes it a classically Asian American film. Though the bulk of the film follows Korean American characters through a night of shenanigans as they try to recoup the money stolen from Sin's father's convenience store, at key turning points, the film compares the oppression of Korean Americans with that of African Americans and other minorities that belong to the multicultural enclave of LA's Koreatown. The film opens with a memory of money, in which Sin, as a child, is taunted by two Latino classmates, who pay for candy using pennies in his father's store. The racial tension established in this opening scene is picked up again later, when a group of young black men enter the store while Sin is working the cash register alone. The scene of the so-called robbery occurs in an impressionistic series of shots: one shot of young black men enter the store, followed by a shot of Sin looking nervously at them, followed by a later scene in which Sin explains that he was robbed. In fact, the robbery never occurs on camera. The film uses constructive editing, or in film school parlance, the "Kuleshov effect," to suggest that a robbery happened by exploiting the viewer's assumption that black men rob Korean convenience stores. Although there are no scenes of altercation or confrontation between Sin and the would-be robbers, the film, through impressionistic montage, plays on the audience's assumptions about the myth of Asian/black relations promulgated by the media circus surrounding several incidents in the 1980s and 1990s, the biggest of which was the Rodney King riots. Min Song says of the riots:

> In popular memory, the main victims of the riots were Korean American, or *kyopo*, merchants. According to one's perspective, these merchants either deserved what they got for their rude behavior—that is, racist disdain for their black customers and participation in a political economy that facilitated capital

extraction from the impoverished neighborhoods in which they worked but did not reside—or were forced by circumstance to absorb the brunt of black resentment against a white-dominated economic elite. Both of these explanations were favorites of the mainstream media, which went out of its way to depict the violence of the riots as racial conflict between blacks and Koreans while simultaneously downplaying the role of Latinos and Latinas.[20]

*Yellow* tries to unravel this highly topical trope of 1990s media, that is, the tension between Koreans and blacks in US inner cities. Sin's father is the prototypical "rude Korean store owner" who gets into arguments with both his son and his customers over money. When two white men wanting a paper bag in addition to a plastic one to carry their beer in, he makes a scene, charging them for the extra bags, explaining condescendingly that bags cost money. Later, an older black man complains about the price of a bottle of antacid medicine to which Sin explains that they cannot sell items at supermarket prices or they would go out of business. Though Sin's explanation is dispassionate, the scene epitomizes the incongruity between the needs of immigrant Korean store owners and those of their customers in South Central Los Angeles. The scene also suggests that if Sin does not find a way out of this life, he will end up like his father—a miserly, miserable, angry man—thereby continuing the cycle of racialized violence and distrust between black and Korean communities.

The fact that Sin's lie depends on our racist assumptions, the very assumptions that demonize both blacks and Koreans in popular narratives of the Rodney King riots, makes *Yellow* a classic example of countermemory. The critique of race in America, as in all Asian American films, is the film's central conflict. However, this topic has notoriously been elided in genre cinema in America. Only the likes of Spike Lee have managed to lift it, if momentarily, out of the margins and into a viable issue in narrative feature film. Ultimately, despite the unevenness that characterizes first feature films, *Yellow*, as its title suggests, is a film that scrutinizes class and race relations, thus carrying on the work of Visual Communications, NAATA, and others in the communal effort to tell stories about race and Asian America.

## *Strawberry Fields* (1997)

Similar to *Yellow* in its social change impulse, Rea Tajiri's *Strawberry Fields* is nominally a genre film, in this case, a countercultural road film whose closest analogues would be *Thelma & Louise* (1991), *Bonnie and Clyde* (1967), and *Easy Rider* (1969) Like these genre classics, *Strawberry Fields* places itself within the mythic context of the American West as well as within the historical context of 1970s counterculture. And like *Yellow* and *Shopping for Fangs*, *Strawberry Fields* also tries to weave the familiar concerns about Asian

American identity through the lenses of sex, generation gap, and family obligation. However, especially important to *Strawberry Fields*' claim to be an authentically Asian American film of countermemory is its relationship to PBS. Intended ideally as a feature film to screen theatrically, it had both the advantage and disadvantage of being funded by CAAM and ITVS, which carried an obligation to air it on PBS (see chapter 2), though *Strawberry Fields* ultimately did not air on television. Tajiri's feature film debut revisits the topic of her acclaimed short essay film, *History and Memory* (1991), but ensconces it within a narrative feature framework.

Set in 1971, coincidentally the year that Bob Nakamura made *Manzanar*, the first internment documentary, *Strawberry Fields* follows Irene Kawai (Suzy Nakamura), a rebellious Japanese American teenager with a penchant for pyromania. In the first scene, Irene discloses that in 1942, shortly before her mother's family was taken to the internment camps, her grandfather burned the family's possessions in a strawberry field behind the house. Irene's younger sister, Terri, dies of a childhood illness, which is followed by her parents' separation. Hanging over these dysfunctions is the fact that Irene's mother, Alice, hides her shame about being interned during World War II by hiding photographs of the past that she deems are "private." It is these photographs, and one in particular of Irene's grandfather standing in front of an internment barracks, that inspires her to find out the source of her family's repression. Outcast by her family and not fitting in at school, where she must withstand classmates who refer to the victims of the war in Vietnam as "gooks," Irene drops out and takes a drug-fueled road trip destined for San Francisco. She is accompanied by her hapa boyfriend, Luke (James Sie), who is an Asian adopted into an American family, and an older Asian American hippie activist couple, Aura (Reiko Mathieu) and Mark (Chris Tashima). On the way, Irene abandons her boyfriend—and with him, the strictures of patriarchy—for a protracted detour to Poston, Arizona, the site of where her mother was interned during the war. In Arizona, Irene confronts the history of the Japanese American internment as well as the repression of painful family memories by blowing up all remnants of them in the desert.

Like many genre films, *Strawberry Fields* engages in universal narrative motifs. For example, fire becomes a thematic link between Irene's pyromania and her grandfather's burning of possessions in anticipation of internment as a way of expressing both feminist angst and the repressed fury about the trauma of the past. The opening scene in which Irene plays with matches as she talks about her grandfather mirrors the last, in which Irene ignites the explosives, originally meant to blow up office buildings in San Francisco, at the Poston internment site. The film is structured as a coming of age story about a rebellious young woman in America in the 1970s; thereby, its touchstone is the discourse of feminism. Beyond Asian American identity politics, *Strawberry*

*Fields* is about the generational rift between Irene and her mother, Alice, who is deeply repressed about the past, keeping mementos of the internment in a box that is forbidden to her daughters. While living in a house with a piano and furniture covered in plastic, symbols of middle-class conformity, she is motivated mostly by hiding her shame over both her past internment and the death of her younger daughter. In running away from Alice, Irene not only discovers the truth about the internment camps, but in bonding with other women with similar stories, she also adopts more productive ways to deal with the past. In the middle of the road trip to San Francisco, Irene abandons her boyfriend and takes off in his truck with Aura. Aura, a glamorous hapa hippie who, in a fit of feminist solidarity, also leaves her paranoid, bomb-wielding, proto-terrorist lover to his own devices, holds a healthier, more open attitude about the internment, which has also touched her family. It is Aura who drives Irene to Poston, where she knows a camp survivor, Takayo. Along this journey, the two women cross the southwest in what is easily a reference to the classic of feminist Hollywood cinema, *Thelma & Louise*. And like that film, which was a celebrated feminist revision of the Western and the road film, *Strawberry Fields* sticks closely to generic formula in order to offer a newly realized version of it.

Though *Strawberry Fields* does present itself successfully as a genre film, and thereby evokes the conventional myths contained therein, the primary concern of the film is to revise US history, namely, the history of the Japanese American internment. Countermemory, so clearly and ingeniously presented in Tajiri's experimental nonfiction film on the same subject, *History and Memory*, also drives the narrative of *Strawberry Fields*. The film forces "revision of existing histories by supplying new perspectives about the past"[21] in two ways—retelling the history of the Japanese American internment as well as the 1970s counterculture. Though Irene's family suffers repression and shame about their imprisonment during World War II, Irene's righteous anger reveals that the internment itself was a violation of civil rights that should not be the source of internalized violence.

The film's narrative is driven by a need to uncover the shame that is generated by Alice, whose excuse for hiding photographic evidence of the internment is that they are "private." That family photographs should be private, even among its members, is the source of division in the Kawai family. Viewed in context with the history of the Japanese American internment, what seems like garden-variety family dysfunction becomes an allegory of how the Office of War Information simultaneously forbade cameras in the camps while producing its own sanitized propaganda films about the camps that showed them to be both necessary and benign. By the 1970s, silence about the Japanese American internment was still a mutually held agreement between the victims and the US government, which represented the imprisonment as a necessary security measure in numerous newsreels produced by the Office of War Information. Against this, *Strawberry Fields* quite literally provides an alternative perspective by continuously blending David Tatsuno's illegal Super 8 home movies of the internment camps in Topaz, Utah. These films are woven into the film as Irene's memories, dreams, and hallucinations but are also literal embodiments of countermemory.

Both *Yellow* and *Strawberry Fields* are examples of the Asian American "roots" film. As "authentic" examples of Asian American media, they are what Sau-ling C. Wong calls texts that express a "commitment to the place where one resides."[22] While ultimately unsuccessful in leading to the creation of a full-fledged genre of Asian American feature film, these films are important in their attempt at maintaining a political engagement with history and place, which are the hallmarks of an Asian American film aesthetics.

## *Shopping for Fangs* (1997)

Unlike *Yellow* and *Strawberry Fields*, *Shopping for Fangs* exemplifies the transnational Asian American feature film and is a key precursor to *Better Luck Tomorrow* in its resolute, global cinephilia. While it adheres to some of the concerns of Asian American identity politics, its overarching narrative, themes, and visual style derive from an unproblematized collapsing of the boundaries between Asian and Asian American identities. Looked at as a precursor to *Better Luck Tomorrow*, *Shopping for Fangs* distinguishes itself from the film of countermemory precisely by offering no overt references to the traumas of Asian American history. Whereas *Yellow* and *Strawberry Fields* are steeped in the countermemorializing of key events in Asian American race politics—the LA riots and the Japanese American internment—*Shopping for Fangs* derives meaning from a recombination of purely cinematic fantasies and seems to exist primarily as a love letter to Hong Kong new wave cinema.

*Shopping for Fangs* was codirected by Justin Lin and Quentin Lee, who met as graduate students UCLA's School of Theater, Film, and Television. Made for under $150,000 and shot on location in Los Angeles and San Gabriel, California, the film received a "three-city theatrical release."[23] Despite these modest circumstances, the film made a minor splash. In their article, "Making Films Asian American," Kent Ono and Sarah Projansky question the terms under which *Shopping for Fangs*' authors Justin Lin and Quentin Lee have been "produced" by the text.[24] The elusiveness of the film—as equal parts homage to Wong Kar Wai and film about Asian American identity politics—stymied journalists' ability to pin them down in definitive ways. In their exhaustive use of labels and assumptions, reviewers did just the opposite—that is, they pointed out the difficulty of labeling

FIG. 10 Clarance and Trinh, from *Shopping for Fangs* (Justin Lin and Quentin Lee, 1997). (Courtesy of Margin Films.)

Lin or Lee in a satisfactory way. In some ways, this is a function of the transnational nature of *Shopping for Fangs*, which self-consciously tries to attract a sense of ambiguity regarding Asian and Asian American identity.

*Shopping for Fangs* is a film that epitomizes the transnational turn in Asian American independent media on many fronts. The film relates three intertwined storylines about three different protagonists. The first, Katherine (Jeanne Chin), is a timid, repressed Southern Californian housewife who suffers from amnesia and split personality disorder. Unbeknownst to everyone in the film including, presumably, the audience, Katherine transforms into her alter ego, Trinh, from time to time in order to disappear from her sterile, suburban life. By contrast, Trinh is a confidently "out" lesbian and waitress who works in a coffee shop in a Chinese American strip mall. Trinh dons the textbook female masquerade, complete with Marilyn Monroe blonde wig, tight-fitting vintage 1950s dresses, cat's-eye sunglasses, and drag-queen attitude. Discovering Katherine's personal effects in a public restroom, where Katherine has just switched over, Trinh falls in love with her(self), courting Katherine through pin-up snapshots that she sends through the mail. The erotic possibility between the split personality of Katherine/Trinh is a feminist metaphor for self-love, the absence of which is the catalyst for Katherine's psychic split. Yet, this identity crisis also becomes a cinematic fantasy of same-sex eroticism that is echoed in Trinh's only confidant, Clarance, himself a young gay Asian man balancing his quest for romantic fulfillment with a struggle to find a home among disparate locales: Taiwan, Singapore, London, and the United States.

That both Trinh and Clarance are defiantly queer (in definitive Gener-Asian X fashion) poses a philosophical roadblock in the heteronormative, unidirectional narrative of desire that structures classical Hollywood narrative. When Trinh and Clarance first meet, a budding relationship between them seems the perfect antidote to Katherine's frigidity, a way for her to find the romance lacking in her marriage. Like May, a fellow waitress who dismisses Trinh's declaration of lesbianism as folly, viewers may also expect something to happen between Trinh and Clarance. Yet, what results is not frustrated desire but kinship, not only as queers drowning in a sea of overdetermined heterosexuality but through the less obvious narrative concern of Asian American identity. Clarance, like Trinh, is also alone, writing letters to his boyfriend in Taiwan. Like Trinh, he is both Asian American and transnational. Though his parents live in Singapore, he chooses to remain in the United States.

There is a strong relationship between the transnational and issues of Asian American identity in the Katherine/Trinh/Clarance storyline in *Shopping for Fangs*. It seems that for these characters, who are both post-1970 immigrants to the United States,[25] the defining aspect of their identity is their shared rootlessness. During the denouement, it is revealed that Katherine's amnesia and personality split is the result of a violent and tragic childhood episode. Under hypnosis induced by her therapist, Katherine reveals that, as a child of war-torn Saigon, her parents put her and her brother alone on a boat to a refugee camp in Bangkok. She is assaulted and robbed, and she witnesses her brother's brutal murder by bandits. The cause of Katherine's trauma, at first suggested to be that of garden-variety gender oppression, turns out to be a childhood trauma, which is specifically identified as a uniquely Asian American experience—that of refugee status brought on by the war in Vietnam. Katherine's amnesia is, like many fictional treatments, one centered on identity. In this case, the forgetting of identity is rooted in nation, race, class, and sexuality. As Trinh, Katherine is able to completely disavow her identity as a repressed, coddled, Southern Californian housewife to become a blonde, queer, sexually confident working-class person. Taking on the feminist problematic of singular points of view explored in the work of filmmaker and scholar Trinh T. Minh-Ha (and clearly paying homage through naming the character after her), Katherine/Trinh's storyline literalizes the necessity of multiple points of view in representing transnational, gendered subjects through the personality split. The splitting of Katherine/Trinh expresses the complexity of representing those who have been deeply traumatized by war as well as by gender discrimination. Only when Katherine is able to connect her repression as an affluent housewife in the United States with her survival of war and immigration is she able to integrate the two sides of her personality.

Another splitting of identity occurs in the film in the unrelated but parallel storyline of Phil, an extremely repressed corporate drone searching for his sexual, ethnic, and philosophical identity. Phil's lack of assertiveness both in his mindless job as an accountant as well as in his pathetic dating life result in violent frustration and excessive hair growth, both of which lead him to believe that he is turning into a werewolf. An allegory about the myth of the emasculated Asian male, Phil's narrative is a fantasy of revenge.

The significance of the transnational comes through not only in *Shopping for Fangs*' narrative, but it is also redolent in the film's visual aesthetic. As mentioned previously, Wong Kar Wai's *Chungking Express* is the most important aesthetic source for *Shopping for Fangs*. From Trinh's masquerade in blonde wig and sunglasses, copied from Brigitte Lin's costume, to Trinh and Clarance's unconsummated date in an anonymous hotel room, to Trinh's waitress friend, May, which is the namesake of Faye Wong's iconic gamine food stall worker, *Shopping for Fangs* is an unabashed love letter to *Chungking Express*. Not only this, *Shopping for Fangs* is littered with references to other Hong Kong films, specifically those of John Woo. The awkward addition of a homicide and a Mexican stand-off à la Woo's *The Killer* (1989) transposes the cinephilic universe of Woo (which is itself littered with French, American, and Italian film references) onto its stylistic surface. This is important in several ways. By referencing Hong Kong cinema, albeit at times in unwieldy and obvious ways, *Shopping for Fangs* sets an important precedent in the marketability-by-proxy of Asian American independent feature films. Although it did not have the impact of *Better Luck Tomorrow*, *Shopping for Fangs* demonstrates the stylistic beginnings of Justin Lin's hybrid Hong Kong–Asian American style, which blends the political, representational concerns of Asian American independent film and video with the marketability of classic and contemporary Hong Kong cinema. It also marks the historical beginning of a trend in Asian American media that continues today—that of the growth of Asian American independent film through its explicit association, as well as blurring of boundaries, with East Asian popular and art house cinema.

Overall, the allure of *Shopping for Fangs* and its relative success compared with the other three films of the 1997 "renaissance" of GenerAsian X filmmakers at the SFIAAFF can be attributed to its narrative and stylistic reliance on foreign art house cinema. Unlike *Yellow* and *Strawberry Fields*, which retells past traumas through countermemory to come to a more nuanced understanding of Asian American history, *Shopping for Fangs* is literally about amnesia and forgetting. The main characters Trinh and Phil are lost and actively forget their pasts in order to move toward a brighter future, perhaps one in which each side of their split identities are integrated without loss. More than the others, *Shopping for Fangs*, with its aggressively marketed homage to Hong Kong cinema anticipates not only the same strategies in American independent film in general but also the strategies of later Asian American feature films.

## *Better Luck Tomorrow* (2003)

From an institutional standpoint, *Better Luck Tomorrow*, which opened both the SFIAAFF and the Asian CineVision Film festival in New York City, follows the trajectory of globalized cinephilia that has informed Asian American media since the 1990s. *Better Luck Tomorrow*'s transnational strategy can be seen as a continuum that begins with his first feature, *Shopping for Fangs*, codirected with Quentin Lee. I see *Better Luck Tomorrow* as the endpoint of a historical trajectory resulting in a dialogue among filmmakers, films, and institutional shifts that began with this new wave of low-budget independent Asian American feature films, referred to as the "Class of 1997" in the film festival discourse. Significantly, *Better Luck Tomorrow*'s appeal lies precisely in the mimicry of a hypermasculine Hong Kong action cinema, which blurs the lines between Asian genre cinema and the identity politics of Asian American media. In other words, rather than seeing *Better Luck Tomorrow*'s success as an isolated endeavor of an individual director, I argue that it is part of a larger trend wherein filmmakers, the discourse of Asian American film festivals, and their audiences have emphasized notions of the transnational in feature films.

My reading of *Better Luck Tomorrow* is one that is in itself transnational. As I have shown throughout this book, Asian American film and video has been known for its struggles in emphasizing its Americanness over its foreignness. Yet, ironically, the most easily and widely recognized film in this genre is a film that is dependent on its highly attuned references to "foreign" cinemas. Therefore, rather than understanding *Better Luck Tomorrow* as an exemplar of Asian American film and video as it has been defined in this book, I want to analyze the film as an homage to and a transnational exemplar of the "heroic bloodshed" genre of Hong Kong action cinema of the 1980s and 1990s. Part of this argument has to do with the "apocalyptic" nature of Hong Kong action films, many of which are helmed by John Woo, Ringo Lam, Johnnie To, and others. These types of films seem most apt to express the rage and violence of institutionalized racism experienced in Asian American life, the seriousness of which had been downplayed during the first years of the increasingly postracial early twenty-first century. Another part of thinking about *Better Luck Tomorrow* as following in the tradition of Hong Kong gunplay films is to understand how the transnational turn in

FIG. 11   Ensemble cast in *Better Luck Tomorrow* (Justin Lin, 2003).

cinema has affected Asian American film and video since the 1990s, which has a lot to do with the global cinephilic turn in the late 1990s that caused a paradigmatic shift in the genre.

Given the history of Asian America, the impulse to analyze Asian American films as reflections on US national identity formation is only natural. In her sustained analysis of *Better Luck Tomorrow*, Margaret Hillenbrand makes this very assumption by her understanding the film as a parody, and therefore critique, of Hollywood film genres:

> *Better Luck Tomorrow*'s most obvious parodic move is to co-opt both these genres—the teen flick and the gangster movie—and to rescript, recast and reedit them for Asian America. This overhaul means transforming Asian American high school students from extras into headliners, to the extent that there are no Caucasians in leading roles whatsoever. It also involves a representation of Asian American criminality that, from the voice-over to the details of the diegesis, breathes real subjectivity into Ben and his gang. The result is an aggressive grab on genre that transforms what Mamber terms "faithful appropriation" into "vengeful revisionism." By slotting Asian American men into these well-worn cinematic models of masculinity, the film gestures powerfully to the absence of any established paradigms that they can call their own. Asian American men have to beg, borrow, and steal a presence on screen because the cultural hegemony continues to deny them more legitimate access.[26]

Hillenbrand's analysis is useful in that it identifies the intertextuality and mimicry of established genres and texts as central to *Better Luck Tomorrow*'s successful strategy. Yet she neglects to mention a key intertext, and that is the film's crucial referencing of the codes of gender, history, and aesthetics from 1980s Hong Kong action cinema or of the transnational turn in Asian American independent filmmaking that preceded *Better Luck Tomorrow*'s box office success. Without discussing these institutional contexts, it is impossible to give the film and the history of Asian American film and video a broader and clearer understanding. Rather than thinking of *Better Luck Tomorrow*'s "most obvious parodic move" as revolving around American gangster films and the teen flick, I'd like to posit an alternative: the possibility of another "obvious" intertextual move, and that is homage. Beyond what others have argued, that the film's asserting of Asian American masculinity through a confrontation with American film genres, I would like to add that the film also, in its referencing of John Woo's classic *A Better Tomorrow*, leans on the hypermasculine yet highly melodramatic representations of brotherhood and redemption through violence of Hong Kong action cinema.

On the surface, *Better Luck Tomorrow* is similar to many other Asian American feature films in that it works to dismantle racist stereotypes, specifically the model-minority myth. The imagery that guides the opening shot says it all: a gate opens like a jail cell door to a residential community lined neatly with identical tract homes while an ice cream truck goes by under a clean, bright Southern California sun. Inside this sterile, upper-middle-class prison lives the film's main character, ambitious high school senior Ben Manibag, who has nothing better to do than play basketball, study for the SAT, and make sure that he racks up points for his college application. Ben lives the model-minority ideal of being conscious of his fortunate place in the capitalist order of things without being greedy or causing a fuss about racism. For all intents and purposes, Ben's existence is a pleasant dream headed for more pleasantness. Trouble comes when he is confronted by his foil, Daric Loo, who introduces Ben to a world of petty crime based largely on his ability, as a model-minority overachiever, to get away with it.

I'd also like to address the issue of the "representational impasse within which Asian American masculinity is locked."[27] The four Asian American male characters of *Better Luck Tomorrow* are sexual and sexualized in unapologetic and unpathological ways. Not only does Ben "get the girl" in the end, an important part of the gambit of becoming criminals is the ability to take part in a time-honored teen male fantasy of hiring prostitutes and being, in parlance, "a pimp." In understanding *Better Luck Tomorrow* to be a homage to Hong Kong action film, one can easily see how its erotic energy emerges out of the screen presence established by stars like Chow Yun Fat, Leslie Cheung, and Ti Lung, all of whom have played gangsters with the attendant masculine empowerment that this lifestyle represents. As many others have argued, the construction of an empowered Asian American masculinity lies at the heart of representational politics in Asian American film and video. It is tempting to read *Better Luck Tomorrow* as a film that primarily extols Asian American race politics, but it is necessary above all to understand that its popularity comes from the pleasure in its play of intertextual surfaces.

What some critics have ignored is that among the intertextual references that are important to the success of *Better Luck Tomorrow* as a cinematic object par excellence is its recourse to a libidinal discourse of Asian men that has never existed in the annals of American cinema and exists in abundance in the popular cinema of Hong Kong. Key to the argument that a transnational aesthetic is crucial to understanding *Better Luck Tomorrow* is the fact that Hong Kong action cinema lives and dies by the libidinal energy of its male matinee idols. From classic Shaw Brothers *wuxia* epics to the Hong Kong handover era "gun fu" masterpieces of John Woo, Ringo Lam, Johnnie To, and others, Hong Kong's action heroes provide a fount of libidinal star power that has been continuously repressed in Hollywood cinema since the days of silent movies, when Sessue Hayakawa in the racist masterpiece *The Cheat* appeared as the last and only Asian matinee idol to grace American screens. By appealing to another source, Hong Kong action film, for this important aspect of cinema, *Better Luck Tomorrow* imbues Asian masculinity with a libidinal energy that goes beyond the model minority.

Much of the libidinal energy imbued in *Better Luck Tomorrow* is tied to violence. A comparative analysis of the uses of violence in *Better Luck Tomorrow* and its Hong Kong namesake, Woo's *A Better Tomorrow*, for example, reveals that Lin's film uses *A Better Tomorrow* as a template to dramatize and allegorize the violence that lay at the heart of institutional racism in a way that no amount of borrowing from US history could yield as effectively. So, politically, the violence and "gun fu" of John Woo's milieu catalyzes the history of Asian American identity politics for the big screen. In the glamorized violence of Hong Kong cinema, Justin Lin finds the language to put Asian American narratives on the grand scale it deserves.[28] The key to understanding *Better Luck Tomorrow*'s gambit as both a deeply transnational film following in the footsteps of John Woo and an important film in the evolution of Asian American film and video is its use of violence.

*Better Luck Tomorrow* was loosely based on the so-called real-life "honor roll killing," in which an Asian American high school student was killed by a gang of his former friends, also Asian American. Though the crux of the violence of *Better Luck Tomorrow* happens within the group of Asian American petty criminals/high-achieving students, the film is structured so that the violent event that triggers the spiral down toward murder is one that is spurred by racial hatred. As Ben and his new gang, Daric, Virgil, and Han begin to work more regularly doing scams, they procure handguns in order to seal their criminal identity. Later at a house party, they are accosted by a group of white students from their high school who taunt them with racist comments, saying, "Bible study is next door," suggesting images of the docile Asian nerd. Han begins a physical scuffle, and in a fit of ironic retaliation, he pulls out his gun, dispelling any illusions about docility and Asian masculinity. The scene ends as Virgil goes into a bloodthirsty hysteria, egging Han on before the four exit the party. As the four drive home in silent contemplation of the possibility of homicide under the conditions of repressed institutional racism, a car drives up next to them containing real gangsters who appear, also, to be Asian. "Real gangsters" in this case refers to the real-life Asian street gangs involved in drug trafficking and other criminal activity in the Southern California region, such as Asian Boyz, a gang whose members are mostly first-generation Cambodian, Vietnamese, Filipino, and Laotian. Ben and his upper-middle-class suburban friends momentarily share nervous sidelong glances with the gang member who briefly brandishes a semiautomatic rifle before riding off into the darkness.

This scene speaks to the multiple layers involving the representation of Asian and Asian American men. On the one hand, Ben and his associates are a world away from the circumstances of first-generation Southeast Asian refugees whose livelihoods depend on crime. The unease with which the film allows for a comparison between the "real" gangsters who kill out of socioeconomic need and the poseurs who are only playing the role becomes painfully clear and is an implicit critique of ethnic and class difference within Asian American identity. At the same time, the scene momentarily juxtaposes upper-middle-class privileged Asian American teens with first-generation Asian refugee gangsters, who awkwardly find common ground through racial oppression. That this mostly wordless exchange follows the film's introduction of guns and violence to the world of Ben and his crew signifies a loss of innocence as much as the reinforcement and reengagement of "Asian American politics" as a response to racial hatred and violence. Earlier in the film, Daric lampooned Asian American identity issues in a scene in which Ben becomes the target of a discrimination case because his basketball coach wouldn't take him off the bench to play as often as the other (non-Asian) players. Later, only after Ben, Daric, Virgil, and Han come face to face with racist violence does their purpose as outlaws begin to contain meaning. There is something to actually fight for and against, despite the misguided and distorted way in which they go about it. The justice sought, especially by Daric, who first brandishes his gun, and Virgil, who expresses distress at a once unavoidable confrontation with racism as well as regret at shattering the possibility of "getting into Princeton," is in racial terms, one of Malcolm X and not Martin Luther King Jr. That is, as in the conundrum offered by Spike

Lee's *Do the Right Thing*, there are two sides to the race problem—violence as never being justified à la King and as necessary for self-defense, and true progress, according to Malcolm. As a plot point, this scene is almost unnecessary, as the key violent event—the killing of one of their own, Steve—is not racially motivated. Yet, there is extra dimension to the use of gun violence that takes a note from the aesthetic of John Woo whose films also grapple with the issue of justifiable and unjustifiable violence. The film asks, is violence a justifiable reaction against racism?

And yet, despite the fact that *Better Luck Tomorrow* takes a political stance in narrating the problem of Asian American identity as one of violence, its appeal ultimately derives less from the history of institutional Asian American film and video and more from its stylistic homage to Hong Action cinema. John Woo has described his desire to realize a truly global cinematic aesthetic blending Hong Kong, American, and European influences. Arguably, Justin Lin's homage to *A Better Tomorrow* is equally hopeful for an Asian American cinema that transcends these global and local boundaries as well. Nevertheless, what is being accomplished in Lin's blending of Hollywood genre tropes with the aesthetic of Hong Kong action cinema lies recalcitrantly on the surface.

Though flawed, *Yellow* and *Strawberry Fields* consistently attempt to stay true to Asian American "roots." These films are faithful to the social change ideals of classic Asian American film and video through the demonstration of a "commitment to the place where one resides" rather than a mythical homeland or an imagined one. By contrast, the strategy of Justin Lin's *Shopping for Fangs*, and later, *Better Luck Tomorrow*, which I would describe as diasporic global cinephilia, squarely inhabits what Wong calls "the potential to glamorize a noncommittal stance in one's land of principal residence," but also, by contrast, according to Marchetti, "the reformulation of increasingly fluid notions of race and gender" which "provides simply one entry into this global transformation of the imagination of identity."[29] Therefore, GenerAsian X as a concept and as a descriptor had an ambivalent effect on the future of Asian American film and video. On the one hand, the bourgeois aspirations of this group of filmmakers enabled their ambitions to move beyond the institutional documentaries and short subjects that were the mainstay of the genre. Yet, their deliberate ambiguity about "roots" encouraged the apolitical forgetting of Asian American media history. These two tendencies provided an impasse in narrative strategies of Asian American film and video, but they also opened the door to a diversity of approaches that revealed its growing complexity.

# 6

# The Post–Asian American Feature Film

The Persistence of Institutionality
in *Finishing the Game:
The Search for a New Bruce Lee*
and *American Zombie*

Whether it is overt or covert, the sign of the "institutional" in Asian American independent film and video is ever present. This sign, which is an acknowledgment or indication of a film's relationship to institutional forms of support—that is, PBS, the Corporation for Public Broadcasting, and the Minority Consortia—is an intrinsic aspect of Asian American film and video. Yet, institutionality is not merely a historical context that is outside of the text but, importantly, also an integral textual element. What this means is that Asian American films are not only "about" the real world—that is, topics and issues—but also about their own material coming into being through various confrontations with institutions. As I have shown in the previous chapters, the sign of institutionality is such an integral discourse that it appears in many guises, even within the text as an overall aesthetic, an inside joke, or as a paratext in the credits. In concluding this book, I refer to the concept of the "post–Asian American" film, that which operates on dual levels: the text that is conventionally "about" Asian American identity issues but also the text that is intertextual and refers explicitly to other Asian American texts. In this vein, I analyze two "fake documentaries"—*Finishing the Game: The Search for a New Bruce Lee* (Justin Lin, 2007) and *American Zombie* (Grace Lee, 2007)—which demonstrate through their intertextual strategies how institutionality is an inextricably embedded, definitive element of the genre.

If the goal of Asian American film and video has been the ability to make a profitable and critically acclaimed feature film, Justin Lin's *Better Luck Tomorrow* (2002) has, arguably, accomplished this. The dual forms of justice according to Nancy Fraser—redistribution and recognition[1]—have been more or less reached with Lin's film. *Better Luck Tomorrow* provided a kind of economic justice in that it "proved" that Asian American film and video could be profitable as well as recognize the problem of the "model minority" through the corrective of a complex rather than simplistic positive/negative representation. Ever since *Hito Hata: Raise the Banner* and *Chan Is Missing*, it has been the implicit goal of Asian American film and video to establish its ability to break out of the margins critically and politically as well as economically. As a consequence of *Better Luck Tomorrow*'s success and the hard-won establishment of Asian American film and video as a recognizable genre, films of all genres, lengths, and modes continue to be made under the auspices of Asian American film and video. Similar to the way that film noir presented a historically contingent cycle that begins with *The Maltese Falcon* (John Huston, 1941) and ends with *Touch of Evil* (Orson Welles, 1960), Asian American film and video can be argued as a cycle strongly tied to historical context. This certainly doesn't mean that Asian American films don't get made anymore. On the contrary, I would argue that this analogy allows us to see the possibility of the "post–Asian American film" in the same way that neo-noir films such as *Chinatown* (Roman Polanski, 1974) and *Blade Runner* (Ridley Scott, 1982) continue to build upon the intertextual formation of the original film cycle. As a conclusion, therefore, I argue for a distinct "post–Asian American film and video" aesthetic that makes institutionality visible and palpable within the text through postmodern strategies of intertextuality and paratextuality in the feature-film "mockumentaries" *Finishing the Game* and *American Zombie*.

The generic identities of both *Finishing the Game* and *American Zombie* as fake documentaries is especially pertinent to the way that Asian American film and video has been associated with public interest media. As this book has revealed, the history of the genre is a history of its relationship to public media. In this way, the fake documentary is the perfect form to enact Asian American film and video's central drama because, as Alexandra Juhasz states:

> The fake documentary is simultaneously and definitively both parody *and* satire, given that satire, according to [Francis] Hutcheson, "has the moral and social in focus." Parodies look first to texts, satires toward the world. As parody, fake documentary "both is and represents" (to use Hutcheson's terms) documentary; as

satire, it also is and feigns documentary's referent, the moral, social, political, and historical. The fake documentary creates a further level of engagement, on top of that already in play with a typical parody, a form that Hutcheson explains speaks doubly: first, its message, and second, the form it mimics. Fake docs—as satire *and* parody—create relations among form, content, style, representation, and the recorded world, and these worlds are multiple and not additive in nature.[2]

The two operative functions of fake documentary—satire and parody—at once address the unique concerns of the history of Asian American independent film and video. The fact that *Finishing the Game* and *American Zombie* parody both the documentary form, ubiquitous in the genre, and ethnic identity—one of the genre's central concerns—shows the fake documentary to be ideal in its ability to comment on both the world (satire) and texts (parody). The fake documentary, as per Juhasz's definition, engages both parody and satire—it's about form as well as about the "world." Since Asian American film and video has been known as a serious genre concerned with the moral and social order, *Finishing the Game* satirizes this seriousness and sense of superiority with the treatment of the relatively trivial world of narcissistic Hollywood wannabes. *American Zombie* parodies the navel-gazing nature of some Asian American documentaries through the cautionary narrative of humanizing zombies, which as the film shows, turns out to be politically correct, but ultimately impossible. Crucially, the reference in both films to institutionality is essential to the parodic/satiric function of the fake documentary because the essence of Asian American film is its relationship to institutional support. In other words, the Asian American fake documentary's simultaneous use of parody and satire reveals in miniature the historical discourse of Asian American independent film and video—its ambivalence between being a "serious" film about fighting racism and being an inconsequential piece of Hollywood entertainment.

*Finishing the Game*, Justin Lin's follow-up to *Better Luck Tomorrow*, is an example of institutionality as textual and paratextual sign. On the surface, it is generically a film "made by and about Asian Americans," yet its highly intertextual and self-referential structure demonstrates how signs of the institution have shaped Asian American independent film and video. Specifically, as the previous chapters have shown, the discourse of the genre—or what filmmakers, critics, and activists talk about when they talk about it—often indicates issues of juggling the responsibility, expectations, and material support necessary to make films under the guise of "Asian American film and video." Therefore, institutionality consistently acknowledges the tension between "authenticity" and "selling out" that is part and parcel of creating art under institutionalized racism and so-called democratic capitalism. In doing intertextual metacommentary about Asian American film and video, *Finishing the Game* is precisely about this idea. Superficially, the content of *Finishing the Game* is, like many Asian American films, about Asian American identity and particularly about the process of *becoming* Asian American. However, what is clear in analyzing the intertextual reverberations of this fake documentary is that *Finishing the Game* problematizes Asian American film and video through a conscious enactment of institutionality. Though others have discussed the way that Asian American films ironically refer to the conventions of cinema as a way of signaling their own marginality,[3] what I suggest is that this ultimately evinces the institutional core of the historical evolution of Asian American media.

*Finishing the Game* is a mockumentary that imagines the completion of Bruce Lee's last and posthumously completed film, *Game of Death* (Robert Clouse, 1978). Following four aspirants to Lee's legendary shoes from audition to screen tests, the film parodies race politics in 1970s Hollywood (and hence contemporary politics of identity) while examining the representation of Asian and Asian American masculinity. The fake documentary follows four would-be Bruce Lees: Cole Kim (Sung Kang), a Korean American naïf from the South looking to be discovered; Breeze Loo (Roger Fan), a narcissistic, professional Bruce Lee imitator who represents the real-life "Bruce Lee clones" of the 1970s, Bruce Li, Bruce Lai, and Dragon Lee; the "half Asian" Tarrick Tyler (McCaleb Burnett), who looks white but is ironically the most politically identified of the Asian American actors; and Troy Poon (Dustin Nguyen), a veteran television actor famous for being a sidekick on a popular cop show, but who subsequently cannot find work, looking for his big break. Poon's character is inspired by Nguyen's own claim to fame in the 1980s cop show *21 Jump Street*, a show that helped catapult its white star Johnny Depp to global cinematic stardom.

*Finishing the Game*, like its predecessor, *Better Luck Tomorrow*, is thematically an attempt to critique representations of Asian American masculinity. By invoking the ghost of the most revered representative of Asian American manhood, Bruce Lee, the film explodes and ridicules Hollywood's capricious yet exacting standards of masculinity and the shifting parameters of its relationship to race. Ironically, it is Bruce Lee himself, who was relegated to playing in background roles as a sidekick—specifically, Kato in TV's *The Green Hornet* (1967–1968). It was only when Lee, a US citizen by birth, returned to Hong Kong, where he was raised and where he experienced instant stardom, that he produced the iconic films that led to his enduring global stardom. Therefore, *Finishing the Game* is, on the one hand, about the inability of Asian American actors to live up to Bruce Lee and, implicitly, about the impossibility of matching his masculine power and star quality. It is also about the impossibility of containing Asian American masculinity in the US context because of its historical representational limitations. The film problematizes the idea that, as Celine Parreñas-Shimizu puts it, Asian American masculinity has been "straitjacketed" into "a racial victimization through lack" in its construction as distanced from representations of white heteronormative masculinity.[4] Yet, as both directors Justin Lin and Grace Lee show, it is a position escapable only through repeated acts of independent filmmaking and returning once again, and in more nuanced, complex ways, to representing Asian Americans on screen.

Given its familiar topic, *Finishing the Game* is ostensibly an Asian American film in terms of its subject matter, authorship, and targeted spectatorship. However, beyond its thematizing about gender and race, the film's ironic and analytical perspective on filmmaking, as subject matter as well as through the frame of the fake documentary itself, presents the problem of Asian American film and video as one that is not only of identity but of the institutional barriers that historically plague Asian American filmmakers and actors. What is significant about Lin's film is that while it fits squarely within Hollywood genre conventions, it contains a covert yet significant nod to the sign of institutionality.

*Finishing the Game*'s opening scene is a cinematic equivalent of what Gérard Genette has termed the "literary paratext." Paratexts are extraneous elements supplied in a published book that frame its content and include illustrations, typeface, cover art, preface, and so on. Genette states, "More than a boundary or a sealed border, the paratext is, rather, a threshold." It is "a zone between text and off-text, a zone not only of transition but also of transaction: a privileged place of pragmatics and a strategy, of an influence on the public, an influence that . . . is at the service of a better reception for the text and a more pertinent reading of it . . . a fringe of the printed text which in reality controls one's whole reading of the text."[5] One cinematic equivalent of a paratext is a film's credits.

*Finishing the Game*'s fake-opening-credits sequence, that is, the credits of the fake documentary being shot in the film-within-the film, references precisely what Genette argues for the subtle yet complete control that this paratext has over the meaning of the text. The film opens with a parody of the PBS credit sequence featuring a 1970s color block graphic in shades of mustard yellow and avocado green with an intertitle that reads, "this film was made possible through the generosity of." Over this, a female voice announces the various fictional supporting entities that follow, which include "The Clayton Townsend Endowment for the Arts," "Bigsby Oil Company ("Driving us toward a better future"), "A Grant from the Bucherer-Wassell Tobacco Company ("seven out of ten doctors prefer smoking Bucherer-Wassell cigarettes"), and "viewers like you." This sequence visually evokes the florid 1970s visual aesthetic as a way to reference that decade's countercultural styles and politics. It also frames the narrative as a film-within-a-film, which is significant to the generic limits of the film as a mockumentary. As a paratext, this fake-credits sequence underlines not only the nature of all Asian American filmmakers' struggles to get out from under the shadow of public support, but "controls one's whole reading of the text"[6] in the way that it underscores the plight of the auditioning actors in the film.

On the one hand, this opening sequence points to many signs that are necessary to the film's exposition. Specifically, it references the aesthetic and naïveté of the 1970s as well as the golden age of PBS, when television identified more strongly as a public sphere and when, especially, it offered a strong articulation of the liberal language of racial equality. Though the sponsors in this spoof are fictional, the last stated sponsor, "viewers like you," is infamously and historically authentic and expressed, in a nutshell, the democratic promise of PBS, which began and flourished in the 1970s. While most Americans are familiar with the utopian televisual experiment of public television, which is rapidly becoming a relic of the past, PBS has a special place in the hearts and minds of people of color, particularly because of its promise to deliver the "diversity" absent in commercial television. As elaborated in chapter 2, public television has been important for Asian American media because as an institution, it was established to address the lack of diversity in the "wasteland" that was American television in the 1960s. And yet, on the other side of this reference to PBS in Lin's film is a jab at the ghettoization of Asian American media on public television, which is, aptly, the subject of this book. *Finishing the Game* reveals that the unlikely bête noire of Asian American media is not racism per se but is, in fact, the institution of public television itself.

*Finishing the Game* is an interesting example of the persistence of institutionality as an enduring hallmark of Asian American independent media. It is not merely a film about Asian Americans, or the politics of identity at large; it is also a film that specifically refers to the unique institutional history of Asian American independent film. Although it is about the making of a Chinese-language movie, because it is being made by an American company, the setting is Hollywood, and the various actors that are brought in as would-be Bruce Lee stand-ins are only Chinese in that they *look* Chinese—that is, somewhat Asian only in the way that audiences would recognize. Again, this points to the institutional marginalization of Asian Americans from Hollywood as well as the practice of yellowface and cross-ethnic casting that has defined the careers of Asian and Asian American actors throughout history.

A useful way of understanding a film's formal dynamics is to compare the opening and closing scenes of a film. The opening scene is a kind of palimpsest—it provides the opening sequence of both the film we are watching and the film-within-the-film, the documentary that is being made about the post-production of *The Game of Death*. In parodying the style of 1970s public television, the film references a period when identity politics and media were embroiled in a much more strongly engaged discourse. It is also telling that the closing credits show a montage of the post–Bruce Lee film careers of the Asian American actors in the film. The careers of two of the actors—doing commercials for a local used-car dealership and starring in and directing a pornographic film—illustrate the epitome of "selling out" in America. What do these bookends tell us about institutionality and Asian American film and video? "Authenticity" is represented by the PBS-sponsored documentary about Bruce Lee and "selling out" is represented by Hollywood and the stardom machine. Inasmuch as it is an Asian American film in the literal sense—a film made by and about Asian Americans—it is also a film that allegorizes the history of Asian American independent film and video. That is, one of the film's covert discourses is about the two distinct possibilities available to Asian American actors and, by association, to Asian American filmmakers.

The film's engagement with the institutional history of Asian American independent film and video demonstrates the epitome of my argument—that what defines the genre is the struggle itself to materially exist. The irony that this commercial independent feature poses as a documentary made for PBS points to the history of that struggle, of Asian American filmmakers striving paradoxically to assert its difference and the assaults of dominant racist culture while simultaneously taking part in it at the same time. Despite Justin Lin's success as one of the very few Asian American filmmakers who has made a profitable Asian American film in Hollywood, the reference to PBS reveals its roots within the institution.

## Asian Americans as Zombies

The parodic is a significant strategy in locating the sign of the institutional in Asian American independent media. In many ways, *American Zombie* is a parody of institutional media, poking fun at the very social change agenda on which Asian American media has been built. Poised as a fake documentary about the forging of "Zombie American identity" in Los Angeles, the film identifies zombies as the latest marginalized group in the identity politics zeitgeist to seek "rights" and "recognition." In fact, *American Zombie* addresses the core issue of marginalization and Asian American media as explored in chapter 2 of this volume—that is, the values of injury and ressentiment as limiting markers of artistic endeavors. To reiterate, injury is what Wendy Brown deems: "Whether one is dealing with the state, the Mafia, parents, pimps, police, or husbands, the heavy price of institutionalized protection is always a measure of dependence and agreement to abide by the protector's rules."[7]

The zombies of *American Zombie* have become dependent on such "institutionalized protection" as a pattern of liberal political response to the "unjust" late capitalist pecking order. The culture of institutionalization— especially of

FIG. 12 Judy, an avid scrapbooker, desperately tries to assimilate among the living in *American Zombie* (2007). (Courtesy of LeeLee Films.)

identity—attempts to normalize zombies as "people like everybody else" who deserve the full rights and privileges of humans. True to fake documentary form, the film follows three undead subjects, Zach (Austin Basis), a twenty-something convenience store clerk; Judy (Suzy Nakamura), a thirty-something Asian American sales rep for a health food company; and Lisa (Jane Edith Wilson), a forty-something florist. The crux of the struggle between the Asian American documentary filmmaker Grace Lee, playing herself, and her codirector John Solomon, also playing himself, is that between portraying the zombies as justifiably "injured" minorities deserving of rights and the notion that this protection from ostracism and marginalization is merely suppressing the true nature of zombies as flesh-eating, inhuman monsters.

Though *American Zombie* is not specifically about Asian Americans, it is a critique of Asian American institutional filmmaking in several respects. Both the film and the film-within-the-film are directed by Grace Lee, who has made several award-winning documentaries, most notably one of the most celebrated Asian American films ever made: *The Grace Lee Project*. Bearing all of the signs and fitting all of the myriad criteria of Asian American film and video, *The Grace Lee Project* is the prototypical "film about Asian Americans made for Asian Americans." In it, Lee seeks the answer to her own identity through an exploration of other women who bear her name: Grace Lee. By seeking these individuals, Lee expects to find connections but finds much more disparity and diversity among the various women named Grace Lee. Classically, Lee's documentary dispels the notion of a certain kind of model-minority, one-size-fits-all assumption about Asian Americans.

*American Zombie* even takes aim at Lee's infamy as a "serious" documentarian by setting her up as part of an odd couple with John Solomon, a slacker filmmaker who declares his reasons for wanting to team up with her even though his personal interest is in horror films. Lee is presented as an award-winning, high-achieving model Asian American. She is seen in real-life clips of her appearance on the national news program *Good Morning America* during the publicity tour for *The Grace Lee Project* and accepting national awards for her film. Solomon, as well the viewer, implicitly understands the value of institutional documentary. It is the epitome of what Daryl Chin calls the "noble and uplifting and boring as hell" Asian American film of social change. "People like that socially conscious stuff," Solomon says disparagingly. Yet the film builds Lee (and Asian American film and video) up only to later tear it down when, after a minor tiff about whether to aggressively confront one of the zombies to reveal the truth of her identity as a flesh eater, Solomon criticizes Lee, saying, "not every movie is about you. Nobody wants to see *The Grace Lee Project, Part 2*." This inside joke on Asian American film and video reads in a number of ways. To outsiders, or the viewer not acculturated to the institutionality inherent to the genre, it reads as a joke about the postfeminist, overachieving narcissism of the model-minority Asian American filmmaker. The character that Lee plays is portrayed as a kind of stock self-absorbed, overly serious, progressive American documentary filmmaker. On the other hand, for viewers who are aware that *The Grace Lee Project* is a film that precisely is about the problem of the model-minority stereotype would see the irony of the inside joke in that Lee's infamous award-winning documentary was about the empty placeholder of stereotypical expectations about Asian American women, that is, not at all about Grace Lee, herself. In this way, *American Zombie* has an ambivalent attitude toward the institution of Asian American film and video. This is evident in the film itself, as all three subjects are portrayed to highlight their normality according to the codes of a certain kind of Asian American documentary whereby subjects are revealed to be "normal," "like everybody else," or happily dispelling the assumptions made about them, à la *The Grace Lee Project*, in which Asian American women defy stereotypes. In the end, all three zombies end up busting out of the safety zones of "protective institutional boundaries" to end up violently attacking and eating people, as is their nature.

Therefore, as *American Zombie* shows, zombies are a perfect metaphor for Asian American film and video, since within that tension between the collective and the individual, it is in the nature of the individual to be independent in order to grow and to truly be him- or herself. If it means eating people alive, making films that have nothing to do with Asian American issues, or daring to be experimental, this is the prerogative and the responsibility of the artist. Though the institution of Asian American film and video has provided the major avenue out of the shadows of marginalization, it is the recognition of the limitations of dependence on the institution that has enabled filmmakers to discover their true independence as filmmakers. While the genre continues in the guise of sophisticated, high-budget, and popular feature films that are growing in distribution numbers and the number of film festivals, its inherent institutionality will remain as its signature and residue to remind us of the reality of the filmmaking enterprise in America and the enduring and indelible place of race in its configuration.

# Afterword

This book has examined the institutional history of Asian American film and video. But more than this, it advocates for the continuation of a dynamic, well-funded public media that must exist in order for diversity to flourish in the United States. Particularly in the current landscape of a so-called postracial, neoliberal media landscape, we must remember the struggles of the past lest we fall back into the institutional racism of the past, but under different guises. This book demonstrates that ultimately, for good or ill, Asian American film and video *is* the public media institution, uniquely entwined unlike in any other film movement or genre. The parodic text allows us to understand the importance of this close relationship in its full historical scope. Through humor, these spoofs reveal not only how Asian American film and video has been shaped by the fight for recognition and equality but how it has been trapped by it, as well. If anything, both *Finishing the Game* and *American Zombie* capture the uncomfortable truth of the genre in that it continues to struggle for freedom from obligations to the state, to identity politics, and to its own history. The struggling Asian American actors of the 1970s in *Finishing the Game* escape Hollywood in the end, and the zombies of *American Zombie* ultimately relinquish their valiant attempts to fit into a civil mode of politically correct citizenship. That the characters in both of these films let go of the struggle represents a fantasy of being able to be oneself (or to make films freely) without the yoke of institutions.

And yet, without these institutions, these parental figures, these motherships, Asian American film and video would not have advanced as it has. The pioneers of the 1970s—Visual Communications, Asian CineVision, and

EthnoCommunications—sought simply to provide images of Asian Americans for a media landscape that was completely devoid of Asian faces, stories, and filmmakers. What followed was the golden age of Asian American film and video during the institution-building era that linked independent Asian American filmmakers with PBS through the Minority Consortia in the 1980s. NAATA became a powerful force in supporting the creation of a vibrant, diverse Asian American filmmaking community. The emergence of ITVS and the globalized film festival pushed the genre into even newer directions that challenged issues of its roots in US civil rights versus transnationality as well as showcasing the role of the avant-garde in redefining the political ethos of Asian American film and video as a movement. The original goal of creating more images of Asians in film and television, particularly in Hollywood feature films, was in many ways realized with Justin Lin's *Better Luck Tomorrow*, though that inevitably created new questions about the legacy of the Asian American film movement.

The commercial feature film in the digital age of affordable production budgets, Internet crowdsourcing, and international cofunding has had greatimpacton Asian American film and video. Even more so in times of threats to the existence of PBS, the history of the social change foundations of public media and its importance to racial diversity in film and television in the United States need to be remembered and fought for. By recalling and referencing this past through humor, *Finishing the Game* and *American Zombie* establish their place as crucial milestones for the body of work of Asian American film and video. And by understanding the historical necessity of public media, the genre's torch bearers show their commitment to continuing the work of social change that began with the original low-budget 8mm documentaries that were humble yet enormous in their aspirations.

Though it seems that the goals of Asian American film and video have been met in some ways, Lin's and Grace Lee's fake documentaries reveal even more deeply what the stakes continue be for the genre in a so-called postracial media environment—that is, the importance not of the positive image or experimental techniques or big-budget feature films but of understanding the singular struggles that have formed and continue to form Asian American film and video's institutional roots.

# Notes

### Introduction: The Shared History of Asian American Film and Video and Public Interest Media

1. Carnegie Commission, *Public Television*.
2. NAATA was renamed CAAM (Center for Asian American Media) in 2005.
3. I use "Asian American media" and "Asian American film and video" interchangeably. The clearinghouse on Asian American film and video is called the Center for Asian American Media, but much of the current scholarship consistently calls it "Asian American film and video." In the age of increasing malleability between formats, distribution, and exhibition, I use both terms equally.
4. The larger context of the Asian American movement and labor can be found in Wei's *Asian American Movement*.
5. Bernard Weinraub, "I Didn't Want to Do Another Chinese Movie," *New York Times*, September 5, 1993.
6. Auteur theory was developed by French film critics in the postwar moment, which the led the way to the establishment of film as an art form. Although auteur theory has largely been relegated as a relic of the past since Roland Barthes's declaration of the "death of the author" and the cultural turn of poststructuralism in the 1970s, the ghost of the authorship lingers on in the popular imagination and in the continued celebration of film directors in the discourse of cinephilia.
7. In his book *Identities in Motion*, Feng defines Asian American film and video as a complex negotiation and movement between the viewer, the film, and prior cinematic constructions. Glen Mimura, on the other hand, defines Asian American film and video as the ghostly remains of Third Cinema in his *Ghostlife of Third Cinema*.
8. Feng, *Identities in Motion*, 214.

## Chapter 1 "Noble and Uplifting and Boring as Hell": Asian American Film and Video, 1971-1982

1. Feng, *Identities in Motion*, 151.
2. See Gong, "A History in Progress," reprinted in Feng, *Screening Asian Americans*, 101–110.
3. Although there are many contemporary Asian American experimental film and video artists, my goal is to relocate the origins of the discourse on form and experimentation in its earlier, formative years. See Oishi, "Bad Asians."
4. Feng, *Identities in Motion*, 2;, James, "Popular Cinemas in Los Angeles," 234.
5. See Jun Okada, "The PBS and NAATA Connection: Comparing the Public Spheres of Asian American Film and Video," *Velvet Light Trap* 55, no. 1 (Spring 2005), 39–51.
6. This discussion is about the experimental video artist Janice Tanaka, not the producer Janice D. Tanaka.
7. James, "Popular Cinemas in Los Angeles," 234.
8. Ibid., 238.
9. Nakamura interview, July 1, 2002.
10. Nichols, *Representing Reality*, 38.
11. Jonas Mekas, "The Changing Language of Cinema," in *Movie Journal: The Rise of the New American Cinema 1959–1971* (New York: Macmillan, 1972), 49.
12. James, "Popular Cinemas in Los Angeles," 238.
13. Nichols, *Representing Reality*, 38.
14. James, "Popular Cinemas in Los Angeles," 237.
15. *Topaz*, a Super 8 film secretly shot with a smuggled camera by internee Dave Tatsuno, is the only known documentary film of the camps. *Topaz* became the second film chosen for preservation by the National Film Registry (the first being the Zapruder film of the JFK assassination).
16. Nakamura interview, July 1, 2002.
17. The Cantonese appellation "Wong Sinsaang" roughly translates to "Mr. Wong."
18. Higashi, *Cecil B. Demille and American Culture*, 61.
19. Daryl Chin, "The Asian American Film Festival," 2.
20. Nakamura interview, July 1, 2002.
21. David James makes the connection between amateur films and worker's film movements of the 1930s in Los Angeles that have many parallels to the Visual Communications of the 1970s in "Popular Cinemas in Los Angeles."
22. James, "Popular Cinemas in Los Angeles," 246.
23. Chin, "After Ten Years," 14.
24. Ibid.
25. Chin, "The Asian American Film Festival," 1.
26. Nakamura interview, July 1, 2002.
27. Chin, "The Asian American Film Festival," 2.
28. Ibid.
29. Chin, "The Critic's Seat," 10.
30. Gong, "Anecdote about *Chan Is Missing*," 37.
31. Chu, "Three Asian American Filmmakers: Wayne Wang," 9.
32. Ibid.
33. See Feng, "Being Chinese American."
34. Wang's post–*Chan Is Missing* career has included *The Joy Luck Club* (1993) as well

as several non–Asian American feature films, including *Slam Dance* (1987), *Smoke* (1995), *Blue in the Face* (1995), and *Maid in Manhattan* (2002).
35. For a detailed analysis of *Hito Hata*, see James, "Popular Cinemas in Los Angeles."
36. Chin, "After Ten Years," 14.
37. James, "Popular Cinemas in Los Angeles," 244.
38. Sturken, "Paradox in the Evolution of an Art Form," 115.
39. Huffman, "Video Art," 85.
40. Ibid., 85–86.
41. About Janice Tanaka, http://www.janicetanaka.com.
42. Marita Sturken, "The Politics of Video Memory: Electronic Erasures and Inscriptions from Resolutions: Contemporary Video Practices," in *Resolutions: Essays on Contemporary Video Practices*, ed. Michael Renov and Erika Suderburg (Minneapolis: University of Minnesota Press, 1995); reprinted in Feng, *Screening Asian Americans*, 173–184.
43. Chin, "After Ten Years," 15.

## Chapter 2    The Center for Asian American Media and the Televisual Public Sphere

1. Habermas refers specifically to a moment in early modern Europe when men of society held discussions in public spaces that often critiqued the ruling state. Habermas, *Structural Transformation of the Public Sphere*.
2. Carnegie Commission on Educational Television, *Public Television*, 18.
3. Hoynes, *Public Television for Sale*, 1.
4. Task Force on Minorities in Public Broadcasting, *A Formula for Change*, xiii.
5. For more about this history see Noriega, *Shot in America*.
6. The National Latino Communications Consortium disbanded in 1998, after which CPB appropriated Minority Consortia funds to the newly formed Latino Public Broadcasting. Pacific Islanders in Communications split from NAATA in 1991.
7. Gong, "A History in Progress," 7.
8. See Corporation for Public Broadcasting, "Annual Report 2003," www.cpb.org, 4 August 2004. These amounts were given to all of the five Minority Consortia that year. CPB's annual appropriation from Congress in 2003 was $362 million, representing the largest single source of funding for public television.
9. For more on *Silk Screen* see Francia, "Asian American Indies Gain PTV Exposure."
10. Coe, "The National Asian American Telecommunications Association."
11. NAATA, "Media Fund Applicants," 1999–2001.
12. Amy Chen interview, July 20, 2002.
13. By nontraditional documentaries, I refer to the sea change that *POV* presented to public television after years of the straight investigative-style documentary endorsed by the program *Frontline*, which was the standard PBS nonfiction program before *POV*. Even before the creation of *POV*, the National Coalition of Independent Public Broadcasting Producers called for the "exclusion of *Frontline* from consideration as 'independent production'" because of its overly bureaucratic and conservative policies, which included the selection of programs without panel review. *POV* welcomed the personal documentary, inviting autobiographical pieces as well as the as-yet-unheard perspectives of marginalized racial, ethnic, sexual, and gendered identities. For more on this history, see Bullert, *Public Television*.

14. Ouellette, *Viewers Like You*, 50.
15. Fraser, "Rethinking the Public Sphere," 111.
16. Aufderheide, "Public Television and the Public Sphere," 169.
17. POV, "About *POV*," last modified August 2004, http://www.pbs.org/pov/utils/aboutpov.html.
18. By contrast, another PBS documentary program, *American Experience*, has shown many fewer NAATA-funded programs, namely, *Daughter from Danang* (2002), a documentary about the experience of an Amerasian woman who tries unsuccessfully to reunite with her Vietnamese family, and Lise Yasui's *A Family Gathering* (1989), a Japanese American internment documentary.
19. Fraser, "Rethinking the Public Sphere," 122.
20. Eddie Wong interview, October 4, 2001.
21. Wendy Brown says of a politics of ressentiment, "Developing a righteous critique of power from the perspective of the injured, it delimits a specific site of blame for suffering by constituting sovereign subjects and events as responsible for the 'injury' of social subordination. It fixes the identities of the injured and the injuring as social positions, and codifies as well the meanings of their actions against all possibilities of indeterminacy, ambiguity, and struggle for resignification or repositioning." Brown, "Injury, Identity, Politics," 27.
22. These include films that complicate a purist notion of Asian American identity with gender, sexuality, class, and humor. These films by directors such as Jon Moritsugu, Patty Chang, Gregg Araki, Richard Fung, Lana Lin, and Ming-Yuen S. Ma would not necessarily fit generically on *POV*, yet the point is that there is no national public sphere for these "bad Asians" and their films, since they don't deal with issues of historical trauma but play with notions of ethnic, racial, and sexual identity. Furthermore, most of their films have been featured at NAATA's film festival. For more about these filmmakers see Oishi, "Bad Asians."
23. Other important Asian American political documentaries that have appeared on *POV* are *Sa-I-Gu* (1992), which aired in the months following the Rodney King riots in 1992, and *Licensed to Kill* (1997), a documentary about gay hate crime directed by Arthur Dong.
24. Nichols, "Historical Consciousness and the Viewer," 56.
25. Feng, *Identities in Motion*, 152.
26. Mimura, "Antidote for Collective Amnesia?" 151.
27. Creef, "The Gendering of Historical Trauma in Internment-Camp Documentary," 169.
28. Nichols, *Representing Reality*.
29. Brown, *States of Injury*, 28.
30. As of 2004's Media Fund Award regulations, awardees are required to "grant to NAATA exclusive domestic public television rights for no more than four years for no additional fee. This means it must premiere on American public television before any other broadcast. After public television broadcast, producer is welcome to take program to cable or other television broadcast entities." NAATA, "Media Fund Award," accessed June 1, 2004, www.naatanet.org.
31. Fraser, "Rethinking the Public Sphere," 123.
32. Tong and Yi, "A New Wave."
33. Marcus, "No 'Ghetto' at the San Francisco International Asian American Film Festival."

## Chapter 3    Pathology as Authenticity: ITVS, *Terminal USA*, and the Televisual Struggle over Positive/Negative Images

1. Feng, *Screening Asian Americans*, 5.
2. Bogle, *Toms, Coons, Mulattoes, Mammies, and Bucks*.
3. Kwon and Au, "Model Minority Myth," 222.
4. Ibid., 223.
5. Historically, though, this has been about only the first wave of Asians immigrating to the United States in the 1960s. In later decades, the model-minority myth was complicated by the waves of immigrants and refugees from Vietnam, Cambodia, and Laos, which were characterized as much more socioeconomically diverse.
6. An infamous example of this was the murder of Vincent Chin, who was killed in 1982 by white auto workers in Detroit who made racially charged comments, while beating him with a baseball bat, referring to the domination by Japanese automakers that led to mass layoffs in the US car industry.
7. Oishi, "Bad Asians," 221.
8. Gray, *Watching Race*, 79.
9. Ibid.
10. E.g., Gray, *Watching Race*; Jhally and Lewis, *Enlightened Racism*; Dyson, "Bill Cosby and the Politics of Race."
11. Gray, *Watching Race*, 79.
12. Ibid., 80.
13. Jhally and Lewis, *Enlightened Racism*, 135.
14. Ibid., 81.
15. Havens, "'The Biggest Show in the World,'" 383.
16. When *The Simpsons* began airing in direct competition with *The Cosby Show*, audience tastes shifted from family sitcom fantasy to family sitcom parody. It has been argued that *The Simpsons*, though animated and putatively "white," were considered to be "more black" than the Huxtables because of their "realistic" working-class milieu and because they parodied many of the fantasy elements that made many incredulous of *The Cosby Show*'s premise.
17. Havens, "'The Biggest Show in the World.'"
18. Palumbo-Liu, *Asian/American*, 174.
19. Marchetti, *Romance and the "Yellow Peril*," 8.
20. Lee, "'Where's My Parade?'"
21. "Rolling with the Punches: Margaret Cho Copes with Critics' Commentary," *USA Today*, September 19, 1994, Final Edition, Life Section, 3D.
22. Benjamin Pimentel, "'All-American Girl' Stirs Debate among Bay Asians: New Sitcom Promotes Distorted View, Some Claim," *San Francisco Chronicle*, November 1, 1994, A17.
23. Matt Roush, "'Girl' Sinks into Sitcom Shtick," *USA Today*, September 14, 1994, 3D.
24. Drickey, "Larry to the Third Power".
25. John Caldwell, "ITVS," http://www.museum.tv/eotv/independentt.htm, accessed April 13, 2014.
26. Ouellette, *Viewers Like You*, 213.
27. Hall, "Encoding/decoding."
28. Caldwell, "Independent Television Service."
29. Stevenson, *Land of a Thousand Balconies*, 133.
30. See http://jonmoritsugu.com/films/awards.php?film=terminal_usa.

31. Lee, "Where's My Parade?" 108.
32. Redpath, "Ultra Low-Budget Feature Filmmakers Explore Youth and Nihilism," Release Print, May 1991, 24.
33. Zedd, "Cinema of Transgression Manifesto (USA 1985)," 88.
34. Kristeva, *Powers of Horror*, 9.
35. Moritsugu's most recent low-budget independent feature, *Pig Death Machine* (2013), was made with funding solicited from the independent crowd-sourcing Web site kickstarter.com.

## Chapter 4   Dismembered from History: Racial Ambivalence in the Films of Gregg Araki

1. Feng, "In Search of Asian American Media," 34.
2. All three have published essays in the first collection of critical, historical, and creative writing about Asian American media, *Moving the Image: Independent Asian Pacific American Media Arts*, edited by Russell Leong.
3. By comparison, Wayne Wang is probably the most famous example of directors who make distinctly different kinds of films, Asian American films and non–Asian American films. Wang continues to make Asian American films on very low budgets while funding them with his Hollywood director-for-hire vehicles.
4. Yutani, "Gregg Araki and the Queer New Wave," 178.
5. Chin, "Girlfriend in a Coma," 104.
6. Redpath, "Ultra Low-Budget Feature Filmmakers," 23.
7. Rich, "New Queer Cinema."
8. Yutani, "Gregg Araki and the Queer New Wave," 175.
9. Araki, "The (Sorry) State of (Independent) Things," 69.
10. Chin, "Girlfriend in a Coma," 107.
11. Hu, "2007 SFIAAFF."
12. Thompson, "Punk Cinema," 49.
13. Ibid.
14. Ibid.
15. Ibid.
16. Araki, quoted in Hu, "2007 SFIAAFF."
17. The discussion of ambiguous race in these films is discussed at length in Jane Park's *Yellow Future: Oriental Style in Hollywood Cinema* and Peter X Feng's "False Consciousness and Double Consciousness: Race, Virtual Reality and the Assimilation of Hong Kong Action Cinema in *The Matrix*."
18. Nakamura, *Mixed Race Hollywood*, 291.
19. James, *The Most Typical Avant-Garde*, 407.
20. Ibid.
21. Marlon Riggs's essay film, *Tongues Untied* (1989), excellently references this problem of white supremacy in gay male culture.
22. It is also quite possibly a product endorsement for Calvin Klein, which makes the situation even weirder.
23. For example, the controversy over the complete lack of romantic consummation between Julia Roberts and Denzel Washington's characters in *The Pelican Brief* and also between Aaliyah and Jet Li's characters in *Romeo Must Die* points to a history of the recalcitrant taboo of white female/black male and black female/Asian male in on-screen couplings.

## Chapter 5  *Better Luck Tomorrow* and the Transnational Reframing of Asian American Film and Video

1. Ebert, "Succeeding at Success," F-08.
2. Hillenbrand, "Of Myths and Men," 51.
3. Interestingly, the SFIAAFF had again changed its name to CAAMfest (Center for Asian American Media Fest), which reflects a branding that hews much more closely to its institutional roots. I believe that this shows an interest, again in the Asian American aspect of the organization, perhaps to stem the tide of postracial sentiments, and less on the global cinephilia that was emphasized in the 1990s and early 2000s.
4. Another feature film that anticipated the proliferation of feature film in 1997 was Quentin Lee's *Flow*, which appeared in 1996 at SFIAAFF. Lee codirected *Shopping for Fangs* with Justin Lin.
5. De Valck, *Film Festivals*, 183.
6. Susan Sontag, "The Decay of Cinema," *New York Times*, February 25, 1996.
7. Center for Asian American Media, "History," http://caamedia.org/festival-info/history-timeline/.
8. Ibid.
9. NAATA, program notes, 13th Annual SFAAIFF (1995).
10. Olds and Yeung, "Pathways to Global City Formation," 505.
11. Wong, "A Film Festival Focuses on 'Gener-Asian X,'" *New York Times*, July 22, 1998.
12. Feng, *Identities in Motion*, 192.
13. Marchetti, "Guests at the Wedding Banquet," 214.
14. Marchetti, "The Gender of GenerAsian X in Clara Law's Migration Trilogy," 71–72.
15. Wong, "Denationalization Reconsidered," 140.
16. Ibid.
17. Lipsitz, *Time Passages*, 212.
18. Sharrett, "End of Story," 319–331.
19. Dennis Harvey, *Variety*, March 24–30, 1997, 36.
20. Song, *Strange Future*, 8.
21. Lipsitz, *Time Passages*, 213.
22. Wong, "Denationalization Reconsidered," 123.
23. Projansky and Ono, "Making Films Asian American," 277.
24. Ibid., 263.
25. After the 1965 Immigration and Nationality Act, there was an unprecedented number of immigrants that arrived in the United States from all over Asia, especially South and Southeast Asia. This added to the Asian American population who had already been in the United States for generations and complicated and diversified the meaning of being Asian American.
26. Hillenbrand, "Of Myths and Men," 64.
27. Hillenbrand, "Of Myths and Men," 51.
28. For more on John Woo's *A Better Tomorrow*, see Karen Fang, *John Woo's "A Better Tomorrow"* (Hong Kong: Hong Kong University Press, 2004).
29. Wong, "Denationalization Reconsidered," 140; Marchetti, "The Gender of GenerAsian X," 71–72.

Chapter 6  The Post-Asian American Feature Film: The Persistence of Institutionality in *Finishing the Game: The Search for a New Bruce Lee* and *American Zombie*

1. Fraser, *Justice Interruptus*, 11.
2. Juhasz and Lerner, *F Is for Fake*, 2.
3. See Feng, *Identities in Motion*, 13.
4. Parreñas-Shimizu, *Straightjacket Sexualities*, 16.
5. Genette, *Paratexts*, 8.
6. Ibid.
7. Wendy Brown, *States of Injury*, 169.

# Bibliography

## Films Discussed

*All-American Girl.* ABC. 1994. DVD. Los Angeles: Shout Factory, 2006.
*American Zombie.* Directed by Grace Lee. 2007. DVD. Burbank, CA: Cinema Libre, 2008.
*Better Luck Tomorrow.* Directed by Justin Lin. 2002. DVD. Los Angeles: Paramount, 2003.
*Chan Is Missing.* Directed by Wayne Wang. 1982. DVD. New York: Koch-Lorber Films, 2006.
*The Chinatown Files.* Directed by Amy Chen. 2001. DVD. New York: Filmmakers Library.
*The Cosby Show.* NBC. 1984–1992. DVD. Los Angeles: First Look Home Entertainment, 2008.
*Days of Waiting: The Life and Art of Estelle Ishigo.* Directed by Steven Okazaki. 1990. DVD. San Francisco: Center for Asian American Media, 2005.
*Doom Generation.* Directed by Gregg Araki. 1995. DVD. Santa Monica: Lions Gate, 2007.
*Finishing the Game: The Search for a New Bruce Lee.* Directed by Justin Lin. 2007. DVD. Los Angeles: Genius Products, 2008.
*First Person Plural.* Directed by Deann Borshay-Liem. 2000. DVD. San Francisco: Center for Asian American Media, 2000.
*Green Card: An American Romance.* Directed by Bruce and Norman Yonemoto. 1982. DVD. New York: Electronic Arts Intermix, 1982.
*Hito Hata: Raise the Banner.* Directed by John Esaki, Duane Kubo, and Robert A. Nakamura. 1980. VHS. San Francisco: Center for Asian American Media, 1995.
*Manzanar.* Directed by Robert A. Nakamura. 1971. DVD. San Francisco: Center for Asian American Media, 2006.
*Nowhere.* Directed by Gregg Araki, 1997. VHS. Los Angeles: New Line Home Video, 1998.
*Shopping for Fangs.* Directed by Quentin Lee and Justin Lin. 1997. DVD. Venice, CA: Pathfinder Home Entertainment, 2009.
*Strawberry Fields.* DVD. Directed by Rea Tajiri. 1997. DVD. Los Angeles: Vanguard Cinema, 2000.

*Superhuman Flights of Submoronic Fancies.* Directed by Janice Tanaka. 1982. DVD. New York: Electronic Arts Intermix.
*Terminal USA.* Directed by Jon Moritsugu. 1994. VHS. San Francisco: Center for Asian American Media, 1994.
*Totally Fucked Up.* Directed by Gregg Araki. 1994. DVD. Culver City: Strand Releasing, 2005.
*Who Killed Vincent Chin?* Directed by Christine Choy and Renée Tajima-Peña. 1988. DVD. New York: Filmmakers Library, 1990.
*Who's Gonna Pay for These Donuts Anyway?* Directed by Janice Tanaka. 1992. VHS. New York: Video Data Bank, 1992.
*Wong Sinsaang.* Directed by Eddie Wong. 1971. VHS. Los Angeles: Visual Communications, 199?.
*Yellow.* Directed by Chris Chan Lee. 1998. DVD. Los Angeles: Phaedra, 2001.

## Secondary Sources

Acham, Christine. *Revolution Televised: Prime Time and the Struggle for Black Power.* Minneapolis: University of Minnesota Press, 2004.
Anbian, Robert. "Phelan Filmmaking Award-Winners Interviewed." *Release Print* (December/January 1988), 7–8, 15–16.
———. "A Room of Our Own? Local Indies Discuss New Pub TV Production Service." *Release Print* (August 1989), 3.
Araki, Gregg. *The Living End.* Screenplay. 1992.
———. "The (Sorry) State of (Independent) Things." In *Moving the Image: Independent Asian Pacific American Media Arts*, ed. Russell Leong, 68–70. Los Angeles: UCLA Asian American Studies and Visual Communications, 1991.
Asian Cine Vision. Program notes, Asian American Film Festival, New York City, February 12–14, 1978.
Aufderheide, Patricia. "Public Television and the Public Sphere." *Critical Studies in Mass Communication* 8 (1991), 168–183.
Bogle, Donald. *Toms, Coons, Mulattoes, Mammies, and Bucks: An Interpretive History of Blacks in American Films.* London: Continuum, 2003.
Bronski, Michael. "Reel Politick." *Z* (September 1992), 73–75.
Brown, Wendy. "Injury, Identity, Politics." In *Multiculturalism?* ed. Avery Gordon and Christopher Newfield. Minneapolis: University of Minnesota Press, 1995.
———. *States of Injury: Power and Freedom in Late Modernity.* Princeton: Princeton University Press, 1995.
Bullert, B. J. *Public Television: Politics and the Battle over Documentary Film.* New Brunswick, NJ: Rutgers University Press, 1997.
Caldwell, John. "Independent Television Service," *Encyclopedia of Television,* 1172–1173. New York: Routledge, 1997.
Carnegie Commission on Educational Television. *Public Television: A Program for Action.* New York: Harper and Row, 1967.
Center for Asian American Media. "History." http://caamedia.org/festival-info/history-timeline/.
Chen, Amy. Personal interview. July 20, 2002.
Chin, Daryl. "After Ten Years: Some Notes on the Asian American International Film Festival." Program notes, 13–19. Asian American Film Festival, Asian CineVision, New York City, June 24–28, 1988.

———. "The Asian American Film Festival." Program notes. Asian American Film Festival, Asian CineVision, New York City, February 12–14, 1978.

———. "The Critic's Seat: An Overview of the Festival." Program notes, 10–12. Asian American Film Festival, Asian CineVision, New York City, June 5, 12, 19, and 26, 1981.

———. "Girlfriend in a Coma: Notes on the Films of Gregg Araki." In *Queer Looks: Perspectives on Lesbian and Gay Film and Video*, ed. Martha Gever, Pratibha Parmar, and John Greyson, 103–107. New York: Routledge, 1993.

———. "Indie? Minority? 'Tain't Easy." *Bridge* 9, no. 3/4 (1984), 6–13.

———. "Removing the Artist, Killing the Messenger." In *Moving the Image: Independent Asian Pacific American Media*, 223–224. Los Angeles: UCLA Asian American Studies Center and Visual Communications, 1991.

Chu, Bernice. "Three Asian American Filmmakers: Wayne Wang." Program notes. Asian American International Film Festival, Asian CineVision, New York City, July 5, 12, 19, and 26, 1981.

Coe, Michelle. "The National Asian American Telecommunications Association." *Independent* (last modified March 1, 1999), http://www.independent-magazine.org/node/603.

Corporation for Public Broadcasting. *Annual Report 2003*. August 4, 2004. www.cpb.org.

Creef, Elena Tajima. "The Gendering of Historical Trauma in Internment-Camp Documentary: The Case of Steven Okazaki's *Days of Waiting*." In *Countervisions: Asian American Film Criticism*, ed. Darrell Hamamoto and Sandra Liu, 163–173. Philadelphia: Temple University Press, 2000.

Daressa, Lawrence. "Objections to Funding of Independent Producers through Stations and Their Consortia." *Independent* (June 1988), 31.

Deaton, Jennifer. "Double Vision: Deann Borshay Liem Unearths Forgotten Memories in *First Person Plural*." *Release Print* (March 2000), 36–38.

de Valck, Marijke. *Film Festivals: From European Geopolitics to Global Cinephilia*. Amsterdam: Amsterdam University Press, 2007.

Drickey, Janice. "Larry to the Third Power: Lawrence Daressa, Laurence Hall, and Lawrence Sapadin." *Current*, December 11, 1989. http://www.current.org/1989/12/larry-to-the-third-power/.

Dyson, Michael. "Bill Cosby and the Politics of Race." *Z Magazine*, September 1989, 26–30.

Ebert, Roger. "Succeeding at Success: Tale of Asian-American Teens Mixes Comedy, Darkness." *Denver Post*, April 25, 2003, F-08.

Espinosa, Julio Garcia. "For an Imperfect Cinema." In *Film and Theory: An Anthology*, ed. Robert Stam and Toby Miller, 287–297. Oxford: Blackwell, 2000.

"The FAF Story." *Release Print* 19, no. 1 (February 1996), 10–12.

Feng, Peter X. "Being Chinese American, Becoming Asian American: *Chan Is Missing*." *Cinema Journal* 35, no. 4 (Summer 1996), 88–118.

———. "False Consciousness and Double Consciousness: Race, Virtual Reality and the Assimilation of Hong Kong Action Cinema in *The Matrix*." In *Chinese Connections: Critical Perspectives on Film, Identity, and Diaspora*, ed. Tam See-Kam, Peter X Feng, and Gina Marchetti, 9–21. Philadelphia: Temple University Press, 2009.

———. *Identities in Motion: Asian American Film and Video*. Durham, NC: Duke University Press, 2002.

———. "In Search of Asian American Media." *Cineaste* 21, no. 1–2 (Winter–Spring 1995), 32–36.

———, ed. *Screening Asian Americans*. New Brunswick, NJ: Rutgers University Press, 2002.

Ferrer, Abe. Personal interview. July 23, 2002.

Figueroa, Pablo. "Beware of False Images, the Proper Subject Matter for Minority Filmmakers." *Independent Film and Video Monthly* (May 1980), 9–10.
*First Person Plural* Adoption Experiences. "I am an (sic) Korean Adoptee too!" *POV Interactive* Message Boards. March 22, 2000.
Fitzgerald, Nora. "Land of the Lost." *Washington City Paper*, October 27, 1995.
Foucault, Michel. "What Is an Author?" In *Language, Counter-Memory, Practice*, trans. Donald F. Bouchard and Sherry Simon, 124–127. Ithaca, NY: Cornell University Press, 1977.
Francia, Luis H. "Asian American Indies Gain PTV Exposure." *Independent* (January/February 1984), 23–24.
Fraser, Nancy. *Justice Interruptus: Critical Reflections on the "Postsocialist" Condition*. London: Routledge, 1997.
———. "Rethinking the Public Sphere." In *Habermas and the Public Sphere*, ed. Craig Calhoun, 109–142. Cambridge, MA: MIT Press, 1992.
Friedman, Lewis. "Five Year Plan for TV Program Fund: And Now a Word from Lewis Friedman." *Independent* (March 1980), 6–8.
Fung, Richard. "Looking for My Penis: The Eroticized Asian in Gay Video Porn." In *How Do I Look? Queer Film and Video*, ed. Bad Object-Choices, 165. Seattle: Bay Press, 1991.
Gee, Bill J. "A History of the Asian American International Film Festival 1978–1997." Program notes, 5–10. Asian CineVision Presents the Twentieth Asian American International Film Festival, '78–'97, New York City, July 18–August 10, 1997.
Genette, Gérard, *Paratexts: Thresholds of Interpretation*. Cambridge: Cambridge University Press, 1997.
Gong, Stephen. "Anecdote about *Chan Is Missing*," Program notes, 37. Asian American International Film Festival, New York City, March 6–13, 2002.
———. "A History in Progress: Asian American Media Arts Centers, 1970–1990." In *Moving the Image: Independent Asian Pacific American Media Arts*, ed. Russell Leong, 1–9. Los Angeles: UCLA Asian American Studies Center and Visual Communications, 1991.
———. "Zen and the Art of Motion Picture Making," Introduction by Hishuru Tori, Program notes, 9–18. Asian American International Film Festival, Asian CineVision, New York City, June 18, 19, 25, and 26, 1982.
Gray, Herman. *Watching Race: Television and the Struggle for Blackness*. Minneapolis: University of Minnesota Press, 1995.
Habermas, Jürgen. *Structural Transformation of the Public Sphere: An Inquiry into a Category of Bourgeois Society*. Trans. Thomas Burger and Frederick Lawrence. Cambridge, MA: MIT Press, 1989.
Hall, Stuart. "Encoding/decoding," In *Culture, Media, Language*, ed. Stuart Hall, Dorothy Hobson, Andrew Lowe and Paul Willis, 128–138. London: Hutchinson, 1980.
Halleck, Dee Dee. "CPB Pays a Visit: Discussion of CPB 'Draft Proposal' on the Issue of Independents and Public Television, The Kitchen, October 16, 1979." *Independent* (November 1979), 6–9.
Hansen, Miriam. "Unstable Mixtures, Dilated Spheres: Negt and Kluge's *The Public Sphere and Experience* Twenty Years Later." *Public Culture* 5, no. 2 (Winter 1993), 171–212.
Havens, Timothy. "'The Biggest Show in the World': Race and the Global Popularity of the Cosby Show." *Media, Culture, and Society* 22 (July 2000), 371–391.
Higashi, Sumiko. *Cecil B. DeMille and American Culture: The Silent Era*. Berkeley: University of California Press, 1994.
———. "Ethnicity, Class, and Gender in Film: DeMille's *The Cheat*." In *Unspeakable Images:*

*Ethnicity and the American Cinema*, ed. Lester D. Friedman, 112–139. Urbana: University of Illinois Press, 1991.

Hillenbrand, Margaret. "Of Myths and Men: *Better Luck Tomorrow* and the Mainstreaming of Asian America Cinema." *Cinema Journal* 47, no. 4 (Summer 2008), 50–75.

Hima B. Personal interview. July 19, 2002.

Hoynes, William. *Public Television for Sale: Media, the Market, and the Public Sphere*. Boulder, CO: Westview Press, 1994.

Hsu, Hua. "Making Luck." *Village Voice*, April 22, 2003, 124.

Hu, Marcus. "2007 SFIAAFF—'Down and Dirty Pictures' Panel Discussion with Gregg Araki, Roddy Bogawa, Jon Moritsugu and Marcus Hu." http://theeveningclass.blogspot.com/2007/03/2007-sfiaaffdown-and-dirty-pictures.html. Accessed April 13, 2014.

Huffman, Kathy Raye. "Video Art: What's TV Got to Do with It?" In *Illuminating Video: An Essential Guide to Video Art*, ed. Doug Hall and Sally Jo Fifer, 81–90. New York: Aperture Foundation, 1990.

James, David E. *Allegories of Cinema: American Film in the Sixties*. Princeton, NJ: Princeton University Press, 1989.

———. *The Most Typical Avant-Garde: History and Geography of Minor Cinemas in Los Angeles*. Berkeley: University of California Press, 2005.

———. "Popular Cinemas in Los Angeles: The Case of Visual Communications." In *The Sons and Daughters of Los: Culture and Community in L.A.*, 231–252. Philadelphia: Temple University Press, 2003

———. "Tradition and the Movies: The Asian American Avant-Garde in Los Angeles." *Journal of Asian American Studies*, vol. 2, no. 2 (1999), 157–175.

Japanese American Citizens League. "About the Japanese American Citizens League." jacl.org/about.html. July 2005.

Jhally, Sut, and Justin Lewis. *Enlightened Racism: The Cosby Show, Audiences, and the American Dream*. Boulder, CO: Westview Press, 1992.

Juhasz, Alexandra, and Jesse Lerner, eds. *F Is for Fake: Fake Documentary and Truth's Undoing*. Minneapolis: University of Minnesota Press, 2006.

Kellner, Douglas. *Television and the Crisis of Democracy*. Boulder, CO: Westview Press, 1990.

Kristeva, Julia. *Powers of Horror: An Essay on Abjection*. Translated by Leon S. Rudiez. New York: Columbia University Press, 1982

Kwon, Hyeyoung, and Wayne Au. "Model Minority Myth." In *Encyclopedia of Asian American Issues Today*, vol. 1, 222. Santa Barbara, CA: ABC-CLIO, 2009.

Lee, Rachel. "'Where's My Parade?': Margaret Cho and the Asian American Body in Space." *Drama Review* 48, no. 2 (Summer 2004), 108–132.

Lee, Robert G. *Orientals: Asian Americans in Popular Culture*. Philadelphia: Temple University Press, 1999.

Leong, Russell, ed. *Moving the Image: Independent Asian Pacific American Media Arts*. Los Angeles: UCLA Asian American Studies and Visual Communications, 1991.

Lewis, Jon. *The Road to Romance and Ruin: Teen Films and Youth Culture*. New York: Routledge, 1992.

Lipsitz, George. *Time Passages: Collective Memory and American Popular Culture*. Minneapolis: University of Minnesota Press, 2001.

Ma, Ming-Yuen S. *Slanted Visions*. Screenplay. 1994.

Marchetti, Gina. "The Gender of GenerAsian X in Clara Law's Migration Trilogy." In *Ladies and Gentlemen, Boys and Girls: Gender in Film at the End of the Twentieth Century*, ed. Murray Pomerance, 71–87. Albany: SUNY Press, 2001.

———. "Guests at the Wedding Banquet: The Cinema of the Chinese Diaspora and the Rise of the American Independents." In *Contemporary American Independent Film: From the Margins to the Mainstream*, ed. Chris Holmlund and Justin Wyatt, 211–225. London: Routledge, 2005.

———. *Romance and the "Yellow Peril": Race, Sex, and Discursive Strategies in Hollywood Fiction*. Berkeley: University of California Press, 1993.

Marcus, Erica. "No 'Ghetto' at the San Francisco International Asian American Film Festival." *Independent* (June 2002), 25–27.

Markey, Representative Edward J., Subcommittee Chair. "The House Subcommittee on Telecommunications and Finance, Energy, and Commerce Committee, March 10, 1988." *Independent* (June 1988), 28.

Mekas, Jonas. "The Changing Language of Cinema." In *Movie Journal: The Rise of the New American Cinema 1959–1971*, 48–50. New York: Macmillan, 1972.

Mills, David. "Korean Images of Torn LA." *Washington Post*, November 14, 1992.

Mimura, Glen Masato. "Antidote for Collective Amnesia? Rea Tajiri's Germinal Image." In *Countervisions: Asian American Film Criticism*, 150–162. Philadelphia: Temple University Press, 2000.

———. *Ghostlife of Third Cinema: Asian American Film and Video*. Minneapolis: University of Minnesota Press, 2009.

Moritsugu, Jon. *Terminal USA*. Screenplay. 1993.

NAATA. "Media Fund Applicants." 1999–2001 (archival document). Center for Asian American Media, San Francisco.

NAATAnet.org. "Media Fund Overview." http://www.naatanet.org/ community/ filmmaker/mediafund/. August 2004.

Nakamura, Eric. "Class of '97." http://youoffendmeyouoffendmyfamily.com/class-of-97/.

Nakamura, Lisa. *Cybertypes: Race, Ethnicity, and Identity on the Internet*. New York: Routledge, 2002.

———. *Mixed Race Hollywood*. New York: NYU Press, 2008.

Nakamura, Robert A. Personal interview. July 1, 2002.

Nakasako, Spencer. Personal interview. July 22, 2002.

"The National Independent Programming Service: A Proposal." *Independent* (June 1988), 15–16.

Nichols, Bill. "Historical Consciousness and the Viewer: Who Killed Vincent Chin?" In *The Persistence of History: Cinema, Television, and the Modern Event*, ed. Vivian Sobchack, 55–68. New York: Routledge, 1996.

———. *Representing Reality*. Bloomington: Indiana University Press, 1991.

Nietzsche, Friedrich. *On the Genealogy of Morals*. Trans. W. Kaufmann and R. J. Hollingdale. New York: Vintage, 1969.

Noriega, Chon A. *Shot in America: Television, the State, and the Rise of Chicano Cinema*. Minneapolis: University of Minnesota Press: 2000.

Oishi, Eve. "Bad Asians: New Film and Video by Queer Asian American Artists." In *Countervisions: Asian American Film Criticism*, ed. Darrell Hamamoto and Sandra Liu, 221–241. Philadelphia: Temple University Press, 2000.

———. Personal interview. July 26, 2002.

Okada, Jun. "The PBS and NAATA Connection: Comparing the Public Spheres of Asian American Film and Video." *Velvet Light Trap* 55, no. 1 (Spring 2005), 39–51.

Olds, Kris, and Henry Wai-Chung Yeung. "Pathways to Global City Formation: A View from the Developmental City State of Singapore." *Review of International Political Economy* 11, no. 3 (August 2004), 489–521.

Omatsu, Glen. "'The Four Prisons' and the Movements of Liberation: Asian American Activism from the 1960's to the 1990's." In *Contemporary Asian America: A Multidisciplinary Reader*, ed. Min Zhou and James Gatewood, 80–113. New York: New York University Press, 2000.
Omi, Michael, and Diane Yamashiro. "Politics with a Human Face." *Bridge* 9, no. 3/4 (1984), 24–29.
Ono, Kent A. "Re/membering Spectators: Meditations on Japanese American Cinema." In *Countervisions: Asian American Film Criticism*, ed. Darrell Hamamoto, 129–149. Philadelphia: Temple University Press, 2000.
Ouellette, Laurie. *Viewers Like You: How Public TV Failed the People*. New York: Columbia University Press, 2002.
Palumbo-Liu, David. *Asian/American: Historical Crossings of a Racial Frontier*. Palo Alto, CA: Stanford University Press, 1999.
Park, Jane Chi Hyun. *Yellow Future: Oriental Style in Hollywood Cinema*. Minneapolis: University of Minnesota Press, 2010.
Parreñas-Shimizu, Celine. *The Hypersexuality of Race: Performing Asian/American Women on Screen and Scene*. Durham, NC: Duke University Press, 2007.
———. *Straitjacket Sexualities: Unbinding Asian American Manhoods in the Movies*. Palo Alto, CA: Stanford University Press, 2012.
POV. "About POV." http://www.pbs.org/pov/utils/aboutpov.html. August 2004.
Projansky, Sarah, and Kent A. Ono. "Making Films Asian American: *Shopping for Fangs* and the Discursive Auteur." In *Authorship and Film*, ed. David A. Gerstner and Janet Staiger, 263–280. New York: Routledge, 2003.
Redpath, Mark. "Ultra Low-Budget Feature Filmmakers Explore Youth and Nihilism." *Release Print* (May 1991), 22–25.
Reid, Mark. *Redefining Black Film*. Berkeley: University of California Press, 1993.
Rich, B. Ruby. "New Queer Cinema." *Sight and Sound* 2, no. 5 (1993), 30–35.
Said, Edward W. *Orientalism*. New York: Vintage, 1978.
Sapadin, Lawrence. "The Hearings." *Independent Film and Video Monthly* (May 1988), 38–41.
———. "Independent Producers and Public Television: An Overview, 1978–1987." *Independent* (June 1988), 14–19.
———. "PBS Fails to Offer Access, Diversity." *Release Print* 10, no. 5 (June 1987), 12.
Sharrett, Christopher. "End of Story: The Collapse of Myth in Postmodern Narrative Film." In *The End of Cinema as We Know It*, ed. Jon Lewis, 319–331. New York: NYU Press, 2001.
Smith, Clairborne. "Newsreel's Second Act: Carrying the Torch after 35 Years." *Independent* (October 2003), 44.
Solanas, Fernando, and Octavio Getino. "Towards a Third Cinema: Notes and Experiences for the Development of a Cinema of Liberation in the Third World." In *Movies and Methods: An Anthology*, ed. Bill Nichols, pp 44–64. Berkeley: University of California Press 1976.
Song, Min. *Strange Future: Pessimism and the 1992 Los Angeles Riots*. Durham, NC: Duke University Press, 2005.
Stack, Peter. "Aim Camera, Push 'Record,' Act Normally." *San Francisco Chronicle*, March 5, 1998, E3.
Stevenson, Jack. *Land of A Thousand Balconies: Discoveries and Confessions of a B Movie Archaeologist*. Manchester: Headpress/Critical Visions, 2003.
Sturken, Marita. "The Absent Images of Memory: Remembering and Reenacting the Japanese Internment." *Positions: East Asia Cultures Critique* 5, no. 3 (Winter 1997), 687–707.

———. "Paradox in the Evolution of an Art Form: Great Expectations and the Making of a History." In *Illuminating Video: An Essential Guide to Video Art*, ed. Doug Hall and Sally Jo Fifer, 101–121. New York: Aperture Foundation, 1990.

Tajima Peña, Renée. "Mississippi Triangle: Three Views on Delta Life." *Bridge* 9, no. 3/ 4 (1984), 19–23.

———. "Moving the Image: Asian American Independent Filmmaking." In *Moving the Image: Independent Asian Pacific American Media Arts*, ed. Russell Leong, 10–33. Los Angeles: UCLA Asian American Studies and Visual Communications, 1991.

———. Personal interview. July 16, 2002.

Takaki, Ronald. *Strangers from a Different Shore: A History of Asian Americans*. New York: Penguin Books, 1989.

Task Force on Minorities in Public Broadcasting. *A Formula for Change: The Report of the Task Force on Minorities in Public Broadcasting*. Washington DC: Corporation for Public Broadcasting, 1978.

Thompson, Stacy, "Punk Cinema." *Cinema Journal* 43, no. 2 (Winter 2004), 47–66.

Tong, Corey, and Paul Yi. "A New Wave: Asian American Films." Program notes, 6–7. 15th Annual SFAAIFF, San Francisco, March 6–13, 1997.

Turner, Tad. "CPB Report." *Independent* (October 1979), 10–11.

"Twenty Years Ago Today (more or less)." *Release Print* (February 1996), 11.

Umemoto, Karen. "'On Strike!' San Francisco State College Strike, 1968–1969: The Role of Asian American Students." In *Contemporary Asian America: A Multidisciplinary Reader*, ed. Min Zhou and James Gatewood, 49–79. New York: New York University Press, 2000.

Waugh, Thomas. "Good Clean Fung." In *Screening Asian Americans*, ed. Peter X Feng, 243–252. New Brunswick, NJ: Rutgers University Press, 2002.

Wei, William. *The Asian American Movement*. Philadelphia: Temple University Press, 1993.

Wong, Eddie. Personal interview. October 4, 2001.

Wong, Edward. "A Film Festival Focuses on 'Gener-Asian X.'" *New York Times*, July 22, 1998.

Wong, Sau-ling C. "Denationalization Reconsidered: Asian American Cultural Criticism at a Theoretical Crossroads." In *Postcolonial Theory and the United States: Race, Ethnicity, and Literature*, ed. Amritjit Singh and Peter Schmidt, 122–148. Jackson: University Press of Mississippi, 2000.

Wu, Robin. "Asian American Filmmaking Today and Tomorrow." Program notes, 3–6. Asian American Film Festival, San Francisco, May 11, 18, 25; June 1, 1979.

Xing, Jun. *Asian America through the Lens: History, Representation, and Identity*. Lanham, MD: Altamira Press, 1998.

Yutani, Kimberly. "Gregg Araki and the Queer New Wave." In *Asian American Sexualities: Dimensions of the Gay and Lesbian Experience*, ed. Russell Leong, 175–180. New York: Routledge, 1996.

Zedd, Nick. "Cinema of Transgression Manifesto (USA 1985)." In *Film Manifestos and Global Cinema Cultures: A Critical Anthology*, ed. Scott Mackenzie, 88–89. Berkeley: University of California Press, 2014.

# Index

AAIAF. *See* Asian American International Film Festival
AAIVF. *See* Asian American International Video Festival
abject: aesthetic of, 70; as resistance, 70–72
AC/DC (musical group), 71
Acham, Christine, 60
ACV. *See* Asian CineVision
aesthetic(s): of abjection, 70; of Asian American film and video, 14, 56; discourse of, 14, 15; global cinematic, 123; inclination in Asian CineVision, 14, 15; punk, 80, 83, 84; queer, 9, 80, 83; strategies in film, 107; transnational, 10, 121
Ahwesh, Peggy, 83
alienation, 74, 80, 88
*All-American Girl* (television show), 56, 57, 69, 70; audience readiness for, 58; comparison to *The Cosby Show*, 58, 59; lack of authenticity on, 62; misunderstanding of function of ethnic sitcom in, 64; premise of defiance on, 64; as sign of normalization of multiculturalism, 59; as standard for commercial television's failure to represent Asian Americans, 61; ultimate failure of, 59, 63
Allen, Tom, 27
American Film Institute, 83
*American Zombie* (Lee, 2007), 10, 11, 130–133, 134, 135; addressing issue of marginalization, 130; ambivalence toward institution of Asian American film and video in, 132; as parody of institutional media, 130–133; satire in, 126
*America So Beautiful* (Shokrian, 2002), 53
Anger, Kenneth, 88, 89
*Anywhere but Here* (Wang, 1999), 6
Araki, Gregg, 8, 51, 79–96, 140n22; ambiguous, pan-sexual sex symbols in films, 89; anti–Asian American media stance, 81, 82, 96; central place in discourse of Asian American film and video, 80, 96; challenges definition of Asian American film and video, 81, 96; confluence of biracial and bisexual identity in films, 86; considered a nonethnic alternative filmmaker, 83; dominant place of whiteness in works of, 85; institutionality in films of, 81; obstacle of whiteness in works, 89; opposition to homophobia in aesthetic of, 87–88; paradoxical position of inclusion/exclusion in Asian American media institution, 80–85; punk and queer aesthetics in films of, 9, 83, 84; question of inclusion of works in Asian American Cinema, 79; race politics in works of, 81, 95; representation of racial ambiguity via sexual ambiguity in films of, 82;

Araki, Gregg (*continued*)
resistance to association with public interest media, 9; resistance to dominant cultural forms; "Teen Apocalypse Trilogy," 85–96; use of aesthetic punk strategies, 80, 83

Asian American film and video: aesthetics of, 56; beginnings of, 3; burden of representation on makers of, 46; as byproduct of rise of public interest media, 2, 7; center-to-periphery structure, 5; changes to through creation of NAATA, 41; collective authorship in, 22–26; commercial feature goal, 4; commitments to style and ideology in, 3; in context, 13–15; conventional strategies of self-representation in, 77; convergence with national public television, 7, 45–51; coterminous with contemporary new wave cinema, 103; defining, 3, 5, 28, 42, 52, 79, 137*n*7; desire to become more visible in mainstream, commercial cinema, 107; documentaries, 33; economic justice and, 125; emergence as recognizable genre, 1, 7, 12–38; emphasis on Americanness over foreignness, 118; evolution of, 110; experimental, 57; filmmaking as a paradigm of center to periphery favoring mainstream, 99; film of global cinephilia, 107; film of "roots," 107, 114, 123; funding for, 42; globalization of, 98; goal of recognition as genre, 11; historical trajectory of, 25; historical trauma, 47, 48; immigrant/transnational directors in, 99; importance of aesthetics and, 14; importance of cinematic form in, 28; importance of feature-length film to, 105; independent feature films, 9; institutional history of, 3, 4, 5, 7; institutional obligations carried by, 54; institutional parameters of, 3; international attention to, 99; lack of major national distribution deals for, 101; limitations of institutionalization of, 85; marginalization by Hollywood, 4; marketability of foreignness in, 99; movement and genre in, 3; at odds with punk aesthetic, 84; political cinema of ethnic identity and, 14; politics of injury in, 69, 130; predominance of positive images in, 13, 14; privileging of "international" over "Asian" and global over local in, 103, 104; production histories of, 13; public television and, 39–54; raced national subject formation in, 74, 75; recognition through capital, 99; relationship to Public Broadcasting Service, 3; relation to avant-garde film, 28; resistance against Hollywood, 7; sitcoms, 57–65; social-political documentaries, 47; sponsorship by public television, 12; transnational reframing of, 9, 97–123; trend toward picked up by mainstream press, 105; zombies as metaphor for, 132

Asian American filmmakers: addressing problem of positive/negative images, 55; Araki, Gregg, 8, 9, 51, 79–96; attempts to achieve commercial mainstream legitimacy, 3; Borshay-Liem, Deann, 48; Chen, Amy, 43; commitment to usurpation of control of images from Hollywood, 3, 7; Dong, Arthur, 42; experimental, 14, 33, 34–38; feature films by, 105; fighting institutional racism by, 7; gay, 79–96; global discourse and, 9; Iimura, Taka, 27, 28, 32, 35; Inada, Lawson, *17*; institutional obligations of, 4, 77; Kawanaka, Nobuhiro, 28; Kondo, Alan, *17*; Kubo, Duane, 15, *17*; Lee, Grace, 10, 11, 131, 132, 135; Lin, Justin, 4, 9, 10, 54, 117, 118–123, 125, 128, 135; making mockumentaries, 10, 11, 124–133; Moritsugu, Jon, 8; Nakamura, Robert, 15, 16, *17*, 18–20, 22, 28, 35, 36, 77, 81, 84, 112; Nakasako, Spencer, 42; Ohashi, Alan, 15; overcoming identity issues, 10; Paik, Nam June, 32, 33; peak period of, 101; political engagement of, 3; politics of ressentiment and, 45–51; post–Asian American, 10; production for wider audiences by, 10; reflections of ethnicities of, 5; refusal to participate in institutional boundaries, 79; risks in acceptance of fiscal support for, 42–45; social change orientation, 3, 5, 7, 8, 14, 15, 16, 24, 27, 31, 32, 107; subjected to proscribed ideological agenda, 39–40; support from associations, 12, 13; Tanaka, Janice, 15, 33, 34–36, 50; use of diverse fiscal strategies, 10; use of dominant cinematic discourses, 13; Wang, Wayne, 6, 12, 29–32; Wong, Eddie, 15, 16, *17*, 20–22;

working in increasingly transnational framework, 100; working outside public funding, 51–54; Yonemoto, Bruce, 15, 33, 36, 37; Yonemoto, Norman, 15, 33, 36, 37; Yu, Jessica, 6

Asian American independent media: countermemory aesthetic strategy, 107, 112, 113; discourse of cinephilia in, 101; as existential dilemma, 82; global cinephilia and, 100–105; growth through explicit association with East Asian popular cinema, 117; impact of Minority Consortia on, 39–54; importance of institutional history in, 78; indications of relationship to institutional forms of support, 124; institutional discourse of, 65; institutionalization of, 39; institutional requirements, 84; institutional schizophrenia of, 46; lack of developed broadcasting outlets for, 43; limitations of concept and application of, 80; microbudgets in, 107; principle of resistance in, 80, 81; restrictive ideological demands of, 90; sign of "institutional" in, 124; transnational aesthetic strategy, 107

Asian American International Film Festival (AAIFF), 15, 103; *Chan Is Missing* at, 30, 32; created by ACV, 27; eclectic film mix, 27, 28

Asian American International Video Festival (AAIVF), 32–34, 34, 37, 38

Asian American Legal Defense and Education Fund, 5

Asian American(s): hate crimes against, 56; institutional marginalization of from Hollywood, 129; labor group formation, 5; masculinity construction, 120; as model minority, 56, 57, 61, 63, 64, 73, 98, 120, 125, 141*n*5; resistance to labeling, 8, 9; stereotypes, 56, 57; stereotypes of consciousness of, 29

Asian Americans for a Fair Media, 5

*Asian America through the Lens* (Xing), 6

Asian CineVision (ACV), 13, 26–29, 102, 134; aesthetic inclination in, 14, 15; Asian American International Film Festival by, 15; *CineVue* journal by, 27; interest in avant-garde cinema, 15; interest in formal abstraction and experimentation, 33; publishes *Bridge* journal, 27; questions premise of social change ideology in filmmaking, 27; support for Asian American communities through media, 26

Asian CineVision Film Festival, 118

Association of Independent Video and Filmmakers, 66

*Atman* (Matsumoto, 1975), 28

Aufderheide, Patricia, 44

auteur theory, 6, 101, 137*n*6


"Bad Asian," 57, 98, 140*n*22

Bakula, Scott, 58

Barthes, Roland, 137*n*6

Basement Workshop, provides generative material for ACV, 26

Basis, Austin, 131

Bay Area Asian American International Film and Video Showcase, 103

Bay Area Asian American International Film Festival, 103

*Beaver Valley* (Tanaka, 1980), 15, 34; construction of femininity in, 35; cultural repression in nuclear age in, 35

*Benson* (television show), 59

Berges, Paul Mayeda, 102

*Better Luck Tomorrow* (Lin, 2000), 10, 54, 110, 118–123, 125, 135; achieves mainstream popularity, 97; as historic marker for Asian American film and video, 107; as homage to Hong Kong action film, 120; libidinal energy in, 120, 121; mimicry of hypermasculine Hong Kong action cinema, 118; mixed genres in, 98; as postmodern mimicry of Hollywood genres, 110; theme of ambivalence toward "selling out" to Hollywood, 97; transnational aesthetic in, 99, 118, 123; understood as parody of Hollywood film genres, 119; uses of violence in, 121, 123; virtues of, 98

*A Better Tomorrow* (Woo, 1986), 120

*Beverly Hills 90210* (television show), 93

Bixby, Bill, 58

*Black Is, Black Ain't* (Riggs, 1994), 67, 68

*Blade Runner* (Scott, 1982), 125

Blanchard, Susan, 58

*Blue in the Face* (Wang, 1995), 6

Bogawa, Roddy, 80, 82, 83

*Bonnie and Clyde* (Penn, 1967), 111

Brakhage, Stan, 71
Brando, Marlon, 89
*The Breakfast Club* (Hughes, 1985), 109
*Bridge* (arts journal), 27
Bronski, Michael, 79
Brown, Wendy, 14, 40, 140*n21*
Bruno, Ellen, 42
Bui, Tony, 99
Buñuel, Luis, 76
Burnett, Charles, 16
Burnett, McCaleb, 127

CAAM. *See* Center for Asian American Media
CAAMfest, 143*n3*
Caldwell, John, 66
Camp Cubes Photo Display, 19, 20
Canadian Council, 105
Carnegie Commission on Educational Television, 1, 40; vision of multiculturalism of, 2
Center for Asian American Media (CAAM), 6, 39, 71, 85, 137*n2*, 137*n3*; funding for *Strawberry Fields* (Tajiri), 112
Chan, Evans, 99
Chang, Patty, 53, 140*n22*
*Chan Is Missing* (Wang, 1982), 6, 9, 29–32, 80, 105, 125; abstraction in, 30; as avant-garde "dialectical" work, 12; box office popularity of, 12; as bridge between Asian American film and American cinema, 30, 31; as move forward in trajectory toward feature filmmaking, 30; neo-noir nature of, 12; reception at festivals, 29, 30, 32; unconventionality of, 29, 30
*The Cheat* (DeMille, 1915), 121
Chen, Amy, 38, 43
Chen Kaige, 103
Cheung, Leslie, 120
Chicago Underground Film Festival, 71
Chin, Daryl, 14, 15, 37, 38, 82, 132; argues against ideological nature of Asian American films, 27, 28; compares ACV with VC, 27; discourse of dissent by, 38; essays for Asian American International Film Festival, 28; film reviews by, 27; interest in vitality of form, 29; on video art, 33; view on conservative direction of Asian American film, 29
Chin, Jeanne, 115
Chin, Vincent, 141*n5*
Chinatown Community Television (CCTV), addressing issues of discrimination through, 26, 27
*Chinatown* (Polanski, 1974), 125
*The Chinatown Files* (Chen, 2001), 43
Cho, Margaret, 56, 57, 58, 61, 62, 63, 64, 70
Chung, Michael, 108
*Chungking Express* (Wong, 1994), 117
Cinema of Transgression, 71
cinephilia: death of as narrow concept, 102; defining, 101; European postwar art cinema and, 102; global, 100–105, 118, 119; resurrected as non-Eurocentric concept, 102
*CineVue* (journal), 27
*City, City* (VC), 22, 23, 26
civil rights movement, 5, 7, 15
"Class of 1997," 118; bent on making narrative feature films, 106; "GenerAsian X" and, 105–108; San Francisco International Asian American Film Festival and, 99
Clouse, Robert, 127
*Come See the Paradise* (Parker, 1990), 50
Conner, Bruce, 71
Corman, Roger, 74
Corporation for Public Broadcasting (CPB), 7, 139*n6*, 139*n8*; commissions task force on minorities, 2, 13, 14; funding by, 40; funds consortia of underrepresented minority groups, 2; provision of funding for Asian American films, 12; support for Asian American independent media, 124
*The Cosby Show* (television show), 56, 57, 58, 70, 141*n16*; ambivalence about, 59; avoidance of representations of struggle on, 60; comparison to *All-American Girl*, 58, 59; as correction for television's historical treatment of African Americans, 60; fantasy projections of, 60, 62, 64; idea that affirmative action not needed in, 60; ideological purposed served by, 62; misrepresentations on, 61
countermemory, 10, 107, 112, 113
*Countervisions* (Hamamoto), 6

*The Courtship of Eddie's Father* (television show), 58
CPB. *See* Corporation for Public Broadcasting
Cross Currents, 41
Cruise, Tom, 88, 89
*Cruisin' J-Town* (VC), 22, 23, 24–26, 27; commitment to communal authorship in, 24–26; dialectical structure of, 25

d'Angelo, Beverly, 92
Daressa, Lawrence, 66
Dash, Julie, 16
*Daughter from Danang* (Dolgin and Franco, 2002), 43, 140*n18*
*Days of Waiting: The Life and Art of Estelle Ishigo* (Okazaki, 1990), 49, 50
Dean, James, 89
Debord, Guy, 71
Depp, Johnny, 127
Derrida, Jacques, 71
de Valck, Marijke, 101, 102
*Diff'rent Strokes* (television show), 59
Dillon, Matt, 88
discourse: of aesthetics and form, 7; cinephilic, 101; circulation of, 44; "death of cinema," 109; of dissent, 38; of diversity, 2, 40; of feminism, 112; global, 9; of inclusion/exclusion, 81–85; of institutionality, 9, 124; libidinal, 121; of model minority, 57; of the "outsider," 80–85; psychoanalytic, 72; public media, 2; racial, 55, 56, 80, 81, 82, 95, 96; on representation in public media, 55; sexual, 86; of transnationality, 9; "yellow peril," 61
discrimination: in Chinatown communities, 26, 27; gender, 116; histories of, 5; racial, 5
diversity: attempts to authentically engage, 65; commitments to, 54; discourse of, 40; ethnic, 69; "excellence in," 2; lack of on commercial television, 1; media activists and, 65; Public Broadcasting Service and, 40–41; public media discourse of, 2
documentaries, 16; expository, 17; fake, 125–133; institutional, 132; internet, 112; non-traditional, 139*n13*; PBS, 9, 10; personal, 139*n13*; political, 140*n23*; social change, 24; traditional, 44
Dong, Arthur, 42, 140*n23*
*Doom Generation* (Araki, 1995), 8, 85–96; critique of classism in, 91; preoccupation with racial subtext, 90
*Do the Right Thing* (Lee, 1989), 110, 123
*Dottie Gets Spanked* (Haynes, 1993), 78
*Double Indemnity* (Wilder, 1944), 90
Duval, James, 85–96

*Easy Rider* (Hopper, 1969), 111
*Eat a Bowl of Tea* (Wang, 1989), 105
Ebert, Roger, 98
*El Mariachi* (Rodriguez, 1992), 105
Elsaesser, Thomas, 102
Emergency School Aid Act (1975), 25, 26
Ethnic Studies movement, transformation of curricula and, 1, 2
EthnoCommunications program, 2, 135; organized by UCLA, 15, 16

*A Family Gathering* (Yasui, 1989), 140*n18*
Fan, Roger, 127
*Feedback* (Kawanaka, 1973), 28
feminism, 112, 113
Feng, Peter X, 2, 6, 13, 79, 137*n7*, 142*n17*
*Ferris Bueller's Day Off* (Hughes, 1986), 109
film, independent feature: of counter-memory, 10, 112, 113; mockumentary, 10, 124–133; post–Asian American, 10; strategies used to identify institutionality in, 10; transnational aesthetic in, 10. *See also* Asian American independent media
film festivals: American Film Institute, 83; Asian American International Film Festival (AAIFF), 15, 27, 28, 103; Asian American International Video Festival (AAIVF), 32–34, 34; Asian CineVision Film Festival, 118; Bay Area Asian American International Film and Video Showcase, 103; Bay Area Asian American International Film Festival, 103; CAAMfest, 143*n3*; Chicago Underground Film Festival, 71; coinciding with cinephilia associated with French new wave, 101;

film festivals (*continued*)
East Coast, 28; ethnic identity-based, 53; making distinction/separation between Asian films and Asian American films, 103; Marathon Film Festival, 27; New Chinese Film Series, 103; New York Underground Film Festival, 71; Pusan International Film Festival, 103; Rotterdam Film Festival, 69; San Francisco International Asian American Film Festival, 2, 9, 42, 43, 52, 53, 54, 71, 99, 100–105, 118, 143*n*3; Sundance Film Festival, 53, 106; supplemented with feature films from Asia, 102; Toronto Film Festival, 69; Toronto International Festival, 53; World Series of Asian Films, 103

film(s): academic criticism of, 28; action, 121; as art form, 137*n*6; articulation of historical injury in, 7, 81; avant-garde, 15, 28, 76; changing global market for, 100; Chinese-language, 9; countercultural, 111; cult, 8; cycles, 3; documentary, 2, 5, 6, 24, 33, 42, 112; on effects of wars on Asian Americans, 5; experimental, 27, 53, 57, 113; exploitation, 74; farm labor, 2, 5; fictional narrative feature, 53; gangster, 110, 120, 122; gay, 80, 82, 83, 85–96; genres, 3; globalization of, 9; "heroic bloodshed" genre, 118; immigrant experience, 2, 5; independent, 2; internment, 2, 5, 17, 18–20, 42, 49, 50, 112, 113; "Kuleshov effect" in, 110; mainstream, 3; marginalized, 101; mockumentaries, 10, 11, 124–133; movements, 3; neo-noir, 125; post–Asian American feature, 4, 124–133; "queersploitation," 86; relocation, 18–20; resistance to racist imagery in, 2, 5; road, 90, 111, 113; social change and, 3, 5, 7, 8, 14, 24, 27, 107; structural, 28, 29; underrepresented minority, 3; used as propaganda for collectivity and community, 25. *See also* Asian American film and video

*Film Strips Number 2* (Iimura, 1969), 27, 28

*Finishing the Game* (Lin, 2007), 10, 11, 134, 135; analytical perspective on filmmaking, 128; Asian American identity and, 127; conscious enactment of institutionality, 127; critique of representations of Asian American masculinity, 127; institutionality as textual and paratextual sign in, 126; as parody, 127; persistence of institutionality and, 67, 129; satire in, 126

*Fire* (Mehta, 1996), 53

*Fire Over Water:* reedited as *Chan Is Missing*, 29–32. *See also Chan Is Missing* (Wang, 1982)

*First Person Plural* (Borshay-Liem, 2000), 42, 48, 49

*First Steps, Experimentally Speaking* program, 71

*Flow* (Lee, 1997), 143*n*4

*A Formula for Change* (Task Force on Minorities in Public Broadcasting), 2, 14, 40

Foucault, Michel, 22, 42

Fournier, Eric Paul, 6, 49

Frampton, Hollis, 28

Fraser, Nancy, 125

Friedrich, Su, 83

Fung, Richard, 140*n*22

*Game of Death* (Clouse, 1978), 127, 129–130

Gehr, Ernie, 28

"GenerAsian X," 101; Class of 1997 and, 105–108

Genette, Gérard, 128

Gerima, Haile, 16

*Ghostlife of Third Cinema* (Mimura), 6, 7

Gibson, Mel, 88

Gidal, Peter, 28

*Gimme a Break* (television show), 59

Godard, Jean-Luc, 29, 71

*The Grace Lee Project* (Lee, 2007), 10, 131, 132

Graham, Heather, 94

Gray, Herman, 59, 64

*A Great Wall* (Wang, 1986), 105

*Green Card: An American Romance* (Yonemoto, 1982), 36

*The Green Hornet* (television show), 127

*Gun Crazy* (Lewis, 1950), 90

*Gung Ho* (television show), 58

Habermas, Jürgen, 39, 44, 139*n*1

Hall, Laurence, 66

Hall, Stuart, 68

Hamamoto, Darrell, 6
Hatta, Kayo, 105, 106
Hayakawa, Sessue, 53, 121
Haynes, Todd, 69, 78, 83
Henry Street Arts for Living Center (NYC), Marathon Film Festival, 27
Hillenbrand, Margaret, 98, 119
Hiroshima (jazz band), 24, 25, 26
*History and Memory* (Tajiri, 1992), 113
*Hito Hata: Raise the Banner* (VC, 1980), 20, 30, 31, 32, 125
HIV-AIDS, 83
Hoang, Nguyen Tan, 53
*Hold Me While I'm Naked* (Kuchar, 1966), 92
Hollywood: encouragement of cult of author in, 22; homophobia of, 88; institutional marginalization of Asian Americans from, 129; "selling out" to, 97; "yellow ceiling" in, 101
Hughes, John, 93, 109
Huston, John, 125
Hutcheson, Francis, 125

*Identities in Motion: Asian American Film and Video* (Feng), 6, 12, 137n7
identity: ambiguity of, 85; ambivalent, 50; American, 74; Asian, 103; Asian American, 45, 46, 47, 51, 53, 74, 77, 122, 123; biracial/bisexual, 86, 87; blurring of lines between Asian and Asian American, 10; crisis, 115; cultural, 24; embedded in national history, 49; ethnic, 14, 126; formation, 76, 119; imagination of, 106; marginalized, 139n13; media, 51; mixed-race, 92; mobilized within spectator, 6; multifaceted, 3; multitudinal, 44; national, 49, 119; "outsider," 49; overcoming issues in, 10; politicization of, 48; politics, 3, 8, 11, 13, 15, 33, 65, 71, 73, 78, 112, 114, 118; post–Asian American, 10; public, 13; racial, 85, 86; repressed, 74; sanctioned, 7; searching for, 117; sexual, 86; splitting, 115, 116, 117; transformation of the imagination of, 106, 123; transnational, 106, 107
Iimura, Taka, 27, 29, 32, 35
images: abject, 70, 72; to break public silences, 20; countercultural, 91; culturally meaningful, 55; distorted, 50; manipulation of electronic, 35; moving, 38; photographic, 36; potential for distortion of, 28; racist, 2, 5; subversion of sanctimoniousness of institutional Asian American film, 98

images, positive/negative, 8, 13, 14, 29, 32, 55; articulation of, 65; of Asian Americans in Hollywood, 61; challenges to divide in, 56; civil rights movement and, 56; connotation of alignment with white, hegemonic values, 59; debates over, 65; forging televisual representations of Asian Americans through, 56; innovative programming and, 65; insidiousness of, 56, 60; problems with in public television, 65–68; representation toward authenticity and, 57
*Imitation of Life* (Sirk, 1959), 36, 37
immigration, 36; quotas, 56; sharing experiences of, 5
Immigration and Nationality Act (1965), 65, 143n25
*I'm the One That I Want* (Coleman, 2000), 58, 61
Inada, Lawson, 17
Independent Television Service (ITVS), 135; attempts at checks and balances of PBS/CPB hierarchy, 8; attempts to reshape PBS to live up to excellence in diversity, 66; challenges to positive image problem in minority media, 68; challenge to PBS diversity mandate, 55–78; conflict with CPB, 66; control of by independent producers, 66; courting of underrepresented viewers, 67, 68; effects of Public Broadcasting Act (1989) on, 8; endowments for direct support for independent films, 41; esoteric content in, 55; fails to change public television, 67; fiscal failure of, 55; funding for *Strawberry Fields* (Tajiri), 112; inability to cater to national audience, 66–67; initial budget received from CPB, 66; intention to innovate, 67; lack of guarantee that films would be shown on PBS, 66; out of touch with average working-class viewer, 68; problem of positive image in public television and, 65–68; public funding for, 44; reinforcement

Independent Television Service (*continued*) of existing social/cultural hierarchies by, 67; run without intervention from Corporation for Public Broadcasting (CPB), 55; use of the "negative image" by, 8

internment, Japanese: Camp Cubes Photo Display and, 19, 20; films dealing with, 2, 5, 18–20, 42; history retold, 113; identity embedded in national history and, 49; illegal films of, 114; memories of, 112, 113; personal reflections of, 24; public commemoration of, 36; relative importance of, 24; shame associated with, 50; silence about, 113, 114

*I Told You So* (VC, 1973), 17, 27

ITVS. *See* Independent Television Service

JACL. *See* Japanese American Citizens League

James, David E., 13, 15, 16, 17, 26, 87, 92, 138*n21*

Japanese American Citizens League (JACL), 15, 20, 26

*The Jeffersons* (television show), 59

*Johnny Mnemonic* (Longo, 1995), 87

Johnson, Lyndon B., 40

Jost, Jon, 87

*The Joy Luck Club* (Wang, 1993), 58

Juhasz, Alexandra, 125, 126

Kang, Sung, 127

Kawanaka, Nobuhiro, 28

*Kelly Loves Tony* (Nakasako, 1998), 42

*The Killer* (Woo, 1989), 117

Kim-Gibson, Dai-sil, 108

King, Rodney, 108, 111, 122

Klein, Calvin, 142*n22*

Kondo, Alan, *17*

Kristeva, Julia, 72

Kubo, Duane, 15, *17*

Kuchar, George, 92

Ladd, Jordan, 94

Lam, Ringo, 118, 121

Landow, George, 28

Lee, Ang, 99, 104, 105, 106

Lee, Bruce, 10, 127

Lee, Chris Chan, 100, 107, 108–111

Lee, Grace, 10, 11, 128, 131, 132, 135

Lee, Helen, 53

Lee, Quentin, 101, 105, 107, 114, 118, 143*n4*

Lee, Rachel, 61

Lee, Spike, 110, 111, 122–123

Léger, Fernand, 71

LeGrice, Malcolm, 28

Leong, Russell, 2, 6

*Licensed to Kill* (Dong, 1998), 42, 140*n23*

Lin, Justin, 4, 9, 10, 54, 118–123, 125, 128, 135; hybrid Hong Kong–Asian American style of, 117; use of transnational aesthetic, 99–123

Lin, Lana, 140*n22*

Lipsitz, George, 107

*The Living End* (Araki, 1992), 8, 82, 83, 90

*The Long Weekend* (Araki, 1989), 83

Lung, Ti, 120

Ma, Ming-Yuen S., 53, 140*n22*

*Maid in Manhattan* (Wang, 2002), 6

*Mai's America* (Poras, 2002), 42, 43

Makavejev, Dusan, 29

Malcolm X, 122

*The Maltese Falcon* (Huston, 1941), 125

*Manzanar* (VC, 1971), 15, 17, 18–20, 35, 36, 74, 81, 112; acknowledgment of racial injustice in, 18–20; done in documentary style, 20; publicizing illegal nature of internment through, 19; social change orientation in, 14; used as device of preservation and documentation, 19

Marchetti, Gina, 106, 123

*Maryam* (Serry, 2001), 53

Mastroiani, Chiara, 92

Mathieu, Reiko, 112

*The Matrix* (Wachowski Brothers, 1999), 87

Matsumoto, Toshi, 28

Mazar, Debi, 92

McGowan, Rose, 90, 95

media: commercial, 4, 77; discourse of diversity in, 2; ethnic, 3; failure to authentically represent Asian Americans, 70; globalized, 87; independent, 7, 8; institutional racism in, 77, 97, 98; mainstream, 7, 111; minority, 53, 54; politics, 80; postmodern, 87; revolutionary activism in, 77; social change, 8

media, Asian American: difficulty in production of feature films, 9; institutionalization of, 8; relegated to PBS documentaries, 9, 10; role of state in development of, 3
media, public interest, 2, 9; relationship to Asian American film and video, 4; significance of, 4; as source of material support, 4; tensions with commercial media, 4
Media Fund, 14, 42–45; constraints imposed on filmmakers by, 42, 43; coveted support from, 42; cutthroat nature of, 43; established through NAATA, 42–45
Media Fund Award, 140*n*30
Mehta, Deepa, 53
Mekas, Jonas, 15, 27
*Memories from the Department of Amnesia* (Tanaka, 1989), 34
memory: collective, 34; cultural, 34; individual, 34; integration with history, 49; irreconcilability between history and, 48; production, 34
Meyer, Russ, 74
Mimura, Glen Masato, 2, 6, 7, 137*n*7
Minh-ha, Trinh T., 53, 83, 116
minority, model, 56, 57, 59, 61, 63, 64, 73, 98, 120, 125, 141*n*5
Minority Consortia, 135, 139*n*6, 139*n*8; addresses question of public television for pluralistic public, 44; creation and funding, 14; criticism for consistent use of "positive" images, 8; development of alternative public spheres by, 52; establishment of, 7; groups in, 40–41; impact on Asian American independent media, 39–54; interest in Public Telecommunications Act (1988), 44; lack of communication with local stations, 43; risks inherent in funding from, 43; support for Asian American independent media, 124; support for diversity mission of public broadcasting and, 39
Min Song, 110
*Mississippi Masala* (Nair, 1991), 105
*Mr. T. and Tina* (television show), 58
mockumentaries: Asian American, 10, 11, 124–133; parody in, 126; satire in, 126

*Mod Fuck Explosion* (Moritsugu, 1994), 72
*Mommy, Mommy Where's My Brain* (Moritsugu, 1986), 71
montage theory, 30
Morita, Pat, 58
Moritsugu, Jon, 55, 56, 57, 65, 68–78, 80, 82, 83, 140*n*22, 142*n*35; bypasses Hollywood and PBS documentary route of films, 70, 71; challenges image problem of Asian Americans, 69; in *First Steps, Experimentally Speaking*, 71; *Mod Fuck Explosion*, 72; *Mommy, Mommy Where's My Brain*, 71; *My Degeneration*, 72; short films of, 72; *Terminal USA*, 67, 69, 70; "underground cinema" of, 71; use of mod teen background, 71; work as ambivalent about institutional expectations, 70
*Moving the Image* (Leong), 6
multiculturalism: commitment to institutional authorship and, 25; diversity in, 1; educational media on, 26; institutional visions of, 2; multiple public spheres and, 52; positive-image, 65; in postmodern globalized media, 87; relationship to identity, 23; utopian vision of, 2
*My Degeneration* (Moritsugu, 1990), 72

NAATA. *See* National Asian American Telecommunications Association
"NAATA Presents" programs, 41, 45, 49
Nair, Mira, 99, 105, 106
Nakamura, Eric, 97
Nakamura, Robert, 15, 16, *17*, 18, 19, 20, 28, 35, 36, 77, 81, 84, 112; in founding of Visual Communications (film collective), 16
Nakamura, Suzy, 112, 131
Nakasako, Spencer, 42
National Asian American Telecommunications Association (NAATA), 2, 135, 139*n*6, 140*n*18, 140*n*30; becomes full-service media arts organization, 41; criteria used to determine which films are funded, 52; definition of Asian American film and video, 52; documentary filmmaking by, 33; educational distribution/public broadcast divisions, 14; establishes Media Fund, 42–45; formation of, 12, 40, 41;

National Asian American Telecommunications Association (*continued*) funding from Corporation for Public Broadcasting (CPB), 12; goal of increasing representation in broadcasting, 14; greater visibility for Asian American film through, 13; growth of, 2; increase in funding to directly support independent film, 41; influence on which films placed on PBS schedule, 42; long-term contracts with a risk for independent filmmakers, 42, 43, 44; obligation to present films appealing to mainstream as well as Asian audience, 46; renamed Center for Asian American Media (CAAM), 39, 137$n2$; transnational shift in festival, 103

National Coalition of Independent Public Broadcasting Producers, 65, 66, 139$n13$

National Film Registry, 138$n15$

Nekes, Werner, 28

New Chinese Film Series, 103

New Queer Cinema movement, 80, 83, 96

*New Relationships* (Wang, 1977), 29

New Wave Cinema, 99, 103, 114

New York Underground Film Festival, 71

Nguyen, Dustin, 127

nihilism, 51, 83, 88, 95

*Nowhere* (Araki, 1997), 8, 85–96; countercultural images in, 91; dependence on variable sexual tastes to spoof straight teen melodrama, 94; interracial and non-heteronormative sexual politics in, 94; politics of resistance in, 91; reliance on racist stereotyping, 94, 95

*Of Civil Wrongs and Rights* (Fournier, 2001), 6, 42, 49

*Ohara* (television show), 58

Ohashi, Alan, 15

Oishi, Eve, 57

Ono, Kent, 3, 114

*Ontogenesis* (Tanaka, 1981), 15, 34; cultural repression in nuclear age in, 35

Ouellete, Laurie, 67

*Out of the Past* (Tourneur, 1947), 90

Paik, Nam June, 32, 33, 35

Palumbo-Liu, David, 61

Park, Jane, 142$n17$

Parker, Alan, 50

Parreñas, Celine, 128

patriarchy, 112

PBS. *See* Public Broadcasting Service

Petersen, William, 56

Phaedra Cinema, 108

Phillippe, Ryan, 94

*Picture Bride* (Hatta, 1994), 105

*Pig Death Machine* (Moritsugu, 2013), 142$n35$

Polanski, Roman, 125

politics: of Asian American identity, 86; gender, 53; identity, 3, 8, 11, 13, 15, 33, 65, 71, 73, 78, 112, 114, 118; of injury, 14, 69, 72, 130; media, 80; racial, 10, 33, 53, 65, 81, 127; of resistance, 76; of ressentiment, 45–51, 140$n21$; subversive, 37

poststructuralism, 137$n6$

*POV* (PBS documentary series), 42, 43, 44, 45, 139$n13$, 140$n22$, 140$n23$; commitment to interactivity with viewers, 45; consistent thematic concern with politics of ressentiment in selection of films, 46, 47; historical trauma films on, 47; importance to Asian American film and video makers, 45, 46; "NAATA Presents" films on, 45, 49; politics of ressentiment and, 45–51; presentation of controversial issues on, 45; social-political documentaries on, 47; "Talking Back" series, 45; as televisual public sphere, 45

*POV: Rabbit in the Moon* (Omori, 1999), 42

*POV Interactive* (website), 45

production: capitalist forms of, 83; commercial, 80; cultural, 26, 27, 38; economics of, 84; ethnic media, 78; independent media, 8; memory, 34; space for, 44; structure, 3

Program Fund: control of, 66

Projansky, Sarah, 114

Public Broadcasting Act (1967), 40

Public Broadcasting Act (1979), 66

Public Broadcasting Act (1988), 66; effects on development of Independent Television Service (ITVS), 8; Independent Television Service and, 55

Public Broadcasting Service (PBS), 135; addresses dearth of diverse content in commercial television, 1, 40; attempts to placate diversity-minded media activists, 65; birth in post–civil rights era, 39; as boon/obstacle to Asian American film and video, 3; budget cuts to, 66; choice of films airing by, 41; as contemporary public sphere, 39; cultural function of, 40; discursive space of, 39; diversity and, 40–41; fails to fulfill diversity mandate, 65; mandate that film be explicitly Asian American, 14; "NAATA Presents," 41, 49; original representation of diversity in single public sphere, 52; relationship to Asian American film and video, 3; scheduling for Asian American film and video on, 42, 43; simplistic use of positive image by, 65; special regard from minorities to, 129; support for Asian American independent media, 124; support for independent minority/ethnic media, 3, 39; use of Asian American documentaries, 9, 10; visibility of Asian American documentaries on, 29. *See also* media, public interest; *POV*

*The Public Enemy* (Wellman, 1931), 110

public sphere: alternative, 52; alternative for dominant commercial systems, 44; as historical phenomenon, 44; ideological imperatives of, 69; incompatibility of Asian American films with formal experimentation in, 69; multiple, 52; public television in, 44, 45; televisual, 45

Public Telecommunications Act (1988), 41, 44

*Public Television: A Program for Action* (Carnegie Commission), 1

punk: aesthetics of, 80, 83, 84; cinema, 83, 84; critique of classism and capitalism of, 85; economics of, 84; lack of support from major studios, 84; material continuity between economics of production and aesthetics, 84, 85; at odds with Asian American film and video, 84; opposition to requirements of institutional attachment, 84; origins in music, 84; sharing marginalization with Asian American film and video, 84; in works of Araki, 9, 83, 84

Pusan International Film Festival, 103

*Pushing Hands* (Lee, 1992), 105

*Rabbit in the Moon* (Omori, 1999), 40, 49, 50

race: ambiguous, 142*n17*; discourses of, 81; fluid notions of, 106; politics, 10, 81; productive discourse on, 56; representation ad, 10

racial: ambiguity, 82, 85–96; conflict, 110, 111; discourse, 82, 95, 96; identity, 85; injustice, 20; marginalization, 15; oppression, 122; order, 59; politics, 53, 65; prejudice, 85; rejection, 89; stereotypes, 120

racism: acknowledgment of, 60; critiques of, 81; different ways of labeling, 74; "enlightened," 56, 57, 58, 59, 68; in gay community, 67; institutional, 5, 7, 56, 60, 61, 77, 89, 97, 101, 118, 122, 134; in internment camps, 18; white, 50

racist: imagery, 2, 5; violence, 122

Reeves, Keanu, 87

*Regret to Inform* (Sonnenborn, 1998), 6, 42

resistance: abject as, 9–72; in Asian American independent media, 80, 81; Asian American worldview of, 81; to association with public interest media, 9; against Hollywood, 7; to labeling, 8, 9; politics of, 76; to racist imagery in film, 2, 5; through remembering, 107

ressentiment: alternatives to, 51–54; politics of, 45–51

Rich, B. Ruby, 83

Riggs, Marlon, 67, 142*n21*

Rodriguez, Robert, 105

*Sacrifice* (Bruno, 1998), 42

*Sa-I-Gu* (Kim-Gibson, 1996), 108, 140*n23*

San Francisco International Asian American Film Festival, 2, 9, 43, 53, 71, 118, 143*n3*; "A Century of the Asian Diaspora in Motion," 103; "Class of 1997" at, 99; as counterpublic sphere, 54; CPB funding, 99; function as counterpublic sphere, 52; global cinephilia and, 100–105; growth of, 54; interest in low-budget independent feature films, 100; name changes in, 103, 104; offerings of themes about varieties of

San Francisco International Asian American Film Festival (*continued*)
  Asian American experiences, 53; promotion of Lin by, 100; showing Media Fund recipients' films at, 42; younger staff in, 103
San Francisco State College, 1
Sapadin, Lawrence, 66
*Scarface* (Hawks and Rossen, 1932), 110
Schaech, Johnathon, 90
Scott, Ridley, 125
Serry, Ramin, 53
Sharits, Paul, 28
Shaw Brothers, 121
Shokrian, Babak, 53
*Shopping for Fangs* (Lin), 99, 100, 101, 107, 114–118, 123, 143*n*4; amnesia/forgetting in, 117, 118; Asian American identity politics in, 114, 115; budget for, 105; lack of overt references to traumas of Asian American history, 114; references to other Hong Kong films in, 117; relationship between transnational and issues of Asian American identity in, 115, 116; seen as precursor to *Better Luck Tomorrow*, 114; shows transnational turn in Asian American independent media, 115
Sie, James, 112
*Silk Screen* (television show), 41
*The Simpsons* (television show), 141*n*16
Sirk, Douglas, 36
*Sixteen Candles* (Hughes, 1984), 109
*Smoke* (Wang, 1995), 6
social: change, 3, 5, 7, 8, 15, 16, 24, 27, 28, 31, 32, 98, 101, 107, 111, 123, 132, 135; exclusion, 50; mobility, 59; order, 52, 59, 126; services, 26, 40
Soe, Valerie, 53
*The Soho Weekly News* (newspaper), 27
Solomon, John, 131, 132
*Something Strong Within* (VC, 1994), 20
Sonnenborn, Barbara, 6, 42
Sontag, Susan, 101, 102
space: for citizens to deliberate, 44; democratic, 44; discursive, 39, 44
spectatorship, theory of, 6
Sternberg, Josef von, 87
*Strawberry Fields* (Tajiri, 1997), 101, 107, 111–114, 123; as coming-of-age story, 112; concerns about Asian American identity in, 111, 112; countermemory in, 112, 113; generational rifts in, 113; in historical context of 1970s counterculture, 111, 112; in mythic context of American West, 111, 112; new perspectives of the past in, 113; relationship to PBS, 112; revisionist US history in, 113; universal narrative motifs in, 112
Sundance Film Festival, 53, 106
*Superhuman Flights of Submoronic Fancies* (Tanaka, 1982), 15, 34, 35

Tajima, Renee, 38
Tajiri, Rea, 101, 107, 111–114
Tanaka, Jack Koto, 50
Tanaka, Janice, 15, 50; concern with manipulation of electronic image, 35; countercultural sentiment in works of, 35; cultural repression in nuclear age and, 35; experimental video art of, 33, 34–36; *Memories from the Department of Amnesia*, 34; *Who's Going to Pay for These Donuts, Anyway*, 34, 49, 50; works categorized as traditional internment documentaries, 34
Tarantino, Quentin, 64
Tashima, Chris, 112
Task Force on Minorities in Public Broadcasting, 2, 13, 14, 40
Tatsuno, David, 114, 138*n*15
Taubin, Amy, 27
"Teen Apocalypse Trilogy" (Araki), 85–96
television: commercial, 1, 40; lack of multicultural diversity on, 1; positive/negative conundrum of racial representation in, 76, 77; racial framework of, 56; video alignment with/revolt against, 33; as "wasteland," 67, 129
television, public: Asian American film and video and, 39–54; creation of one-dimensional definition for Asian American film by, 47; as democratic space for equality for all voices, 44; and disappearance of collective authorship, 25, 26; exclusion of films addressing complexities of Asian American identity, 47; funding for, 139*n*8; idea of "public sphere" in, 44; KQED, 34; minimal outlets for independent Minority Consortia–funded films on, 43; problems with positive image in,

65–68; reform in, 44; relationship of minority media to, 54; set up with rigid standards of diversity, 67; as theater for noncommercial representation of ideas, 44; WGBH, 34; WNET, 34. *See also* Public Broadcasting Service (PBS)

*Terminal USA* (Moritsugu, 1993), 8, 55, 56, 57, 65, 67, 68–78; appropriation of negative image by, 70; critiquing Asian American film and video, 74; example of incompatibility of race and innovation on television, 68–70; as high camp, 72–73; presentation of thinking about purpose of public television's mission of diversity, 69; rejection of by local public television stations, 69; seen as corrective to enlightened racism, 69; use of aesthetic of abjection, 70, 72; use of positive/negative images to dismantle model minority myth, 72–78

*Thelma & Louise* (Scott, 1991), 111, 113

Third Cinema, 6, 7, 137*n*7

Third World Liberation Front, 1

Thompson, Stacy, 84, 85

*Three Bewildered People in the Night* (Araki, 1987), 83

To, Johnnie, 118, 121

Tong, Corey, 103

Tong, Nancy, 38

*Tongues Untied* (Riggs, 1989), 67, 142*n*21

*Topaz* (Tatsuno, 1945), 138*n*15

Toronto International Festival, 53

*Totally Fucked Up* (Araki, 1993), 8, 85–96; alienation of gay male culture's preference for whiteness in, 88, 89, 90; artificial environment of, 87; as example of spatially informed, minor cinema, 87; racial difference in, 88; shows society's intolerance to queer teens, 89

*Touch of Evil* (Welles, 1960), 125

*Toyo Miyatake: Infinite Shades of Gray* (VC, 2001), 20

True, Rachel, 92, 95

*TV Families* (ITVS series), 55, 68, 78

Umeki, Miyoshi, 58

*Un Chien Andalou* (Buñuel, 1929), 76

University of California, Berkeley, 1

University of California at Los Angeles: establishment of EthnoCommunications program at, 1, 2; School of Theater, Film, and Television, 114

Uyeki, Bob, 102

Van Sant, Gus, 83

VC. *See* Visual Communications

video: aligned with/revolting against television, 33; art, 15, 33, 34; Asian American International Video Festival (AAIVF), 32; deconstruction of spatial continuity in, 15; divergence from social change documentaries in, 33, 107; emphasis on irony in, 33; experimental, 33; form as mode of expression, 34; guerrilla, 33; properties of, 33; queer experimental, 38; relationship to modernism, 33; repressed imagery in, 35; soap operas, 36; structural, 15. *See also* Asian American film and video

Visual Communications (VC) (film collective), 2, 5, 13, 81, 134, 138*n*21; attempt at feature-length film, 26; community in, 22; *Cruisin' J-Town*, 22, 24–26; documentary films of, 16; grassroots filmmaking by, 99, 100; *Hito Hata: Raise the Banner*, 20, 30, 31, 32; ideological social change mission of, 14; *Manzanar*, 18–20; opposition to mainstream art world by, 15–17, 28; preoccupation with relationship between identity and multiculturalism, 23; promotion of awareness of issues in Asian communities, 15; replacement of function of individual author with institutional authorship, 22; revolutionary activism in, 77; seeking solutions to racism in, 17; social ideology of collective authorship in, 22–26; use of camera image to break public silences, 20; use of grant funding for educational media, 25, 26; *Wataridori: Birds of Passage*, 20, 22, 23–24; *Wong Sinsaag*, 20–22

Walsh, Jack, 83

Wang, Peter, 105

Wang, Wayne, 6, 29–32, 105, 106, 142*n*3; *Chan Is Missing*, 29–32; choice of

Wang, Wayne (*continued*)
conventional narrative form in film, 31; *The Joy Luck Club*, 58; non–Asian American career of, 31
Watanabe, Gedde, 58
*Wataridori: Birds of Passage* (VC, 1974), 20, 22, 23, 24; documentation of first-generation immigrant laborers, 23; rearrangement of iconic status of internment in, 23; as revision of *Manzanar*, 23, 24
*Webster* (television show), 59
*The Wedding Banquet* (Lee, 1993), 105
Weiss, Marc, 45
Welles, Orson, 125
*Who's Going to Pay for These Donuts, Anyway* (Tanaka, 1992), 34, 49, 50
Willemen, Paul, 102
Wilson, Jane Edith, 131
Wong, B. D., 62
Wong, Eddie, 15, *17*, 20, 77, 81, 84; in founding of Visual Communications (film collective), 16
Wong, Frank, *21*
Wong, Garret, 63
Wong Kar Wai, 117
Wong, Sau-ling C., 106, 107
*Wong Sinsaag* (VC, 1971), 15, 17, 20–22, 27, 74, 81; critique of racist imagery in, 20–22; deconstructs stereotypes of Asian Americans, 20–22; social change orientation in, 14; visual/aural dialectic in, 22

Woo, John, 117, 118, 120, 121, 123
World Series of Asian Films, 103
Wynborny, Klaus, 28

Xing, Jun, 2, 6

Yasui, Lisa, 140*n18*
*Yellow* (Lee, 1998), 100–101, 107, 108–111, 123; black-Korean relations in, 108, 111; commitment to narrativizing racial conflict, 110; communal effort in, 111; film of ressentiment, 108; as postmodern mimicry of Hollywood genres, 110; principle of "allusionism" in, 109
Yi, Paul, 103
Yonemoto, Bruce, 15; experimental video art of, 33, 34, 35, 36; *Green Card*, 36; notions of love in works, 36; use of video to deconstruct classical narrative cinema, 36
Yonemoto, Norman, 15; experimental video art of, 33, 34, 35, 36; notions of love in works, 36; use of video to deconstruct classical narrative cinema, 36
Yu, Jessica, 6
Yu, Ruan Ling, 53

Zhang Yimou, 103

## About the Author

JUN OKADA is an assistant professor of English and Film Studies at State University of New York, Geneseo. She has published essays and reviews in *Film Quarterly, Velvet Light Trap, Quarterly Review of Film and Video, Asian Studies Journal*, and *Cinema Journal*. Born in Tokyo, Japan, she has lived in Berkeley and Los Angeles, California, and Paris and currently resides in Rochester, New York, where she writes and teaches about cinema, culture, and ethnic and gender studies.

CPSIA information can be obtained
at www.ICGtesting.com
Printed in the USA
LVHW092145141118
597156LV00001B/9/P